Communications in Computer and Information Science 548

Commenced Publication in 2007
Founding and Former Series Editors:
Alfredo Cuzzocrea, Dominik Ślęzak, and Xiaokang Yang

More information about this series at http://www.springer.com/series/7899

Fabien Gandon · Elena Cabrio
Milan Stankovic · Antoine Zimmermann (Eds.)

Semantic Web Evaluation Challenges

Second SemWebEval Challenge at ESWC 2015
Portorož, Slovenia, May 31 – June 4, 2015
Revised Selected Papers

 Springer

Editors

Fabien Gandon
Inria
Sophia Antipolis
France

Milan Stankovic
Université Paris-Sorbonne
Paris
France

Elena Cabrio
INRIA Sophia-Antipolis Méditerranée
Sophia Antipolis
France

Antoine Zimmermann
École des Mines de Saint-Étienne
Saint-Étienne
France

ISSN 1865-0929   ISSN 1865-0937   (electronic)
Communications in Computer and Information Science
ISBN 978-3-319-25517-0   ISBN 978-3-319-25518-7   (eBook)
DOI 10.1007/978-3-319-25518-7

Library of Congress Control Number: 2015951390

Springer Cham Heidelberg New York Dordrecht London
© Springer International Publishing Switzerland 2015

Printed on acid-free paper

Springer International Publishing AG Switzerland is part of Springer Science+Business Media
(www.springer.com)

Preface

Common benchmarks, established evaluation procedures, comparable tasks, and public datasets are vital to ensure reproducible, evaluable, and comparable scientific results. To assess the current state of the art and foster the systematic comparison of contributions to the Semantic Web community, open challenges are now a key scientific event of the Semantic Web conferences. After last year's success, we organized the second edition of the "Semantic Web Evaluation Challenge" as an official track of the ESWC 2015 conference (held in Portorož, Slovenia, from May 31 to June 4 2015), one of the most important international scientific events for the Semantic Web research community. The purpose of challenges is to showcase the maturity of the state of the art in tasks common to the Semantic Web community and adjacent academic communities, in a controlled setting of rigorous evaluation. In particular, this second edition focused on four areas: Open Knowledge Extraction (OKE-2015), Semantic Publishing (SemPub2015), Concept-Level Sentiment Analysis (CLSA-2015), and Schema-Agnostic Queries over Linked Data (SAQ-2015). A total of 19 teams were accepted to compete in different challenges (four participants for OKE-2015, nine for Sem-Pub2015, four for CLSA-2015, and two for SAQ-2015). The event attracted several attendees, many of whom came to the conference specifically to attend the challenge, indicating that Semantic Web Evaluation Challenges were much welcomed by the community and brought added value to the conference.

This book includes the descriptions of all methods and tools that competed at "Semantic Web Evaluation Challenge 2015," together with a detailed description of the tasks, and evaluation procedures and datasets, offering to the community a snapshot of the advancement in those areas at that moment in time, and material for replications of results. The editors have divided the book content into four chapters, each dedicated to one area (and challenge). The first chapter refers to "Open Knowledge Extraction," the second chapter to "Semantic Publishing," the third to "Concept-Level Sentiment Analysis," and the fourth to "Schema-Anostic Queries over Linked Data." Each chapter includes an introductory section by the Challenge Chairs providing a detailed description of the challenge tasks, the evaluation procedure, and associated datasets.

We would like to thank the challenges chairs, who worked hard during the organization of the 2015 edition of the Semantic Web Challenges. Thanks to their work, we experienced a successful and inspiring scientific event, and we are now able to deliver this book to the community.

August 2015

Fabien Gandon
Elena Cabrio
Milan Stankovic

Organization

Organizing Committee

General Chair
Fabien Gandon   Inria, France

Program Chairs
Marta Sabou   Vienna University of Technology, Austria
Harald Sack   Hasso Plattner Institute for IT Systems Engineering, University of Potsdam, Germany

Local Chair
Marko Grobelnik   Jožef Stefan Institute Ljubljana, Slovenia

Workshops Chairs
John Breslin   National University of Ireland, Galway, Ireland
Catherine Faron   University of Nice, Sophia Antipolis, France

Poster and Demo Chairs
Christophe Guéret   Data Archiving and Networked Services, The Netherlands
Serena Villata   Inria, Sophia Antipolis, France

Tutorials Chairs
Elena Simperl   University of Southampton, UK
Antoine Isaac   Vrije Universiteit Amsterdam, The Netherlands

PhD Symposium Chairs
Claudia d'Amato   Università degli Studi di Bari, Italy
Philippe Cudré-Mauroux   University of Fribourg, Switzerland

Challenge Chairs
Elena Cabrio   Inria, Sophia Antipolis, France
Milan Stankovic   Sépage and STIH, Université Paris-Sorbonne, France

Semantic Technologies Coordinators
Andrea Giovanni Nuzzolese   University of Bologna/STLab ISTC-CNR, Italy
Luca Costabello   Fujitsu, Galway, Ireland

Lionel Medini   University of Lyon, France
Fuqi Song   Inria, Sophia Antipolis, France
Anna Lisa Gentile   University of Sheffield, UK

EU Project Networking Session Chairs

Frédérique Segond   Viseo, Grenoble, France
Jun Zhao   Lancaster University, UK
Erik Mannens   Multimedia Lab - iMinds - Ghent University, Belgium
Sergio Consoli   STLab ISTC-CNR, Italy

Publicity Chair

Mauro Dragoni   Fondazione Bruno Kessler, Italy

Sponsor Chair

Blaž Fortuna   Ghent University, Belgium

Web Presence

Serge Tymaniuk   STI International, Austria

Proceedings Chair

Antoine Zimmermann   École nationale supérieure des mines de Saint-étienne,
                             France

Treasurer

Ioan Toma   STI International, Austria

Local Organization and Conference Administration

Špela Sitar   Jožef Stefan Institute Ljubljana, Slovenia
Monika Kropej   Jožef Stefan Institute Ljubljana, Slovenia

Program Committee

Program Chairs

Marta Sabou   Vienna University of Technology, Austria
Harald Sack   Hasso Plattner Institute for IT Systems Engineering,
                             University of Potsdam, Germany

Track Chairs

Silvio Peroni   University of Bologna, Italy and National Research
                             Council, Italy
Pavel Shvaiko   Informatica Trentina SpA, Italy
Pascal Hitzler   Wright State University, USA
Stefan Schlobach   Vrije Universiteit Amsterdam, The Netherlands

Sören Auer	University of Bonn, Germany
Stefan Dietze	L3S Research Center, Germany
Miriam Fernandez	Knowledge Media Institute, The Open University, UK
Markus Strohmaier	GESIS and University of Koblenz-Landau, Germany
Olivier Curé	Université Pierre et Marie Curie, France
Axel Polleres	Vienna University of Economics and Business, Austria
Kalina Bontcheva	University of Sheffield, UK
Simone Paolo Ponzetto	University of Mannheim, Germany
Bettina Berendt	Katholieke Universiteit Leuven, Belgium
Heiko Paulheim	University of Mannheim, Germany
Alasdair Gray	Heriot-Watt University, UK
Terry Payne	University of Liverpool, UK
Carlos Pedrinaci	Knowledge Media Institute, The Open University, UK
Aba-Sah Dadzie	The HCI Centre, The University of Birmingham, UK
Andreas Nürnberger	Otto von Guericke University Magdeburg, Germany
Lora Aroyo	Vrije Universiteit Amsterdam, The Netherlands
Gianluca Demartini	University of Sheffield, UK
Vanessa Lopez	IBM Research, Ireland
Giovanni Tumarello	SindiceTech/Fondazione Bruno Kessler, Italy

Steering Committee

Chair

John Domingue	The Open University, UK and STI International, Austria

Members

Claudia d'Amato	Università degli Studi di Bari, Italy
Grigoris Antoniou	FORTH, Greece
Philipp Cimiano	Bielefeld University, Germany
Oscar Corcho	Universidad Politécnica de Madrid, Spain
Marko Grobelnik	Jožef Stefan Institute Ljubljana, Slovenia
Axel Polleres	Vienna University of Economics and Business, Austria
Valentina Presutti	STLab ISTC-CNR, Italy
Elena Simperl	University of Southampton, UK

Challenges Organization

Challenge Chairs

Elena Cabrio	Inria, Sophia Antipolis, France
Milan Stankovic	Sépage and STIH, Université Paris-Sorbonne, France

Open Knowledge Extraction Challenge

Andrea Giovanni Nuzzolese	University of Bologna/STLab ISTC-CNR, Italy
Anna Lisa Gentile	University of Sheffield, UK

Valentina Presutti	STLab ISTC-CNR, Italy
Aldo Gangemi	Université Paris 13, France and CNR-ISTC, Italy
Darío Garigliotti	Sapienza University of Rome, Italy
Roberto Navigli	Sapienza University of Rome, Italy

Semantic Publishing Challenge

Angelo Di Iorio	University of Bologna, Italy
Anastasia Dimou	Ghent University, Belgium
Christoph Lange	University of Bonn and Fraunhofer IAIS, Germany
Sahar Vahdati	University of Bonn, Germany

Schema-Agnostic Queries over Large-schema Databases Challenge

André Freitas	University of Passau, Germany and Insight, Ireland
Christina Unger	Bielefeld University, Germany

Concept-Level Sentiment Analysis Challenge

Mauro Dragoni	Fondazione Bruno Kessler, Italy
Valentina Presutti	STLab ISTC-CNR, Italy
Diego Reforgiato Recupero	STLab ISTC-CNR, Italy

Sponsoring Institutions

STI · INNSBRUCK

xLiMe – crossLingual crossMedia knowledge extraction

Contents

Open Knowledge Extraction Challenge (OKE-2015)

Open Knowledge Extraction Challenge

Andrea Giovanni Nuzzolese[1]($\boxtimes$), Anna Lisa Gentile[2], Valentina Presutti[1],
Aldo Gangemi[1], Darío Garigliotti[3], and Roberto Navigli[3]

[1] Semantic Technology Lab, ISTC-CNR, Rome, Italy
andrea.nuzzolese@istc.cnr.it
[2] Department of Computer Science, University of Sheffield, Sheffield, UK
[3] Department of Computer Science, Sapienza University of Rome, Rome, Italy

Abstract. The Open Knowledge Extraction (OKE) challenge is aimed
at promoting research in the automatic extraction of structured content
from textual data and its representation and publication as Linked Data.
We designed two extraction tasks: (1) *Entity Recognition, Linking and
Typing* and (2) *Class Induction and entity typing*. The challenge saw the
participations of four systems: CETUS-FOX and FRED participating to
both tasks, Adel participating to Task 1 and OAK@Sheffield participating to Task 2. In this paper we describe the OKE challenge, the tasks,
the datasets used for training and evaluating the systems, the evaluation
method, and obtained results.

1 Introduction

The vision of the Semantic Web (SW) is to populate the Web with machine
understandable data so as to make intelligent agents able to automatically interpret its content - just like humans do by inspecting Web content - and assist users
in performing a significant number of tasks, relieving them of cognitive overload.
The Linked Data movement [1] kicked-off the vision by realising a key bootstrap
in publishing machine understandable information mainly taken from structured
data (typically databases) or semi-structured data (e.g. Wikipedia infoboxes).
However, most of the Web content consists of natural language text, e.g., Web
sites, news, blogs, micro-posts, etc., hence a main challenge is to extract as much
relevant knowledge as possible from this content, and publish it in the form of
Semantic Web triples.

There is huge work on knowledge extraction (KE) and knowledge discovery
contributing to address this problem, and several contests addressing the evaluation of Information Extraction systems. Hereafter we shortly list some of the
most popular initiatives which have contributed to the advancement of research
on automatic content extraction:

MUC-6. The Message Understanding Conferences is a series of conferences
designed to evaluate research in information extraction. MUC-6 [7] was the
first to define the "named entity" task, where the participants had to identify
the names of all the people, organizations, and geographic locations in a
collection of textual documents in English.

F. Gandon et al. (Eds.): SemWebEval 2015, CCIS 548, pp. 3–15, 2015.
DOI: 10.1007/978-3-319-25518-7_1

HUB-4. The Hub-4 Broadcast News Evaluation[1] included a MUC-style evaluation for Named Entity Recognition, but with the focus on speech input in the domain of broadcast news.

MUC-7 and MET-2. The main difference between MUC-7/MET-2[2] to previous MUC is the introduction of multilingual NE evaluation, using training and test articles from comparable domains for all languages.

CONLL. The CoNLL-2002 and CoNLL-2003 shared task focused on language independent named entity recognition. The evaluation focused on entities of four types: persons (PER), organizations (ORG), locations (LOC) and miscellaneous (MISC) and the task was performed on Spanish and Dutch for CoNLL-2002 and German and English for CoNLL-2003 [12,13].

ACE. The Automatic Content Extraction program evaluates methods to extract (i) entities, (iii) relations among these entities and (iii) the events in which these entities participate. In the first edition extraction tasks were available in English, Arabic and Chinese . In the entity detection and tracking (EDT) task, all mentions of an entity, whether a name, a description, or a pronoun, are to be found. ACE defines seven types of entities: Person, Organization, Location, Facility, Weapon, Vehicle and Geo-Political Entity (GPEs). Each type is further divided into subtypes (for instance, Organization subtypes include Government, Commercial, Educational, Non-profit, Other) [4]. ACE started in 2004 with following successful editions[3].

TAC. The Text Analysis Conference[4] is a series of evaluation workshops on Natural Language Processing, with several specific tasks (known as "tracks"). The Knowledge Base Population (KBP) task[5] is present since 2009 and has the goal to populate knowledge bases (KBs) from unstructured text. The current KB schema consists of named entities that can be a person (PER), organization (ORG), or geopolitical entity (GPE) and predefined attributes (or slots) to fill for those named entities.

TREC-KBA. The Knowledge Base Acceleration (KBA) track[6] ran in TREC 2012, 2013 and 2014. It evaluates systems that filter a time-ordered corpus for documents and slot fills that would change an entity profile in a predefined list of entities. The focus is therefore on spotting novelty and changes for predefined entities.

SemEval-2015 Task 13. The Multilingual All-Words Sense Disambiguation (WSD) and Entity Linking (EL) are tasks that address the lexical ambiguity of language, but they use different meaning inventories: EL uses encyclopedic knowledge, while WSD uses lexicographic information. The main goal of this

---

[1] http://www.itl.nist.gov/iad/mig/publications/proceedings/darpa99/html/ie5/ie5.htm.

[2] http://www.itl.nist.gov/iaui/894.02/related_projects/muc/proceedings/muc_7_proceedings/overview.html.

[3] https://www.ldc.upenn.edu/collaborations/past-projects/ace/annotation-tasks-and-specifications.

[4] http://www.nist.gov/tac/tracks/index.html.

[5] http://www.nist.gov/tac/2015/KBP.

[6] http://trec-kba.org/.

combined task is to treat the two problems holistically using a resource that integrates both kinds of inventories (i.e., BabelNet 2.5.1).

Despite the numerous initiatives for benchmarking KE systems, there is lack of a "genuine" SW reference evaluation framework for helping researchers and the whole community to assess the state of the art in this domain. In fact, results of Knowledge Extraction systems are usually evaluated against tasks that do not focus on specific Semantic Web goals. For example, tasks such as named Entity Recognition, Relation Extraction, Frame Detection, etc. are certainly of importance for the SW, but in most cases such tasks are designed without considering the output design and formalisation in the form of Linked Data and OWL ontologies. This makes results of existing methods often not directly reusable for populating the SW, until a translation from linguistic semantics to formal semantics is performed.

The OKE challenge, inspired by [9], has the ambition to provide a reference framework for research on *Knowledge Extraction from text for the Semantic Web* by re-defining a number of tasks (typically from information and knowledge extraction) by taking into account specific SW requirements.

2 Tasks

The OKE challenge defines two tasks. This section provides their detailed description.

2.1 Task 1: Entity Recognition, Linking and Typing for Knowledge Base population

This task consists of (i) identifying Entities in a sentence and create an OWL individual (owl:Individual statement) representing it, (ii) link (owl:sameAs statement) such individual, when possible, to a reference Knowledge Base (i.e., DBpedia [2]) and (iii) assigning a type to such individual (rdf:type statement) selected from a set of given types. In this task by Entity we mean any discourse referent (the actors and objects around which a story unfolds), either named or anonymous that is an individual of one of the following DOLCE Ultra Lite classes[7] [5], i.e., dul:Person[8], dul:Place, dul:Organization, and dul:Role. By entities we also refer to anaphorically related discourse referents. Hence, anaphora resolution is part of the requirements for the identification of entities. As an example, for the sentence:

> *Florence May Harding studied at a school in Sydney, and with Douglas Robert Dundas , but in effect had no formal training in either botany or art.*

we want to recognize the entities reported in Table 1.

---

[7] http://stlab.istc.cnr.it/stlab/WikipediaOntology/.

[8] The prefix dul: stands for the namespace http://www.ontologydesignpatterns.org/ont/dul/DUL.owl.

Table 1. Task 1: example.

Recognized Entity	Generated URI	Type	SameAs
Florence May Harding	oke:Florence_May_Harding	dul:Person	dbpedia:Florence_May_Harding
school	oke:School	dul:Organization	
Sydney	oke:Sydney	dul:Place	dbpedia:Sydney
Douglas Robert Dundas	oke:Douglas_Robert_Dundas	dul:Person	

Sentences were provided in input to systems as RDF by using the NIF notation[9] [8]. The following is an example of input for the previous sentence.

```
oke:task-1/sentence-1#char=0,146
        a                       nif:RFC5147String, nif:String, nif:Context;
        nif:beginIndex          "0"^^xsd:nonNegativeInteger;
        nif:endIndex            "146"^^xsd:nonNegativeInteger;
        nif:isString            "Florence May Harding studied at a school in Sydney, and with
                                Douglas Robert Dundas, but in effect had no
                                formal training in either botany or art."@en.
```

System were asked to provide recognised entities by using a NIF-compliant output as shown in the following example.

```
...
oke:Florence_May_Harding
        a                       owl:Individual, dul:Person;
        rdfs:label              "Florence May Harding"@en;
        owl:sameAs              dbpedia:Florence_May_Harding.

oke:task-1/sentence-1#char=0,20
        a                       nif:RFC5147String, nif:String;
        nif:anchorOf            "Florence May Harding"@en;
        nif:beginIndex          "0"^^xsd:nonNegativeInteger;
        nif:endIndex            "20"^^xsd:nonNegativeInteger;
        nif:referenceContext    oke:task-1/sentence-1#char=0,146;
        itsrdf:taIdentRef       oke:Florence_May_Harding.
```

The RDF above[10] is an example of possible output for annotating the string that represents the entity *Florence May Harding* in the original sentence. This string is typed as a `nif:RFC5147String` and is related to a reference context (cf., property `nif:referenceContext`), which identifies the input sentence, and to an `owl:Individual` (cf., property `itsrdf:taIdentRef`), which represents the entity within the dataset. This entity is further typed as `dul:Person` and linked to its corresponding entity in DBpedia (cf. property `owl:sameAs`). The namespace prefix `oke:` is used to identify the URIs of recognised entities. There is not a given rule for generating these URI, thus any system can implement its own algorithm for generating URIs. The linking to DBpedia can be omitted in

---

[9] http://persistence.uni-leipzig.org/nlp2rdf/.

[10] The prefixes `nif:`, `itsrdf:`, `dul:`, and `dbpedia:` identify the namespaces http://persistence.uni-leipzig.org/nlp2rdf/ontologies/nif-core, http://www.w3.org/2005/11/its/rdf, http://www.ontologydesignpatterns.org/ont/dul/DUL.owl, and http://dbpedia.org/resource/ respectively.

case a system is not able to identify a corresponding entity in such a dataset. This means that it might be possible to have entities that cannot be linked to any DBpedia entities. This is always the case occurring when dealing with anonymous entities. For example, given the sentence:

> *She was appointed as Senator for Life in Italy by the President Carlo Azeglio Ciampi.*

We want to recognise the term *She* an as anonymous entity within our dataset and to type it as `owl:Individual` and `dul:Person`. However, we do not want any linking to DBpedia because it would introduce an error.

2.2 Task 2: Class Induction and Entity Typing for Vocabulary and Knowledge Base Enrichment

This task was designed for producing `rdf:type` statements for an entity, given its definition as natural language text. The participants were provided with a dataset of sentences, each defining an entity (known a priori). More in detail the task required the participants to (i) identify the type(s) of the given entity as they are expressed in the given definition, (ii) create a `owl:Class` statement for defining each of them as a new class in the target knowledge base, (iii) create a `rdf:type` statement between the given entity and the new created classes, and (iv) align the identified types, if a correct alignment is available, to a set of given types from a subset of DOLCE+DnS Ultra Lite classes. Table 2 shows the complete list of these types[11]

For example, given the entity `dbpedia:Skara_Cathedral` and its definition

> *Skara Cathedral is a church in the Swedish city of Skara.*

the types that the systems were asked to recognise are reported in Table 3.

Target entities, i.e. the entities to type, along with their definition in natural language were provided as RDF by using the NIF notation. The following is an example of input for the previous example.

```
oke:task-2/sentence-1#char=0,150>
      a                  nif:RFC5147String, nif:String, nif:Context;
      nif:isString       "Brian Banner is a fictional villain from the Marvel Comics Universe
                         created by Bill Mantlo and Mike Mignola and first
                         appearing in print in late 1985.";
      nif:beginIndex     "0"^^xsd:int;
      nif:endIndex       "150"^^xsd:int.

oke:task-2/sentence-1#char=0,12
      a                  nif:RFC5147String, nif:String;
      nif:anchorOf       "Brian Banner"@en;
      nif:referenceContext  oke:task-2/sentence-1#char=0, 150;
      nif:beginIndex     "0"^^xsd:int;
```

---

[11] Prefixes `d0:` and `dul:` stand for namespaces http://ontologydesignpatterns.org/ont/wikipedia/d0.owl and http://www.ontologydesignpatterns.org/ont/dul/DUL.owl respectively.

```
nif:endIndex          "12"^^xsd:int;
itsrdf:taIdentRef     dbpedia:Brian_Banner.

dbpedia:Brian_Banner
rdfs:label            "Brian Banner"@en.
```

Table 2. The subset of DOLCE+DnS ultra lite classes used for typing entities in the Task 2.

Class	Description
dul:Abstract	Anything that cannot be located in space-time
d0:Activity	Any action or task planned or executed by an agent intentionally causing and participating in it
dul:Amount	Any quantity, independently from how it is measured, computed, etc
d0:Characteristic	An aspect or quality of a thing
dul:Collection	A container or group of things (or agents) that share one or more common properties
d0:CognitiveEntity	Attitudes, cognitive abilities, ideologies, psychological phenomena, mind, etc
dul:Description	A descriptive context that creates a relational view on a set of data or observations
d0:Event	Any natural event, independently of its possible causes.
dul:Goal	The description of a situation that is desired by an agent
dul:InformationEntity	A piece of information, be it concretely realized or not: linguistic expressions, works of art, knowledge objects
d0:Location	A location, in a very generic sense e.g. geo-political entities, or physical object that are inherently located
dul:Organism	A physical object with biological characteristics, typically able to self-reproduce
dul:Organization	An internally structured, conventionally created social entity such as enterprises, bands, political parties, etc
dul:Person	Persons in commonsense intuition
dul:Personification	A social entity with agentive features, invented or conceived through a cultural process
dul:PhysicalObject	Any object that has a proper space region, and an associated mass: natural bodies, artifacts, substances
dul:Process	Any natural process, independently of its possible causes.
dul:Process	Any natural process, independently of its possible causes
dul:Role	A concept that classifies some entity: social positions, roles, statuses
dul:Situation	A unified view on a set of entities, e.g. physical or social facts or conditions, configurations, etc
hline d0:System	Physical, social, political systems
dul:TimeInterval	A time span.
d0:Topic	Any area, discipline, subject of knowledge

Table 3. Task 2: example.

Recognized string for the type	Generated Type	Subclass of
fictional villain	oke:FictionalVillain	dul:Personification
villain	oke:Villain	oke:FictionalVillain, dul:Person

Participants were asked to complete the RDF snippet above with the following information about typing by using the NIF notation:

```
...
oke:FictionalVillain
        a                     owl:Class;
        rdfs:label            "fictional villain"@en;
        rdfs:subClassOf       dul:Personification.

oke:Villain
        a                     owl:Class;
        rdfs:label            "villain"@en;
        rdfs:subClassOf       oke:FictionalVillain, dul:Person.

oke:sentence-1#char=18,35
        a                     nif:RFC5147String, nif:String;
        nif:anchorOf          "fictional villain"@en;
        nif:referenceContext  oke:task-2/sentence-1#char=0, 150;
        nif:beginIndex        "18"^^xsd:int;
        nif:endIndex          "35"^^xsd:int;
        itsrdf:taIdentRef     oke:FictionalVillain.

oke:sentence-1#char=28,35>
        a                     nif:RFC5147String, nif:String;
        nif:anchorOf          "villain"@en;
        nif:referenceContext  oke:task-2/sentence-1#char=0, 150;
        nif:beginIndex        "28"^^xsd:int;
        nif:endIndex          "35"^^xsd:int;
        itsrdf:taIdentRef     oke:Villain.
```

We designed the task in order to ask participants to report as `rdfs:label` the string recognised within a definition as a valid type for a given entity. Additionally, we asked participants to record span indexes for such strings with respect to the original definition by using `nif:beginIndex` and `nif:endIndex`. Namely, `nif:beginIndex` and `nif:endIndex` were used to identify the initial and final span index respectively.

3   Training and Evaluation Datasets

We built two separate datasets for each task in order to distinguish between a (i) a dataset to be used for training purposes and (ii) another one to use for evaluating the systems. In next sections we describe how we built such datasets for each task and we provide details about them.

3.1   Task 1

The training and the evaluation datasets for Task 1 were built by manually annotating a set of 196 sentences. These sentences were selected from Wikipedia

Table 4. Figures about the training and the evaluation datasets for Task 1.

Parameter	Training dataset	Evaluation dataset
# of sentences	95	101
# of annotated entities	290	428
Avg # of annotated entities per sentence	3.51	5.37
# of entities linked to DBpedia	255	321

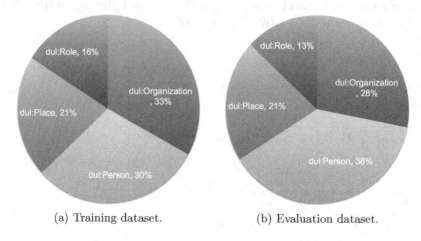

(a) Training dataset.   (b) Evaluation dataset.

Fig. 1. Distribution of entities according to their DOLCE type.

articles reporting biographies of scholars. This choice comes from the observation that biographies about scholars typically contain entities about people (e.g., the scholar that is subject of the given Wikipedia article, her collegues, her relatives, etc.), locations (e.g., the places the scholar lived in), organisations (e.g., the universities the scholar worked for) and roles (e.g., the academic roles held by the scholar during her career). Hence, we split the 196 into the training and the evaluation datasets by taking care to have:

- no overlap of sentences between the two datasets;
- a comparable number of sentences in both datasets;
- as much as possible an equal distribution of DOLCE entity types (i.e., Person, Place, Organization, and Role) within the datasets.

Therefore, the training dataset for Task 1 is composed of 95 sentences while the evaluation dataset for the same task counts 101 sentences. Table 4 shows the details about the two datasets in terms of the number of sentences, the overall number of annotated entities, the average number of annotated entities per sentence, and the number of entities linked to DBpedia.

Figure 1 shows the distribution of entities with respect to the four DOLCE types used for typing in Task 1. More in detail, Fig. 1(a) and (b) show the distribution in the training dataset and the evaluation dataset respectively.

Table 5. Figures about the training and the evaluation datasets for Task 2.

Parameter	Training dataset	Evaluation dataset
# of sentences	99	99
# of rdfs:subClassOf axioms	166	282
# of annotated classes	165	186

Both datasets are available on-line as TURTLE for download[12].

3.2 Task 2

For Task 2, similarly to Task 1, we built a training and an evaluation dataset by manually annotating a set of 198 sentences, using the NIF notation. Each sentence provided a definition of a DBpedia entity expressed as natural language. The number of sentences for the two datasets was split in order to have the training dataset and the evaluation dataset composed of 99 sentences each. Table 5 reports the details about the training and the evaluation datasets for Task 2 in terms of (i) number of sentences annotated, (ii) number of rdfs:subClassOf axioms used within the datasets and (iii) number of classes extracted from the natural language and used for typing the DBpedia entities. It is worth remarking that each sentence provided a definition for a single DBpedia entity only, meaning that the number of sentences and the number of DBpedia entities in the datasets were the same.

Figure 2(a) and (b) show the distribution of entities over the subset of DOLCE Ultra Lite classes used for Task 2, for the training and the evaluation datasets respectively.

Both datasets are available on-line as TURTLE for download[13].

4   Results

The evaluation of the challenge was enabled by designing a dedicated version of GERBIL [14], which was used as benchmarking system for evaluating precision, recall and F-measure for both tasks. For Task 1 GERBIL was designed in order to evaluate systems with respect to (i) their ability to recognize entities using the NIF offsets returned by the systems (only full matches were counted as correct, e.g., if the system returned "Art School" instead of "National Art School", this was counted as a miss), (ii) their ability to assign the correct type among the 4

---

[12] The training dataset is available at https://github.com/anuzzolese/oke-challenge/blob/master/GoldStandard_sampleData/task1/dataset_task_1.ttl. Similarly, the evaluation dataset is available at https://github.com/anuzzolese/oke-challenge/blob/master/evaluation-data/task1/evaluation-dataset-task1.ttl.

[13] The training dataset is available at https://github.com/anuzzolese/oke-challenge/blob/master/GoldStandard_sampleData/task2/dataset_task_2.ttl. Similarly, the evaluation dataset is available at https://github.com/anuzzolese/oke-challenge/blob/master/evaluation-data/task2/evaluation-dataset-task2.ttl.

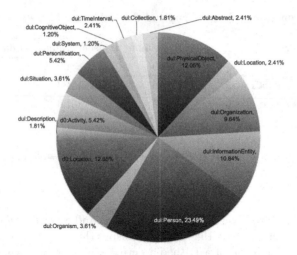

(a) Training dataset.

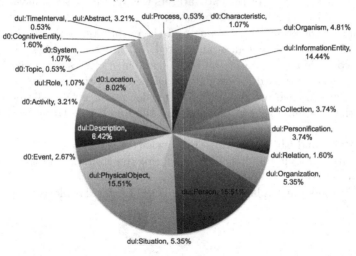

(b) Evaluation dataset

Fig. 2. Distribution of entities over the subset of DOLCE ultra lite classes used for Task 2.

target DOLCE types (cf. Sect. 2.1), and (iii) their ability to link individuals to DBpedia 2014. Instead, for Task 2 GERBIL was designed in order to evaluate systems with respect to (i) their ability to recognize strings (i.e., linguistic evidences) in the definition that identify the type of a target entity (i) their ability to align identified types to a the subset of DOLCE Ultra Lite classes (cf. Table 2 in Sect. 2.2).

We received four submissions: two of them participated to one task only and the other two participated to both tasks of the challenge. Table 6 lists the systems

Table 6. Systems participating to the challenge.

System	Description	Participating to Task
CETUS-FOX [11]	A Baseline Approach to Type Extraction	1-2
Adel [10]	A Hybrid Approach for Entity Recognition and Linking	1
FRED [3]	Named Entity Resolution, Linking and Typing for Knowledge Base population	1-2
OAK@Sheffield [6]	Exploiting Linked Open Data to Uncover Entity Types	2

Table 7. Task 1 results

Annotator	Micro F1	Micro Precision	Micro Recall	Macro F1	Macro Precision	Macro Recall
Adel	0.6075	0.6938	0.5403	0.6039	0.685	0.54
FOX	0.4988	0.6639	0.4099	0.4807	0.6329	0.4138
FRED	0.3473	0.4667	0.2766	0.2278	0.3061	0.1814

Table 8. Task 2 results

Annotator	Micro F1	Micro Precision	Micro Recall	Macro F1	Macro Precision	Macro Recall
CETUS	0.4735	0.4455	0.5203	0.4478	0.4182	0.5328
OAK@Sheffield	0.4416	0.5155	0.39	0.3939	0.3965	0.3981
FRED	0.3043	0.2893	0.3211	0.2746	0.2569	0.3173

participating to the challenge by providing the names and the short descriptions of the systems, and the tasks they are involved in.

The winner for Task 1 was Adel, which obtained micro F1 and macro F1 of 0.6075 and 0.6039 respectively. The exhaustive results for all the system involved in Task 1 is reported in Table 7.

The winner for Task 2 was CETUS-FOX, which obtained micro F1 and macro F1 of 0.4735 and 0,4478 respectively. The exhaustive results for all the system involved in Task 2 are reported in Table 8.

5   Conclusions

The Open Knowledge Extraction challenge attracted four research groups coming from the Knowledge Extraction (KE) and the Semantic Web (SW) communities. Indeed, the challenge proposal was aimed at attracting research groups from these two communities in order to further investigate existing overlaps between KE and the SW. Additionally, one of the goals of the challenge was to foster the collaboration between the two communities, to the aim of growing further the SW community. To achieve this goal we defined a SW reference evaluation framework, which is composed of (i) two tasks, (ii) a training and evaluation dataset for each task, and (iii) an evaluation framework to measure the accuracy of the systems.

Although the participation in terms of number of competing systems remained quite limited, we believe that the challenge is a breakthrough in the hybridisation of Semantic Web technologies with Knowledge Extraction methods. As a matter of fact, the evaluation framework is available on-line[14] and can be reused by the community and for next editions of the challenge.

References

1. Bizer, C., Heath, T., Berners-Lee, T.: Linked data - the story so far. Int. J. Semantic Web Inf. Syst. **5**(3), 1–22 (2009)
2. Bizer, C., Lehmann, J., Kobilarov, G., Auer, S., Becker, C., Cyganiak, R., Hellmann, S.: DBpedia - a crystallization point for the web of data. J. Web Sem. **7**(3), 154–165 (2009)
3. Consoli, S., Reforgiato, D.: Using fred for named entity resolution, linking and typing for knowledge base population. In: Gandon, F., Sabou, M., Sack, H., Cabrio, E., Stankovic, M., Zimmermann, A. (eds.) ESWC 2015 Challenges, CCIS, pp. 40–50. Springer International Publishing, Switzerland (2015)
4. Doddington, G.R., Mitchell, A., Przybocki, M.A., Ramshaw, L.A., Strassel, S., Weischedel, R.M.: The automatic content extraction (ace) program-tasks, data, and evaluation. In: LREC (2004)
5. Gangemi, A., Guarino, N., Masolo, C., Oltramari, A., Schneider, L.: Sweetening ontologies with DOLCE. In: Gómez-Pérez, A., Benjamins, V.R. (eds.) EKAW 2002. LNCS (LNAI), vol. 2473, pp. 166–181. Springer, Heidelberg (2002)
6. Gao, J., Mazumdar, S.: Exploiting linked open data to uncover entity types. In: Gandon, F., Sabou, M., Sack, H., Cabrio, E., Stankovic, M., Zimmermann, A. (eds.) ESWC 2015 Challenges, CCIS, pp. 51–62. Springer International Publishing, Switzerland (2015)
7. Grishman, R., Sundheim, B.: Message understanding conference-6: a brief history. In: Proceedings of the 16th Conference on Computational Linguistics, COLING 1996, vol. 1, pp. 466–471. Association for Computational Linguistics, Stroudsburg, PA, USA (1996)
8. Hellmann, S., Lehmann, J., Auer, S., Brümmer, M.: Integrating NLP using linked data. In: Alani, H., Kagal, L., Fokoue, A., Groth, P., Biemann, C., Parreira, J.X., Aroyo, L., Noy, N., Welty, C., Janowicz, K. (eds.) ISWC 2013, Part II. LNCS, vol. 8219, pp. 98–113. Springer, Heidelberg (2013)
9. Petasis, G., Karkaletsis, V., Paliouras, G., Krithara, A., Zavitsanos, E.: Ontology population and enrichment: state of the art. In: Paliouras, G., Spyropoulos, C.D., Tsatsaronis, G. (eds.) Multimedia Information Extraction. LNCS, vol. 6050, pp. 134–166. Springer, Heidelberg (2011)
10. Plu, J., Rizzo, G., Troncy, R.: A hybrid approach for entity recognition and linking. In: Gandon, F., Sabou, M., Sack, H., Cabrio, E., Stankovic, M., Zimmermann, A. (eds.) ESWC 2015 Challenges, CCIS, pp. 28–39. Springer International Publishing, Switzerland (2015)
11. Röder, M., Usbeck, R., Ngonga Ngomo, A.-C.: Cetus - a baseline approach to type extraction. In: Gandon, F., Sabou, M., Sack, H., Cabrio, E., Stankovic, M., Zimmermann, A. (eds.) ESWC 2015 Challenges, CCIS, pp. 16–27. Springer International Publishing, Switzerland (2015)

---

[14] https://github.com/anuzzolese/oke-challenge.

12. Tjong Kim Sang, E.F.: Introduction to the conll-2002 shared task: language-independent named entity recognition. In: Proceedings of the 6th Conference on Natural Language Learning, COLING-02, vol. 20, pp. 1–4. Association for Computational Linguistics, Stroudsburg, PA, USA (2002)
13. Iordache, O.: Introduction. In: Iordache, O. (ed.) Polystochastic Models for Complexity. UCS, vol. 4, pp. 1–16. Springer, Heidelberg (2010)
14. Usbeck, R., Röder, M., Ngomo, A.N., Baron, C., Both, A., Brümmer, M., Ceccarelli, D., Cornolti, M., Cherix, D., Eickmann, B., Ferragina, P., Lemke, C., Moro, A., Navigli, R., Piccinno, F., Rizzo, G., Sack, H., Speck, R., Troncy, R., Waitelonis, J., Wesemann, L.: GERBIL: general entity annotator benchmarking framework. In Gangemi, A., Leonardi, S., Panconesi, A. (eds.) Proceedings of the 24th International Conference on World Wide Web, WWW 2015, pp. 1133–1143. ACM (2015)

CETUS – A Baseline Approach to Type Extraction

Michael Röder[✉], Ricardo Usbeck, René Speck,
and Axel-Cyrille Ngonga Ngomo

University of Leipzig, Leipzig, Germany
{roeder,usbeck,speck,ngonga}@informatik.uni-leipzig.de

Abstract. The concurrent growth of the Document Web and the Data Web demands accurate information extraction tools to bridge the gap between the two. In particular, the extraction of knowledge on real-world entities is indispensable to populate knowledge bases on the Web of Data. Here, we focus on the recognition of types for entities to populate knowledge bases and enable subsequent knowledge extraction steps. We present CETUS, a baseline approach to entity type extraction. CETUS is based on a three-step pipeline comprising (i) offline, knowledge-driven type pattern extraction from natural-language corpora based on grammar-rules, (ii) an analysis of input text to extract types and (iii) the mapping of the extracted type evidence to a subset of the DOLCE+DnS Ultra Lite ontology classes. We implement and compare two approaches for the third step using the YAGO ontology as well as the FOX entity recognition tool.

1 Introduction

Both the Document and the Data Web grow continuously. This is a mixed blessing, as the two forms of the Web grow concurrently and most commonly contain different forms of information. Modern information systems must thus bridge this gap to allow a holistic access to the Web. One way to bridge the gap between the two forms of the Web is the extraction of structured data from the growing amount of unstructured information on the Document Web. While extracting structured data from unstructured data allows the development of powerful information system, it also requires high-quality knowledge extraction tool chains to lead to useful results. However, standard document processing pipelines miss the opportunity to gain insights from semantic entities novel to the underlying knowledge base (KB). That is, most known tool chains recognize entities based on linguistic models and link them to a KB or null if they are emerging entities. Assigning a type to these entities is a well known task [10] and has been in the focus of several recent challenges, e.g., the TAC KBP Entity Linking challenge 2014[1], the Micropost workshop series[2] and the OKE challenge 2015[3].

---

[1] http://nlp.cs.rpi.edu/kbp/2014/.
[2] http://www.scc.lancs.ac.uk/microposts2015/.
[3] http://2015.eswc-conferences.org/important-dates/call-OKEC.

© Springer International Publishing Switzerland 2015
F. Gandon et al. (Eds.): SemWebEval 2015, CCIS 548, pp. 16–27, 2015.
DOI: 10.1007/978-3-319-25518-7_2

In this article, we present CETUS, a pattern based entity type extraction tool for identifying the type of a given entity inside a given text and linking this type to a KB, i.e., to the DOLCE+DnS Ultra Lite ontology classes[4]. CETUS is a fast and easy to implement baseline approach to path a way to novel research insights. CETUS' pipeline is divided into three subsequent parts: (i) an a-priori pattern extraction, (ii) a grammar-based analysis of the input document and (iii) mapping the type evidence to the DOLCE+DnS Ultra Lite classes. CETUS implements two approaches for the third step using the YAGO ontology as well as the FOX entity recognition tool. We will explain these parts in detail in the Sects. 3, 4, 5 and 6 respectively, before we are summarizing the results of the OKE Challenge in Sect. 7 and conclude in Sect. 8. The source code of CETUS can be found at https://github.com/AKSW/Cetus.

2   Related Work

Next to the above mentioned challenges about entity linking, several tools have been introduced with the ability to type entities, e.g., FOX [13]. However, most of these systems differ in several major aspects compared to CETUS. First, most of the existing tools comprise a complex work flow and are using techniques ranging from supervised and semi-supervised to unsupervised learning methods [10]. Thus, these tools can not serve as a baseline with a simple approach. Second, CETUS marks the part of a given document that contains the type evidence, i.e., a string indicating the chosen type. Third, in contrast to the most other tools, CETUS uses the DOLCE+DnS Ultra Lite ontology classes for typing and is, thus, able to take part the OKE Challenge 2015.

Our approach is mainly based on patterns inspired by Hearst Patterns [4]. Those patterns match text parts describing hyponym relations between two nouns. There have been several other tools that are using patterns to identify the parts of a document containing the type of an entity, e.g., Snow et al. [12]. However, these tools differ in terms of complexity. While some of them are using a predefined set of patterns or rules, other approaches try to discover new patterns from a given corpus using bootstrapping. Since CETUS should serve as an easy to implement baseline for the OKE Challenge, we decided to use a straight forward a-priori iterative, incremental pattern extraction process described in Sect. 3.

3   Pattern Extraction

The patterns used for identifying the type of an entity inside a document, are generated semi-automatically in an iterative manner. First, CETUS identifies phrases containing entities and their types in a given document corpus (here we use the DBpedia 2014 abstracts) and extracts them. After sorting these

---

[4] See http://stlab.istc.cnr.it/stlab/WikipediaOntology/. Throughout this paper, we use the prefix `dul` for types of this ontology.

phrases according to the string in between the entity and its type, we analyze them and create the patterns in an incremental process. The progress of our pattern extraction is measured by the amount of phrases that are covered by our patterns. In the following, these steps are described in more detail.

3.1   Sentence Part Extraction

For extracting the phrases containing entities and their types, we used the abstracts of the English DBpedia 2014 abstracts dump file. Every abstract describes the entity it belongs to and, thus, contains the label of the entity and its type. We assume, abstracts are written properly and thus contain both information.

First, CETUS preprocesses each abstract individually. Our approach removes the text written in brackets, e.g., pronunciations. Afterwards, we use the Stanford CoreNLP [8] library for part-of-speech tagging and lemmatization as well as the Stanford Deterministic Coreference Resolution System [6] to replace pronouns with their coreferenced words, e.g., *He studied physics* with *Albert Einstein studied physics*. The last step of the preprocessing is the splitting of the abstracts into single sentences.

Second, sentences containing the entity label and at least one label of one of its types (`rdf:type`) are processed further. CETUS extracts the part of the sentence between the entity label and the type label and stores additionally the words, their lemmas and part-of-speech tags of the extracted phrase.

After analysing all abstracts, CETUS counts the different phrases. Table 1 shows examples of extracted phrases and their counts how often they have been found inside the English DBpedia. The words inside these parts are encoded as `<word>_<lemma>_<pos-tag>`.

Delving into the extracted phrases reveals insights into the structure of entity type descriptions in DBpedia abstracts. It can be seen that the formulation "`<entity>` *is a* `<type>`" occurs most often. The second most common formulation uses a type preceding the entity and is listed as the second example in Table 1. The third example is a variant of the first one containing the determiner "an" instead of "a". The fourth example shows that some abstracts contain more complex formulations like "`<entity>` *is a* `<type>` *of* `<type>`" while the last example contains an additional adjective that was not a part of the types label, i.e., "flowering".

3.2   Grammar Construction

The aim of creating a grammar is to generate a parser that is able to identify the part of a sentence describing an entities type given the position of the entity inside the sentence. For generating a parser based on our grammar, we are using the ANTLR4 library[5].

Our grammar is based on the following assumptions:

---

[5] http://www.antlr.org/.

Table 1. Examples of sentence parts found between an entity and its type.

Extracted phrase	Count
`<entity> is_be_VB a_a_DT <type>`	242 806
`<type> <entity>`	107 082
`<entity> is_be_VB an_an_DT <type>`	12 981
`<entity> is_be_VB a_a_DT species_species_NN of_of_IN <type>`	12 554
`<entity> is_be_VB a_a_DT species_species_NN` `of_of_IN flowering_flower_JJ <type>`	4 069

1. A sentence contains an entity and a type. Otherwise the sentence is not part of our grammar language.
2. A type should contain at least one noun, but can contain additional words that are specifying the meaning of the noun, e.g., adjectives. If a noun could not be found, a single adjective can be used as type as well.

The first assumption simplifies the task of defining a grammar since we can focus on the sentences that are important for our task and ignore all others. The second assumption contains the definition of a type surface form. It might seem to be contradictory w.r.t. the last example of Table 1 but for the extraction it is important that we extract all words that *could* be part of the types surface form. Following this assumptions, we can define a type inside the grammar with the rule in Listing 1.1.[6]

```
type :  (ADJ|VERB|ADVERB|CD)* FOREIGN? NOUN+ (ADJ NOUN)*
     |  ADJ;
```

Listing 1.1. The grammar rule defining a type surface form.

A surface form of a type can contain a number of adjectives, verbs or adverbs as well as a foreign word, e.g., the latin word "sub". Additionally, a type has one or more nouns.

As mentioned above, the construction of the grammar is designed to be an iterative, incremental, self-improving process. We start with the simple *is-a* pattern that matches the most common phrase "`<entity>` *is a* `<type>`". The definition of this pattern is shown in Listing 1.2.

With this simple grammar, we try to match all phrases extracted beforehand and create a list containing all those phrases that have not been matched so far. Using this list, we extend our grammar to match other phrases. In our example, we extend the simple *is-a* pattern towards matching different temporal forms of the verb "be" and different determiners, e.g., "a" and "an", see Listing 1.3.

```
is_a_pattern :  ENTITY is_be_VB a_a_DT type;
```

Listing 1.2. First simple version of the *is-a* pattern. `ENTITY` is a marking for the entities position.

---

[6] Abbreviations in Listing 1.1: ADJ = adjective, CD = cardinal number.

```
1 is_a_pattern : ENTITY FORM_OF_BE DETERMINER type;
2 FORM_OF_BE : ~[ \t\r\n]+ '_be_VB' ~[ \t\r\n]?;
3 DETERMINER : ~[ \t\r\n]+ '_' ~[ \t\r\n]+ '_DT';
```

Listing 1.3. Extended version of the *is-a* pattern.

With this iterative, incremental process, we further extended the grammar until we covered more than 90 % of the extracted phrases.[7]

4   Type Extraction

The pattern-based type extraction can be separated into two steps. The first step extracts type evidence strings from the text, while the second step creates a local type hierarchy based on the extracted string. In the following, we describe both steps in more detail.

4.1   Type String Extraction

To identify the type evidence string for a certain entity, CETUS extracts the string containing the type of a given entity from a given text using the grammar from above. Let us assume the following running example: CETUS processes the document as input with "Albert Einstein" marked as entity.

> In 1921, **Albert Einstein** got the Nobel Prize in Physics. He was a German-born theoretical physicist.

First, the Stanford Deterministic Coreference Resolution System is applied to replace the pronoun of the second sentence by "Albert Einstein".

> In 1921, **Albert Einstein** got the Nobel Prize in Physics. **Albert Einstein** was a German-born theoretical physicist.

After that, the text is split into sentences and the surface form of the entity is replaced by a placeholder.

> In 1921, **ENTITY** got the Nobel Prize in Physics.
> **ENTITY** was a German-born theoretical physicist.

A parser based on the grammar from Sect. 3.2 is applied to every sentence. While the first sentence is identified as not contained in the language of the grammar, the second sentence is identified to be in the language. Moreover, the parser identifies "German-born theoretical physicist" as evidence type string.

4.2   Local Type Hierarchy

Based on the extracted evidence type string, CETUS creates a local type hierarchy and links the given entity to the hierarchy. The type hierarchy comprises

---

[7] The complete grammar can be found in the projects source code repository.

classes that are generated automatically from the extracted string based on the second assumption of Sect. 3.2. Each class is generated by concatenating the words found in the extracted string using camel case. After a class has been created, the first word is removed and the next class is created. Every following class is a super class of the classes generated before. Finally, the entity is connected to all generated classes.

For our example, three classes would be generated and linked to the entity as shown in Fig. 1 and Listing 1.4[8].

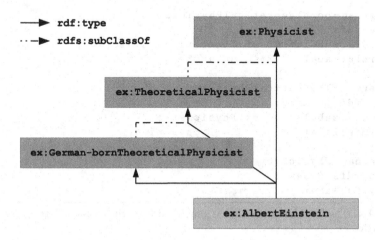

Fig. 1. Schema of the generated local hierarchy of the example.

5   Entity Type Linking Using YAGO

The linking of the generated classes to a KB can be done in two different ways. Our first approach, CETUS$_{YAGO}$, uses the labels of the automatically generated classes to find a matching class inside another, well-known KB. CETUS uses the YAGO ontology [7] which comprises a large class hierarchy and, thus, increases the chance to match one of these classes. YAGO itself contains more than 10 mio. entities and exceeds 350.000 classes.

First, we created an index containing the surface forms of the YAGO classes with a mapping to the class URIs. Second, for every class that has been generated during the extraction step described in Sect. 4, CETUS retrieves all YAGO classes with a label equal to the label of the generated class. All retrieved classes are linked to the local generated class using a `owl:equivalentClass` predicate.

After that, we are using a predefined mapping from the YAGO ontology to the DOLCE+DnS Ultra Lite ontology[9] to iterate through the class hierarchy

---

[8] The `rdfs` prefix stands for http://www.w3.org/2000/01/rdf-schema while the prefix `ex` could stay for every user defined vocabulary, e.g., http://example.com/.

[9] This mapping can be found inside the git repository of the project at https://github.com/AKSW/Cetus/blob/master/DOLCE_YAGO_links.nt.

from the linked classes to the root of the DOLCE ontology. The lowest DOLCE classes on these paths to the root are used as super type for the local generated classes and, thus, are used as types for the entity. The result for our running example can be seen in Fig. 2.[10]

```
1  ex:AlbertEinstein
2      a ex:German-bornTheoreticalPhysicist ,
3          ex:TheoreticalPhysicist , ex:Physicist .
4
5  ex:German-bornTheoreticalPhysicist
6      a rdfs:Class ;
7      rdfs:subClassOf ex:TheoreticalPhysicist ;
8      rdfs:label "German-born theoretical physicist" .
9
10 ex:German-TheoreticalPhysicist
11     a rdfs:Class ;
12     rdfs:subClassOf ex:Physicist ;
13     rdfs:label "theoretical physicist" .
14
15 ex:German-Physicist
16     a rdfs:Class ;
17     rdfs:label "physicist" .
```

Listing 1.4. The local hierarchy that is generated from the extracted string expressed using turtle.

6   Entity Type Linking Using FOX

A second approach for a type extraction baseline is the usage of one of the various, existing entity typing tools. For our second version CETUS$_{FOX}$, we are using FOX [13].

FOX is a framework based on ensemble learning for named entity recognition, an approach to increase the performance of state-of-the-art named entity recognition tools. It integrates four named entity recognition tools for the English language so far: the Stanford Named Entity Recognizer [8], the Illinois Named Entity Tagger [11], the Ottawa Baseline Information Extraction [9] and the Apache OpenNLP Name Finder [1]. It has been shown that the ensemble learning of named entity recognition tools with a Multilayer Perceptron lead to an increased performance. Unfortunately, FOX identifies only persons, locations and organizations in its current version.

CETUS$_{FOX}$ sends the given document to the FOX web-service for retrieving annotations. If the entity inside the document is found and typed by FOX, the type is used to choose one of the DOLCE+DnS Ultra Lite classes, see Table 2. The chosen class is used as super class for the automatically created classes.

---

[10] Throughout this paper, we use the prefix **yago** for http://yago-knowledge.org/resource/.

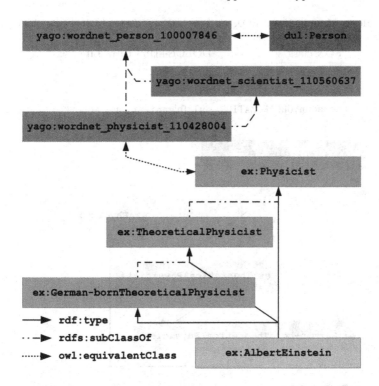

Fig. 2. Resulting type hierarchy that is created based on the YAGO ontology.

With respect to our running example, the FOX tool marks "Albert Einstein" as a person. Thus, the created classes would be defined as subclasses of dul:Person as shown in Fig. 3.

7   Evaluation

FOX and two other tools—Adel [5] and FRED [2]—participated in the first task, CETUS and two other tools—FRED [2] and OAK [3]—participated in the second task of the OKE Challenge 2015. The dataset of the first task used for the evaluation contains 101 documents and 99 documents for the evaluation of the second task.

7.1   OKE Challenge 2015 Task 1

First, we employed the off-the-shelf framework FOX to show that FOX is able to identify the relevant DOLCE types. The evaluation results of the first task are shown in Table 3 and the sub tasks for FOX are depicted in Table 4.

In the entity recognition sub task, FOX performs well (with a micro precision of ~ 0.96 and a macro precision of ~ 0.92) and reaches nearly the recall of the best system Adel. Unfortunately, FOX supports only three of the four

Table 2. Mapping from FOX classes to DOLCE+DnS Ultra Lite classes.

FOX class	DOLCE+DnS Ultra Lite class
scmsann:PERSON	dul:Person
scmsann:LOCATION	dul:Place
scmsann:ORGANIZATION	dul:Organization

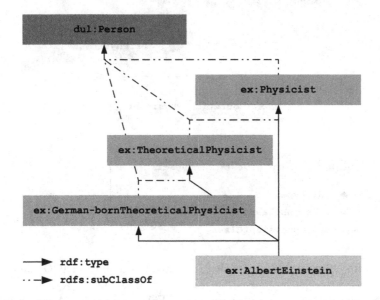

Fig. 3. Resulting type hierarchy that is created based on the results of FOX.

entity types in the OKE challenge in its current version. Thus, the recall and consequently the F1 score for entity linking and typing are low. We assume that the lack of supported entity types leads to FOX' inability to reach the best performance in the OKE Challenge 2015 task 1.

7.2 OKE Challenge 2015 Task 2

For evaluating the different systems, a local modified version of GERBIL [14] has been used. Since the official results contained only the results of CETUS$_{YAGO}$[11] we set up an instance of GERBIL and repeated the evaluation for both versions of CETUS. The results can be seen in Table 5. The tables show that both versions of CETUS outperform the other participants regarding the F1 score.

Table 6 shows the detailed results of the two steps of CETUS. It can be seen, that the pattern based recognition of the string containing the type of an entity performs well with a micro F1 measure of õ.7. However, there is still space for

---

[11] The results of the challenge can be found at https://github.com/anuzzolese/oke-challenge#results.

Table 3. Results of the OKE Challenge 2015 task 1

System	Micro			Macro		
	F1	Prec.	Recall	F1	Prec.	Recall
Adel	**0.61**	**0.69**	**0.54**	**0.60**	**0.69**	**0.54**
FOX	0.50	0.66	0.41	0.48	0.63	0.41
FRED	0.35	0.47	0.28	0.23	0.31	0.18

Table 4. Results for the different sub tasks of task 1

System	Micro			Macro		
	F1	Prec.	Recall	F1	Prec.	Recall
FOX (Entity Recognition)	0.68	0.96	0.52	0.65	0.92	0.53
FOX (Entity Linking)	0.50	0.70	0.38	0.46	0.65	0.38
FOX (Entity Typing)	0.35	0.35	0.35	0.37	0.37	0.37

Table 5. Results of the OKE Challenge 2015 task 2

System	Micro			Macro		
	F1	Prec.	Recall	F1	Prec.	Recall
$CETUS_{YAGO}$	**0.47**	0.45	**0.52**	**0.45**	0.42	**0.53**
$CETUS_{FOX}$	0.46	0.45	0.46	0.44	**0.42**	0.47
OAK@Sheffield	0.44	**0.52**	0.39	0.39	0.40	0.40
FRED	0.30	0.29	0.32	0.27	0.26	0.32

Table 6. Results for the different sub tasks of task 2

System	Micro			Macro		
	F1	Prec.	Recall	F1	Prec.	Recall
CETUS (Type Recognition)	0.70	0.69	0.70	0.66	0.64	0.72
$CETUS_{YAGO}$ (Type Linking)	0.25	0.20	0.34	0.23	0.20	0.34
$CETUS_{FOX}$ (Type Linking)	0.22	0.21	0.22	0.22	0.21	0.22

improvement. A large problem for this approach are formulations that have a different grammatical structure than those inside the DBpedia abstracts. Thus, a system with a better understanding of the internal structure of the sentence, e.g., by using parse trees, could avoid these problems.

Comparing both type linking approaches, it can be seen that both have a similar precision (see Table 6). But the YAGO-based approach has a higher recall leading to a slightly higher F1 score. The FOX-based type linking lacks the identification of types different to persons, organizations and locations. The YAGO-based type linking suffers from two main problems. First, some of the extracted local types cannot be matched to YAGO types. This might be solved by using a better search strategy for finding YAGO types with a similar label, e.g., trigram similarity. The second point of failure is the mapping from YAGO to DOLCE types. For some YAGO types there are no linked DOLCE types while for others the linked DOLCE types are very high inside the hierarchy leading to a coarse typing result and, thus, to a lower precision. A further improvement of the mapping between YAGO and DOLCE types could reduce these problems.

8   Conclusion

We presented CETUS—a pattern based type extraction that can be used as baseline for other approaches. Both versions—CETUS$_{YAGO}$ and CETUS$_{FOX}$— have been explained in detail and we showed the performance of FOX also on task 1. We showed how the first one uses a label matching for determining a super type for the automatically generated classes while the second is based on one of the various, existing entity typing tools. Both versions outperformed the competing systems during the OKE Challenge 2015. However, the evaluation pointed out several possibilities for further improvement.

Acknowledgements. This work has been supported by the FP7 project GeoKnow (GA No. 318159) and the BMWI Project SAKE (Project No. 01MD15006E).

References

1. Baldridge, J.: The opennlp project (2005)
2. Consoli, S., Reforgiato, D.: Using fred for named entity resolution, linking and typing for knowledge base population. In: Gandon, F., Sabou, M., Sack, H., Cabrio, E., Stankovic, M., Zimmermann, A. (eds.) Proceedings of the OKE Challenge 2015 co-located with the 12th Extended Semantic Web Conference (ESWC 2015). Springer International Publishing, Switzerland (2015)
3. Gao, J., Mazumdar, S.: Exploiting linked open data to uncover entity type. In: Gandon, F., Sabou, M., Sack, H., Cabrio, E., Stankovic, M., Zimmermann, A. (eds.) Proceedings of the OKE Challenge 2015 co-located with the 12th Extended Semantic Web Conference (ESWC 2015), pp. 51–62. Springer International Publishing, Switzerland (2015)
4. Hearst, M.A.: Automatic acquisition of hyponyms from large text corpora. In: COLING (1992)
5. Plu, G.R.J., Troncy, R.: An hybrid approach for entity recognition and linking. In: Gandon, F., Sabou, M., Sack, H., Cabrio, E., Stankovic, M., Zimmermann, A. (eds.) Proceedings of the OKE Challenge 2015 co-located with the 12th Extended Semantic Web Conference (ESWC 2015), pp. 28–39. Springer International Publishing, Switzerland (2015)
6. Lee, H., Chang, A., Peirsman, Y., Chambers, N., Surdeanu, M., Jurafsky, D.: Deterministic coreference resolution based on entity-centric, precision-ranked rules. Comput. Linguist. **39**(4), 885–916 (2013)
7. Mahdisoltani, F., Biega, J., Suchanek, F.: YAGO3: a knowledge base from multilingual Wikipedias. In: CIDR (2014)

8. Manning, C.D., Surdeanu, M., Bauer, J., Finkel, J., Bethard, S.J., McClosky, D.: The stanford CoreNLP natural language processing toolkit. In: Proceedings of 52nd Annual Meeting of the Association for Computational Linguistics: System Demonstrations, pp. 55–60 (2014)

9. Nadeau, D.: Balie-baseline information extraction: Multilingual information extraction from text with machine learning and natural language techniques. Technical report, University of Ottawa (2005)

10. Nadeau, D., Sekine, S.: A survey of named entity recognition and classification. Lingvisticae Investigationes **30**(1), 3–26 (2007)

11. Ratinov, L., Roth, D.: Design challenges and misconceptions in named entity recognition. In: Proceedings of the Thirteenth Conference on Computational Natural Language Learning, CoNLL 2009, pp. 147–155. Association for Computational Linguistics, Stroudsburg, PA, USA (2009)

12. Snow, R., Jurafsky, D., Ng, A.Y.: Learning syntactic patterns for automatic hypernym discovery. In: Advances in Neural Information Processing Systems (NIPS 2004), November 2004

13. Speck, R., Ngonga Ngomo, A.-C.: Ensemble learning for named entity recognition. In: Mika, P., et al. (eds.) ISWC 2014, Part I. LNCS, vol. 8796, pp. 519–534. Springer, Heidelberg (2014)

14. Usbeck, R., Röder, M., Ngomo, A.-C.N., Baron, C., Both, A., Brümmer, M., Ceccarelli, D., Cornolti, M., Cherix, D., Eickmann, B., Ferragina, P., Lemke, C., Moro, A., Navigli, R., Piccinno, F., Rizzo, G., Sack, H., Speck, R., Troncy, R., Waitelonis, J., Wesemann, L.: GERBIL - general entity annotation benchmark framework. In: 24th WWW conference (2015)

A Hybrid Approach for Entity Recognition and Linking

Julien Plu[✉], Giuseppe Rizzo, and Raphaël Troncy

EURECOM, Sophia Antipolis, France
{julien.plu,giuseppe.rizzo,raphael.troncy}@eurecom.fr

Abstract. Numerous research efforts are tackling the entity recognition and entity linking tasks resulting in a large body of literature. One could roughly categorize the proposed approaches in two different strategies: linguistic-based and semantic-based methods. In this paper, we present our participation to the OKE challenge, where we experiment with a hybrid approach, which combines the strength of a linguistic-based method augmented by a high coverage in the annotation obtained by using a large knowledge base as entity dictionary. The main goal of this hybrid approach is to improve the extraction and recognition level to get the best recall in order to apply a pruning step. On the training set, the results are promising and the breakdown figures are comparable with the state of the art performance of top ranked systems. Our hybrid approach has been ranked first to the OKE Challenge on the test set.

Keywords: Entity recognition · Entity linking · Entity filtering · Learning to rank · OKE challenge

1 Introduction

The first task of the Open Knowledge Extraction (OKE) challenge organized at ESWC 2015 aims to advance research in entity extraction, typing (recognition) and linking for Knowledge Base population. In this paper, we present a hybrid approach for extracting, typing and linking entities from textual documents, to a targeted knowledge base that has been indexed beforehand.

Following the challenge requirements, we make use of the 2014 snapshot of DBpedia as the targeted knowledge base. Our proposed workflow is broken down into three tasks: entity recognition, entity linking and entity pruning. Entity recognition is composed of two subtasks: (*i*) entity extraction that refers to the task of spotting mentions that can be entities in the text and (*ii*) entity typing that refers to the task of assigning them a proper type. In the following, we use the terms extraction and typing to refer to those two subtasks. Entity linking refers to the task of disambiguating the mention in a targeted knowledge base, and it is also often composed of two subtasks: generating candidates and ranking them according to various scoring functions. Entity pruning aims to filter out candidates that are unlikely to be relevant for the domain considered.

© Springer International Publishing Switzerland 2015
F. Gandon et al. (Eds.): SemWebEval 2015, CCIS 548, pp. 28–39, 2015.
DOI: 10.1007/978-3-319-25518-7_3

The remainder of this paper is structured as follows. We first present some recent related work for both the entity recognition and the entity linking tasks (Sect. 2). Next, we describe the modular architecture (Sect. 3) and we detail its current implementation (Sect. 4). We present our experiment settings and we provide preliminary results on the OKE challenge training dataset (Sect. 5). Finally, we conclude and outline some future work (Sect. 6).

2   Related Work

In this section, we present several top-performing systems that recognize and link entities in text. We distinguish the approaches proposed for the entity recognition (Sect. 2.1) and the entity linking (Sect. 2.2) steps.

2.1   Entity Recognition

Numerous approaches have been proposed to tackle the task of recognizing entities in a text. Amongst the recent and best performing systems, WAT builds on top of TagME algorithms and follows the three steps approach we are advocating: extraction, linking and pruning [9]. For the extraction, a gazetteer that contains wiki-anchors, titles and redirect pages with a list of all their possible links ranked according to a probability score is used. The extraction performance can also be tuned with an optional binary classifier (SVM with linear or RBF kernel) using statistics (features) for each entity referenced in the gazetteer. For typing the entities, WAT relies on OpenNLP NER with the types `PERSON`, `LOCATION` and `ORGANIZATION`. One limitation of this method is that anything matching an entry in the gazetteer, including terms that are common words such as verbs or prepositions, is extracted. Furthermore, the recognition of an entity is limited to the kind of mentions that can be typed by OpenNLP NER. If a mention does not exist in Wikipedia, it cannot be extracted by the WAT system.

Similar to WAT, DBpedia Spotlight uses a gazetteer containing a set of labels from the DBpedia lexicalization dataset for the extraction step [7]. More precisely, the LingPipe Exact Dictionary-Based Chunker with the Aho-Corasick string distance measure is being used. Extracts that only contain verbs, adjectives, adverbs and prepositions can be detected using the LingPipe part-of-speech tagger and then discarded. For the typing step, DBpedia Spotlight re-uses the type of the link provided by DBpedia. The limitation of this method is again the DBpedia dependency, since mentions that do not exist in this knowledge base cannot be extracted nor recognized.

A different kind of approach is the one developed by AIDA [5]. For the recognition step, AIDA uses Stanford NER. A limitation of this approach is that it becomes dependent of the specific model used by the CRF algorithm of Stanford NER. A comparable approach to ours is the one used in Babelfy [8]. For the extraction step, a part-of-speech tagger is used in order to identify the segments in the text which contain at least one noun and that are substring of the entities referenced in BabelNet. For the typing step, the Babelnet categories are used.

The limitation of this approach is that only entities appearing in BabelNet can be extracted which prevents to recognize "emerging" entities [4].

2.2 Entity Linking

Once recognized (extracted and typed), entities are linked (disambiguated) according to a reference knowledge base. Various approaches are again reported in the literature. The WAT system uses two methods, namely voting-based and graph-based algorithms [9]. The voting-based approach assigns one score to each entity. The entity having the highest score is then selected. The graph-based approach builds a graph where the nodes correspond to mentions or candidates (entities) and the edges correspond to either mention-entity or entity-entity relationships, each of these two kinds of edges being weighted with three possible scores: (i) identity, (ii) commonness that is the prior probability $Pr(e|m)$ and (iii) context similarity that is the BM25 similarity score used by Lucene[1]. The goal is to find the subgraph that interlinks all the mentions.

AIDA uses a similar approach than the graph-based method of WAT. The graph is built in the same way but only one score for each kind of edge (mention-entity or entity-entity) is proposed. The score used to weight the mention-entity edges is a combination of similarity measure and popularity while the score used to weight the entity-entity edges is based on a combination of Wikipedia-link overlap and type distance [5]. Another graph-based approach is the one used by Babelfy. Two main algorithms have been developed: random walk and a heuristic for finding the subgraph that contains most of the relations between the recognized mentions and candidates. The nodes are pairs (mention,entity) and the edges correspond to existing relationships in BabelNet which are scored. The semantic graph is built using word sense disambiguation (WSD) that extracts lexicographic concepts and entity linking for matching strings with resources described in a knowledge base.

In contrast, DBpedia Spotlight relies on the so-called TF*ICF (Term Frequency-Inverse Candidate Frequency) score computed for each entity. The goal of this score is to show that the discriminative strength of a mention is inversely proportional to the number of candidates it is associated with. This means that a mention that commonly co-occurs with many candidates is less discriminative.

The limitation of systems such as AIDA, Babelfy and DBpedia Spotlight is that they do not include a pruning step that would remove possible false positive candidates. This requires a strong entity recognition system since precision and recall can only fall down at the linking stage.

3   A Hybrid Approach for Entity Recognition and Linking

Our proposed system implements a three steps approach: (i) named entity recognition, (ii) named entity linking, and (iii) named entity pruning. In the following, we detail each of those steps.

---

[1] http://lucene.apache.org/.

Table 1. List of features contained in the index and used by the pruning algorithm

ID	Feature	Definition
1	title	the title of the entity
2	URI	the URI associated to the entity
3	redirects	the list of all the redirect pages associated to the entity
4	disambiguation	the title of the disambiguation pages associated to the entity if there is at least one
5	types	the full type hirarchy of the entity, from the highest to the fine-grained type
6	pageRank	the PageRank score of the DBpedia resource corresponding to the entity
7	hits	the HITS score of the DBpedia resource corresponding to the entity
8	inlinks	the number of inLinks of the DBpedia resource corresponding to the entity
9	outlinks	the number of outLinks of the DBpedia resource corresponding to the entity
10	length	the length in number of characters of the associated Wikipedia page of the entity
11	numRedirects	the number of redirects links associated to the entity
12	surfaceForms	the different surface forms used to call the entity in all the Wikipedia articles
13	quotes	the direct outbound links and the number of time they appear in the article of the corresponding entity

3.1 Named Entity Recognition

We rely on a linguistic approach for the first stage of the system. More precisely, we rely on the grammatical meaning of the mentions that are spotted and typed in a text. This ensures a robust performance for well-written texts. Those linguistic approach are:

1. Part-Of-Speech tagging system where we will only keep the singular and plural proper nouns.
2. Named Entity Recognition system to extract and type the named entities.
3. Gazetteers to re-enforce the extraction bringing a robust spotting for well-known mentions.

3.2 Named Entity Linking

This step is composed of three sub-tasks: (*i*) entity generation, where an index is built on top of both DBpedia2014[2] and a dump of the Wikipedia articles[3] dated

---

[2] http://wiki.dbpedia.org/services-resources/datasets/datasets2014.
[3] https://dumps.wikimedia.org/enwiki/.

from October 2014 to get possible candidates; (*ii*) filtering candidates based on direct inbound and outbound links from Wikipedia; (*iii*) entity ranking based on a proposed ranking function. If an entity does not have an entry in the knowledge base, we normally link it to NIL following the TAC KBP convention [6]. However, for the OKE challenge, we do not make use of NIL but we instead create a new URI to describe not-in-the-knowledge-base entities in order to populate DBpedia.

The core of this part grounds on the index created on top of the DBpedia 2014 Knowledge Base and the Wikipedia dump. Each record of the index has a key which corresponds to a DBpedia resource, while the features are listed in Table 1.

For each mention, we have potentially many candidates, while some of them have to be filtered out because they are not related to the context. With all the candidates of each mention, we create a graph and we find the densest graph between all of these candidates, similarly to [8]. Our approach is, however, slightly different: we use the feature number 13 (quotes) described in the Table 1 and not BabelNet in order to build the graph. The edges of the graph are weighted according to the number of occurrence of the link between each candidates. For example, given the Wikipedia article describing the Eiffel Tower, if there is one outbound link to Paris in Texas and three to Paris in France, both candidates (Paris in Texas and Paris in France) will be kept. However, the weight of Paris in France will be higher than the one of Paris in Texas. In case all candidates of a mention do not have any relation with any other candidate of the other mentions, all its candidates are kept.

To create those pairs, we used an in-house library to parse the Wikipedia dump. We first tried several libraries that parse Wikipedia such as Sweble[4], GWTWiki[5] and wikipedia-parser[6]. However, these libraries are either too complex to use for the simple extraction we need or too greedy in terms of memory. We have therefore developed our own library in order to extract the pairs (Wikipedia article title, number of times the title appears in the article).

Given an extracted mention, we implement a ranking algorithm based on a string similarity measure between the extracted mention and the title of the link, the set of redirect and the set of disambiguation pages. The rank score of the link, computed by the rank function $r(l)$, is then weighted by a Page Rank score of the referenced resources.

$$r(l) = (a \cdot L(m, title) + b \cdot max(L(m, R)) + c \cdot max(L(m, D))) \cdot PR(l) \quad (1)$$

where $a = \frac{4}{7}, b = \frac{1}{7}, c = \frac{2}{7}$ are empirically defined. In our experiment, L corresponds to the Levenshtein distance, R and D are respectively the set of redirect and disambiguation pages and PR refers to the PageRank score of the link.

---

[4] http://sweble.org/.
[5] https://code.google.com/p/gwtwiki/.
[6] https://github.com/Stratio/wikipedia-parser.

3.3 Named Entity Pruning

At this stage, each extracted mention has been either linked to a DBpedia resource or to NIL. Applying a supervised learning approach, we plan to increase the precision of the system by discarding mentions that are not in the scope of the ones observed in the labeled data. The prediction model is built using the features from 6 to 11 listed in Table 1 and the rank function $r(l)$.

4 System Implementation

We derived three different pipelines of the proposed system that we name respectively **Pipeline_1**, **Pipeline_2** and **Pipeline_3**. In the reminder of this section, we describe the different configurations of those pipelines. The entity linking and entity pruning steps are the same for all the three pipelines while the entity recognition step has a different configuration for the three pipelines: **Pipeline_1** favors a linguistic approach with gazetteer, **Pipeline_2** uses a supervised NER model and **Pipeline_3** combines the two approaches.

4.1 Pipeline_1

We generate candidates by selecting the proper noun in the singular (NNP) and the plural form (NNPS) of the part-of-speech tagging. Our POS tagging system is the Stanford NLP POS Tagger [10] with the model *english-bidirectional-distsim* trained on WSJ[7] sections 0-18 using a bidirectional architecture and including word shape and distributional similarity features.

To increase the coverage of the system in correctly annotating `dul:Role` entities, the current pipeline implements two gazetteers for job names and nationalities. The two gazetteers are built using the list of jobs and nationalities from the corresponding English Wikipedia pages. This process generates the types of the extracted entities, and they are linked to them.

Each proper noun is then looked up in the index, and a set of matching links are retrieved. Those links are then sorted according to the ranking function $r(l)$, and the first one is considered to be the entity link of the mention. The index is built using Lucene v5 and requires 44 h to be built on a 20 core CPU at 2.5 Ghz with 64 GB RAM machine. A possible improvement could be to parallelize, or distribute this process in order to decrease the index building time.

At this stage, the entities typed are the `dul:Role` ones. For the others, a set of manual alignment drives the typing process. The alignments are meant to map the DBpedia types with the entities typed as `dul:Person`, `dul:Location` and `dul:Organization`. Often, in retrieving the whole hierarchy of the fine-grained type from a DBpedia resource, the type given is this hierarchy. Traversing the T-Box, we label the entity with the type in the hierarchy learned from the manual alignment process. The `dul` types used have the same name than the one used by DBpedia so the alignment is quite simple: `dul:Place` $\sim$

---

[7] http://www.wsj.com.

dbpedia:Place, dul:Person ∼ dbpedia:Person and dul:Organization ∼ dbpedia:Organisation.

To favor the precision, we filter out the entities that do not follow the ones observed in the labeled data. We use the so-called pruning stage, which relies on a properly trained KNN classifier [1] with the features set listed in Sect. 3.3. To train this classifier, we annotate each value coming from the results as false if they do not appear in the gold standard (training set) and as yes if they appear.

4.2 Pipeline_2

A properly trained Stanford NER [3] is used as a named entity recognizer. The type is statistically predicted according to the observed labels in the training data.

The linking step follows the same strategy than the one described for the Pipeline_1. Hence, each named entity is looked up in the index, and a set of matching links are retrieved which are again sorted according to the rank function $r(l)$. Similarly, we use the so-called pruning stage (using a KNN classifier trained with the features set listed in Sect. 3.3) to increase the precision.

4.3 Pipeline_3

This pipeline presents a hybrid approach which implements both an annotation mechanism leaded by a properly trained supervised learning entity recognizer, Stanford NER [3], and a re-enforced mechanism of NNP/NNPS detection, Stanford POS tagger [10] trained with newswire content.

We do make use of our two previously defined gazetteers for job names and nationalities in order to increase the coverage of the system in correctly extracting dul:Role entities.

Sometimes, at least two extractors (Stanford NER, Stanford POS tagger or the gazetteer) extract overlapped mentions. For example, given the two extracted mentions *States of America* from Stanford NER and *United States* from Stanford POS tagger (both with the settings described in the previous sections), we detect that there is an overlap between both mentions, so we take the union of both boundaries to create a new mention and we remove the two others. We obtain the mention *United States of America* with the type provided by Stanford NER. In the case that one mention is included in another one (nested mentions) we take the longest one. For example, if *United States* and *States* are extracted, only the first one will be kept while the second one will be removed. If the one removed comes from Stanford NER, the original type associated to the removed mention is kept.

The linking step follows again the same strategy than in the previous two pipelines where we use our index to look up entities and to return matching links. The same pruning stage is also used for increasing precision.

5 Experimental Settings and Results

5.1 Statistics of the Oracle

The training dataset provided by the OKE challenge organizers is composed of a set of 95 annotated sentences using the NIF ontology[8]. The average length of the sentences is 124 chars. In total, the dataset contains 337 mentions corresponding to 290 distinct entities that belong to one of the four types: dul:Place, dul:Person, dul:Organization and dul:Role. 256 entities (88 %) are linked within DBpedia, while 33 (12 %) are not. The breakdown of those annotations per type is provided in the Table 2.

Table 2. Statistics of the oracle

Type	nb mentions	nb entities	nb mentions disambiguated (%)	nb entities disambiguated (%)
dul:Place	62	61	58 (93 %)	57 (93 %)
dul:Person	126	87	110 (87 %)	71 (81 %)
dul:Organisation	98	95	88 (90 %)	85 (89 %)
dul:Role	51	47	47 (92 %)	43 (91 %)
Total	337	290	303 (90 %)	256 (88 %)

5.2 Experimental Settings

We applied a 4-fold cross validation of the released training set. In each fold of the cross validation, a train and a test sets are generated and respectively used for building the supervised learning models and for benchmarking the output of the model with the expected results of the test set.

5.3 Results on the Training Set

We have tested the three pipelines against the OKE training set provided. We only consider strict match for the extraction (exact boundaries), recognition (exact type) and linking (exact disambiguation uri) tasks. We use the neleval scorer[9] to compute our performance, given the measures detailed in Table 3.

The results are divided in two parts: Table 4 shows the results obtained for each of our three pipelines without running the pruning step while the Table 5 shows the results obtained when running the pruning step for each pipeline.

We can see that the pruning step increases significantly the precision but at the cost of decreasing tremendously the recall. Overall, it performs poorly as it removes too many mentions to get good results at the linking stage. Nevertheless, it provides correct results at the recognition stage. This idea has been inspired by the WAT system [9]. However, the features we choose probably differ from the ones used in WAT resulting in this serious performance drop.

---

[8] http://persistence.uni-leipzig.org/nlp2rdf/ontologies/nif-core.
[9] https://github.com/wikilinks/neleval.

Table 3. Measures used in the evaluation for each task

Task	Measure
Extraction	strong_match_mention
Recognition	strong_typed_mention_match
Linking	strong_link_match

Table 4. Breakdown figures per task on the OKE challenge training set for the three pipelines without the pruning. Higher values per row for each metric are in bold.

Task	Pipeline_1			Pipeline_2			Pipeline_3		
	P	R	F_1	P	R	F_1	P	R	F_1
Extraction	49.48	65	56.18	**93.43**	85.95	**89.53**	83.55	**93.5**	88.2
Recognition	30.6	40.25	34.75	**93.05**	85.63	**89.15**	81.65	**91.38**	86.23
Linking	35.83	50.53	41.95	**65.98**	43.13	**52.13**	53.7	**46.63**	49.9

Table 5. Breakdown figures per task on the OKE challenge training set for the three pipelines with the pruning. Higher values per row for each metric are in bold.

Task	Pipeline_1			Pipeline_2			Pipeline_3		
	P	R	F_1	P	R	F_1	P	R	F_1
Extraction	44.18	12.6	19.58	**94.53**	**49.63**	**64.75**	88.78	41.93	56.7
Recognition	25.18	7.1	11.08	**93.93**	**49.3**	**64.33**	87.28	41.23	55.75
Linking	32.93	9.98	15.3	**69.98**	19.18	29.95	55.98	**21.13**	**30.6**

We stay positive on the fact that a pruning step can typically help increasing the precision when a real high recall at the recognition level is obtained. In terms of recall at the recognition level, the *Pipeline_3* without pruning provides the best results. This means that our hybrid approach (mix between NLP, NER and gazetteer approaches) is the most appropriate one to get a high recall at the recognition level enabling to apply a pruning strategy to improve the precision. We observe that there is still a margin of progress to correct the performance drop between the recognition stage and the final results at the linking stage.

5.4 Comparison with Other Tools on the Training Set

We have developed a process to evaluate the performance of three other tools on the same dataset, namely AIDA[10], TagMe[11], DBpedia Spotlight[12] and Babelfy[13]. The results are presented in the Table 6. The recognition level is not evaluated since the tested tools does not provide the types used by the challenge.

---

[10] https://gate.d5.mpi-inf.mpg.de/webaida/.
[11] http://tagme.di.unipi.it/.
[12] http://dbpedia-spotlight.github.io/demo/.
[13] http://babelfy.org/.

Table 6. Breakdown figures per task on the OKE challenge training set for AIDA, Tagme, DBpedia Spotlight and Babelfy. Higher values per row for each metric are in bold.

Task	AIDA			TagMe			DBpedia Spotlight			Babelfy		
	P	R	F_1	P	R	F_1	P	R	F_1	P	R	F_1
Extraction	**69.4**	49.65	57.78	49.15	**85.6**	**62.43**	35.55	52.18	42.25	4.5	18.83	7.2
Linking	**54.23**	43.1	47.98	42.43	**82.43**	**55.98**	22.95	37.35	28.4	3.8	16.18	6.15

Table 7. Breakdown figures per task on the OKE challenge test set for the pipeline 3 with and without the pruning step

Task	without pruning			with pruning		
	P	R	F_1	P	R	F_1
Extraction	78.2	65.4	71.2	83.8	9.3	16.8
Recognition	65.8	54.8	59.8	75.7	8.4	15.1
Linking	49.4	46.6	48	57.9	6.2	11.1

Table 8. Breakdown figures per task on the OKE challenge test set for AIDA, Tagme, DBpedia Spotlight and Babelfy. Higher values per row for each metric are in bold.

Task	AIDA			TagMe			DBpedia Spotlight			Babelfy		
	P	R	F_1	P	R	F_1	P	R	F_1	P	R	F_1
Extraction	**55.7**	49.1	**52.2**	39.7	61.7	48.3	40.3	52.6	45.6	21.4	**62**	31.9
Linking	**51.6**	43.9	**47.4**	28.5	**54.9**	37.5	28.3	45.7	34.9	25.4	54.5	34.7

We used the public API of those systems while applying the default settings for each one.

TagME clearly outperforms all systems at the linking level. Nevertheless, the results show that our hybrid approach provides the best results at the extraction stage, motivating the need for researching better linking strategy.

5.5 Results on the Test Set

The official figures of the challenge are published at https://github.com/anuzzolese/oke-challenge#results. The figures provided on the official web site do not provide a breakdown view that we propose in the Table 7 computed with the nelevel scorer. We have cleaned the test set in order to correct visible errors such as mix of links and phrases for the same entity, missing extracted entities, wrong type, etc. The pipeline used is the *Pipeline_3* with and without the pruning step (Table 7).

5.6 Comparison with Other Tools on the Test Set

As for the training set, we have also computed the performance of AIDA, TagMe, DBpedia Spotlight and Babelfy on the test set using the same standard settings

(Table 8). Contrarily to the training set, this time, our approach slightly out-performs (in terms of F1) the best performing tool (AIDA) at the linking stage. This is largely due to our excellent performance at the extraction stage.

6 Conclusion and Future Work

In this paper, we have described three different pipelines of a hybrid system we have developed to address the OKE challenge. We show that a successful app-roach relies on effectively using a hybrid approach, which exploits both linguistic features and semantic features as one can extract and index from a large Knowl-edge Base such as DBpedia. As future work, we plan to focus on improving the linking task by doing better graph based algorithms with a more accurate rank-ing function and to further develop our pruning strategy by reviewing the list of feature used to show the full potential of our hybrid approach. We plan as well to improve the way we build and make use of gazetteers in order to further increase the recall at the extraction stage.

Acknowledgments. This work was partially supported by the EIT Digital 3cixty project and by French National Research Agency (ANR) within the WAVE Project, under grant number ANR-12-CORD-0027.

References

1. Aha, D., Kibler, D.: Instance-based learning algorithms. Mach. Learn. **6**, 37–66 (1991)
2. Cano, A.E., Rizzo, G., Varga, A., Rowe, M., Milan, S., Dadzie, A.-S.: Making sense of microposts (#microposts2014) named entity extraction & linking challenge. In: 4th International Workshop on Making Sense of Microposts, Seoul, South Korea (2014)
3. Finkel, J.R., Grenager, T., Manning, C.: Incorporating non-local information into information extraction systems by gibbs sampling. In: 43rd Annual Meeting on Association for Computational Linguistics (ACL), pp. 363–370, Stroudsburg, PA, USA (2005)
4. Hoffart, J., Altun, Y., Weikum, G.: Discovering emerging entities with ambiguous names. In: 23rd International Conference on World Wide Web (WWW), pp. 385–396, Seoul, Korea (2014)
5. Hoffart, J., Yosef, M.A., Bordino, I., Fürstenau, H., Pinkal, M., Spaniol, M., Taneva, B., Thater, S., Weikum, G.: Robust disambiguation of named entities in text. In: 8th Conference on Empirical Methods in Natural Language Processing (EMNLP), pp. 782–792, Stroudsburg, PA, USA (2011)
6. Ji, H., Nothman, J., Hachey, B.: Overview of TAC-KBP2014 entity discovery and linking tasks. In: Text Analysis Conference (TAC), Gaithersburg, USA (2014)
7. Mendes, P.N., Jakob, M., García-Silva, A., Bizer, C.: DBpedia spotlight: shed-ding light on the web of documents. In: 7th International Conference on Semantic Systems (I-Semantics), pp. 1–8 (2011)
8. Moro, A., Raganato, A., Navigli, R.: Entity linking meets word sense disambigua-tion: a unified approach. TACL **2**, 231–244 (2014)

9. Piccinno, F., Ferragina, P.: From TagME to WAT: a new entity annotator. In: 1st ACM International Workshop on Entity Recognition & Disambiguation (ERD), pp. 55–62, Gold Coast, Australia (2014)

10. Toutanova, K., Christopher, D.: Enriching the knowledge sources used in a maximum entropy part-of-speech tagger. In: North American Chapter of the Association for Computational Linguistics (HLT-NAACL), pp. 252–259, Edmond, Canada (2003)

11. Usbeck, R., Röder, M., Ngonga Ngomo, A.-C., Baron, C., Both, A., Brümmer, M., Ceccarelli, D., Cornolti, M., Cherix, D., Eickmann, B., Ferragina, P., Lemke, C., Moro, A., Navigli, R., Piccinno, F., Rizzo, G., Sack, H., Speck, R., Troncy, R., Waitelonis, J., Wesemann, L.: GERBIL - general entity annotation benchmark Framework. In: 24th World Wide Web Conference (WWW), Florence, Italy (2015)

Using FRED for Named Entity Resolution, Linking and Typing for Knowledge Base Population

Sergio Consoli and Diego Reforgiato Recupero$^{(\boxtimes)}$

STLab-ISTC Consiglio Nazionale Delle Ricerche, Catania, Italy
`diego.reforgiato@istc.cnr.it`

Abstract. FRED is a machine reader for extracting RDF graphs that are linked to LOD and compliant to Semantic Web and Linked Data patterns. We describe the capabilities of FRED as a semantic middleware for semantic web applications. In particular, we will show (i) how FRED recognizes and resolves named entities, (ii) how it links them to existing knowledge base, and (iii) how it gives them a type. Given a sentence in any language, it provides different semantic functionalities (frame detection, topic extraction, named entity recognition, resolution and coreference, terminology extraction, sense tagging and disambiguation, taxonomy induction, semantic role labeling, type induction) by means of a versatile user-interface, which can be recalled as REST Web service. The system can be freely used at http://wit.istc.cnr.it/stlab-tools/fred.

1 Introduction

The vision of the Semantic Web (SW) is to populate the Web with machine understandable data so that intelligent agents are able to automatically interpret its content, just like humans do by inspecting Web content, and assist users in performing a significant number of tasks, relieving them of cognitive overload. The Linked Data movement [1] kicked-off the vision by realising a key bootstrap in publishing machine understandable information mainly taken from structured data (typically databases) or semi-structured data (e.g. Wikipedia infoboxes). However, most of the Web content consists of natural language text, hence a main challenge is to extract as much relevant knowledge as possible from this content, and publish them in the form of Semantic Web triples.

In this paper we employ *FRED* [15], a machine reader for the Semantic Web, to address the first two tasks of the Open Knowledge Extraction (OKE) Challenge at the European Semantic Web Conference (ESWC) 2015, which focuses on the production of new knowledge aimed at either populating and enriching existing knowledge bases or creating new ones. The first task defined in the Challenge focuses on extracting concepts, individuals, properties, and statements that not necessarily exist already in a target knowledge base whereas the second task addresses entity typing and class induction. Then results for the two tasks are represented according to Semantic Web standard in order to be directly injected

© Springer International Publishing Switzerland 2015
F. Gandon et al. (Eds.): SemWebEval 2015, CCIS 548, pp. 40–50, 2015.
DOI: 10.1007/978-3-319-25518-7_4

in linked datasets and their ontologies. This is in line with available efforts in the community[1] to uniform results of existing knowledge extraction (KE) methods to make them directly reusable for populating the SW. Indeed, most of the work addressed so far in the literature on knowledge extraction and discovery are focused on linking extracted facts and entities to concepts already existing on available Knowledge Bases (KB).

The described system, FRED, is a Semantic Web machine reader able to produce a RDF/OWL frame-based representation of a text. Machine reading generally relies on bootstrapped, self-supervised Natural Language Processing (NLP) performed on basic tasks, in order to extract knowledge from text. Machine reading is typically much less accurate than human reading, but can process massive amounts of text in reasonable time, can detect regularities hardly noticeable by humans, and its results can be reused by machines for applied tasks. FRED performs a hybrid (part of the components are trained, part are rule-based), self-supervised variety of machine reading that generates RDF graph representations out of the knowledge extracted from text by tools dedicated to basic NLP tasks. Such graph representations extend and improve NLP output, and are typically customized for application tasks.

FRED integrates, transforms, improves, and abstracts the output of several NLP tools. It performs deep semantic parsing by reusing Boxer [2], which in turn uses a statistical parser (C&C) producing Combinatory Categorial Grammar trees, and thousands of heuristics that exploit existing lexical resources and gazetteers to generate structures according to Discourse Representation Theory (DRT) [10], i.e. a formal semantic representation of text through an event (neo-Davidsonian) semantics.

The basic NLP tasks performed by Boxer, and reused by FRED, include: event detection (FRED uses DOLCE+DnS[2] [4]), semantic role labeling, first-order logic representation of predicate-argument structures, logical operators scoping (called *boxing*), modality detection, tense representation, entity recognition using TAGME[3], word sense disambiguation (the next version is going to use BabelNet[4]), DBpedia for expanding tacit knowledge extracted from text, etc. All is integrated and semantically enriched in order to provide a Semantic Web-oriented reading of a text.

FRED reengineers DRT/Boxing discourse representation structures according to SW and linked data design practices in order to represent events, role labeling, and boxing as typed n-ary logical patterns in RDF/OWL. The main class for typing events in FRED is dul:Event[5]. In addition, some variables created by Boxer as discourse referents are reified as individuals when they refer to something that has a role in the formal semantics of the sentence.

Linguistic Frames [12], Ontology Design Patterns [7], open data, and various vocabularies are reused throughout FRED's pipeline in order to resolve, align,

---

[1] E.g. http://aksw.org/Projects/GERBIL.html.

[2] D. U. L. Ontology. http://www.ontologydesignpatterns.org/ont/dul/dul.owl.

[3] http://tagme.di.unipi.it/.

[4] http://babelnet.org/.

[5] Prefix dul: stands for http://www.ontologydesignpatterns.org/ont/dul/dul.owl#.

or enrich extracted data and ontologies. The most used include: VerbNet[6], for disambiguation of verb-based events; WordNet-RDF[7] and OntoWordNet [6] for the alignment of classes to WordNet and DOLCE; DBpedia for the resolution and/or disambiguation of named entities, as well as for enriching the graph with existing facts known to hold between those entities; schema.org (among others) for typing the recognized named entities. For Named Entity Recognition (NER) and Resolution (a.k.a. Entity Linking) FRED relies on TAGME [3], an algorithmic NER resolver to Wikipedia that heavily uses sentence and Wikipedia context to disambiguate named entities.

Besides the graph visualization[8] displayed using Graphviz[9], and the triple output, FRED can be recalled also as a REST API with RDF serialization in many syntaxes so that everyone can build online end-user applications that integrate, visualize, analyze, combine and infer the available knowledge at the desired level of granularity.

FRED is also accessible by means of a Python API, namely *fredlib*. It exposes features for retrieving FRED graphs from user-specified sentences, and managing them. More specifically, a simple Python function hides details related to the communication with the FRED service and returns to the user a FRED graph object that is easily manageable. FRED graph objects expose methods for retrieving useful information, including the set of individual and class nodes, equivalences and type information, categories of FRED nodes (events, situations, qualities, general concepts) and categories of edges (roles and non roles). *fredlib* supports *rdflib*[10] (for managing RDF graphs) and *networkx*[11] (for managing complex networks) libraries. It can be freely downloaded[12].

Additional visual interfaces to FRED can be experienced in the Sheldon[13] framework. Potentially, each stakeholder interested in semantic aggregate information for multilingual text could be a customer of the system. As FRED has been successfully applied [5,6,8,9,11,14–17] in the past in several domains, we want to move forward towards the market uptake exploitation; in fact, the foundation of a start-up exploiting FRED's technology (with only commercially-viable components) as one of its main cutting-edge products is currently on-going.

The rest of this paper is organized as follows: Sect. 2 introduces FRED and shows how it works. Section 3 discusses how we addressed the first two tasks requirements of the challenge; in particular, Sect. 3.1 shows the capabilities of FRED that we used to solve task 1 requirements (named entity resolution, linking, typing for knowledge base population) whereas Sect. 3.2 shows FRED's capabilities for solving task 2 (entity typing and knowledge base enrichment). Section 4 include the description of the datasets and the evaluation of the challengers' systems (including the one we propose in this paper) on those

---

[6] T. V. project. http://verbs.colorado.edu/~mpalmer/projects/verbnet.html.

[7] http://www.w3.org/TR/wordnet-rdf/.

[8] Available at http://wit.istc.cnr.it/stlab-tools/fred/.

[9] Graphviz - Graph Visualization Software, http://www.graphviz.org/.

[10] http://code.google.com/p/rdflib/.

[11] https://networkx.github.io/.

[12] http://wit.istc.cnr.it/stlab-tools/fred/fredlib.

[13] Sheldon - available at http://wit.istc.cnr.it/stlab-tools/sheldon/.

datasets for the two tasks mentioned above. Section 5 draws conclusions and sketches out future directions where we are headed.

2   FRED at Work

FRED has a practical value to either general Web users or application developers. General Web users can appreciate the graph representation of a given sentence using the visualization tools provided, and semantics expert can analyze the RDF triples in more detail. More important, application developers can use the REST API for empowering applications using FRED capabilities. Developers of semantic technology applications can use FRED by automatically annotating text, by filtering FRED graphs with SPARQL, and by enriching their datasets with FRED graphs, and with the knowledge coming from linkable datasets.

FRED's user main interface, available at http://wit.istc.cnr.it/stlab-tools/fred/, allows users to type a sentence in any language, to specify some optional features, and to decide the format of the output to produce. Available formats include RDF/XML, RDF/JSON, TURTLE, N3, NT, DAG, and the intuitive graph visualization using Graphviz.

The reader will notice that FRED will always provide the results in English, although Bing Translation APIs[14] have been used and embedded within FRED to support users specifying their input sentence in any desired language. If the used language of the sentence is different than English, then the tag $<BING\_LANG : lang>$ needs to precede the sentence, where *lang* indicates a code for the language of the current sentence[15]. For example, the sentence:

$<BING\_LANG : it>$*Nel Febbraio 2009 Evile iniziò il processo di pre-produzione per il loro secondo album con Russ Russell.*

Would be a valid Italian sentence to be processed. The English translation for this sentence is *In February 2009 Evile began the pre-production process for their second album with Russ Russell.* Figure 1 shows the produced output for this sentence. As shown, FRED produces as output an RDF graph with several associated information (detected DBpedia entities, events and situations mapped within DOLCE, WordNet and VerbNet mapping, pronoun resolution).

Additionally, FRED reuses the Earmark vocabulary and annotation method [13] for annotating text segments with the resources from its graphs[16]. For example, in the example sentence of Fig. 1, the term "Evil", starting from the text span "17" and ending at the text span "22" denotes the entity `fred:Evil`[17] in the FRED graph G. This information is formalised with the following triples[18]:

---

[14] http://www.microsoft.com/web/post/using-the-free-bing-translation-apis.

[15] check http://msdn.microsoft.com/en-us/library/hh456380.aspx for the list of language codes.

[16] These triples are not returned in the graph-view result of FRED at http://wit.istc.cnr.it/stlab-tools/fred/, they are returned with all other serialization output options.

[17] Prefix `fred:` stands for http://www.ontologydesignpatterns.org/ont/fred/.

[18] Prefix `pos:` stands for http://www.essepuntato.it/2008/12/earmark#, `semio:` stands for http://ontologydesignpatterns.org/cp/owl/semiotics.owl#, `rdfs:` stands for http://www.w3.org/2000/01/rdf-schema# and `xmls:` stands for http://www.w3.org/2001XMLSchema#.

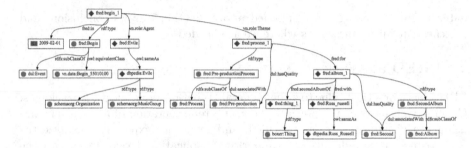

Fig. 1. Machine reader output for the sentence: *In February 2009 Evile began the pre-production process for their second album with Russ Russell.*

```
fred:offset_17_22_Evil
        a    pos:PointerRange;
        rdfs:label"Evil"^^xmls:string;
        semio:denotes fred:Australia;
        pos:begins  "17"^^xmls:nonNegativeInteger;
        pos:ends    "22"^^xmls:nonNegativeInteger;
```

The RDF/OWL graph reported in Fig. 1 is a typical representative output of FRED. It is enriched with verb senses to disambiguate frame types, DBpedia entity resolutions, thematic roles played by DBpedia entities participating in frame occurrences, and entity types. FRED's user interface returns an interactive RDF graph as output that can be used by an user for browsing the resulting knowledge. When clicking on each DBpedia entity node displayed in a graph, for example, a pop-up appears showing the visualization of that entity's page on DBpedia.

The user interface allows also to show the complete list of RDF triples (syntactic constructs, offset between words and input sentence, URIs of recognized entities, text span markup specification support using Earmark [13], relations between source and translated text) that FRED outputs by choosing a view (RDF/XML, RDF/JSON, Turtle, N3, NT, DAG) other than the Graphical View item which is set by default.

Within the options at the bottom of the produced graphs it is possible to export the graph as a PNG or JPEG image, to see the augmented knowledge for the identified DBpedia entities from FRED using a nice GUI built on top of RelFinder[19].

3   Addressing the Open Knowledge Extraction Challenge

The Open Knowledge Extraction Challenge focuses on the production of new knowledge aimed at either populating and enriching existing knowledge bases or creating new ones. This means that the defined tasks focus on extracting concepts, individuals, properties, and statements that not necessarily exist already

---

[19] http://www.visualdataweb.org/relfinder.php.

in a target knowledge base, and on representing them according to Semantic Web standard in order to be directly injected in linked datasets and their ontologies.

In this direction, the tasks proposed in the OKE Challenge are structured following a common formalisation; the required output is in a standard SW format (specifically the Natural Language Interchange (NIF) format) and the evaluation procedure is then produced in a publicly way by using a standard evaluation framework.

The OKE challenge is opened to everyone from industry and academia and it is aimed at advancing a reference framework for research on Knowledge Extraction from text for the Semantic Web by re-defining a number of tasks (typically from information and knowledge extraction) by taking into account specific SW requirements. Systems are evaluated against a testing dataset for each task. Precision, recall, F-measure for all the tasks are computed automatically by using GERBIL[20], a state of the art benchmarking tool. In the following we will show how we have addressed the first two tasks of the challenge that we have considered.

3.1 Task 1: Named Entity Resolution, Linking and Typing for Knowledge Base Population

This task consists of:

1. identifying Named Entities in a sentence and create an OWL individual (`owl:Individual`[21]) statement representing it;
2. link (`owl:sameAs` statement) such individual, when possible, to a reference KB (DBpedia);
3. assigning a type to such individual (`rdf:type`[22] statement) selected from a set of given types (i.e., a subset of DBpedia).

In this task by "Entity" we mean any discourse referent (the actors and objects around which a story unfolds), either named or anonymous that is an individual of one of the following *DOLCE Ultra Lite classes* [4]:

- Person;
- Place;
- Organization;
- Role.

Entities also include anaphorically related discourse referents[23].

To address this task, we have implemented a web application, available at http://wit.istc.cnr.it/stlab-tools/oke-challenge/index.php, relying upon FRED's capabilities. The system requires to upload a file in NIF format, as requested by the OKE Challenge, containing a set of sentences to process.

---

[20] E.g. http://aksw.org/Projects/GERBIL.html.

[21] Prefix `owl:` stands for http://www.w3.org/2002/07/owl#.

[22] Prefix `rdf:` stands for http://www.w3.org/1999/02/22-rdf-syntax-ns#.

[23] Hence, anaphora resolution has to be take into account for addressing the task.

Each sentence is then processed independently by means of FRED, producing as output a set of triples, again in NIF format. The result includes the offsets of recognized entities for the processed sentence and can be downloaded by the user.

As an example, given the sentence:

Florence May Harding studied at a school in Sydney, and with Douglas Robert Dundas, but in effect had no formal training in either botany or art.

the system recognizes four entities[24]:

Recognized Entity	Generated URI	Type	SameAs
Florence May Harding	oke:Florence_May_Harding,	dul:Person	dbpedia:Florence_May_Harding
school	oke:School	dul:Organization	
Sydney	oke:Sydney	dul:Place	dbpedia:Sydney
Douglas Robert Dundas	oke:Douglas_Robert_Dundas	dul:Person	

The evaluation of task 1 includes the following three aspects:

- *Ability to recognize entities* - it is checked whether all strings recognizing entities are identified, using the offsets returned by the systems.[25]
- *Ability to assign the correct type* - this evaluation is carried out only on the selected four target DOLCE types, as already stated above.
- *Ability to link individuals to DBpedia 2014* - entities need to be correctly linked to DBpedia, when possible (in the sentence above, for example, the referred "Douglas Robert Dundas" is not present within DBpedia; therefore, obviously, no linking is possible).

Precision, recall and F1 for these three subtasks of task 1 are calculated by using GERBIL, as already mentioned above. Initial experiments of our tool with the provided Gold Standard showed precision and recall close to 70 %.

3.2 Task 2: Class Induction and Entity Typing for Vocabulary and Knowledge Base Enrichment

This task consists in producing rdf:type statements, given definition texts. A dataset of sentences are given as input, each defining an entity (known a priori); e.g. the entity: dpedia:Skara_Cathedral, and its definition: *Skara Cathedral is a church in the Swedish city of Skara.*

Task 2 requires to:

1. identify the type(s) of the given entity as they are expressed in the given definition;

---

[24] Prefix oke: stands for http://www.ontologydesignpatterns.org/data/oke-challenge/task-1/, dul: stands for http://www.ontologydesignpatterns.org/ont/dul/DUL.owl# and dbpedia: stands for http://dbpedia.org/resource/.

[25] Only full matches are counted as correct (e.g. if the system returns "Art School" instead of "National Art School" is counted as a miss).

2. create a `owl:Class` statement for defining each of them as a new class in the target knowledge base;
3. create a `rdf:type` statement between the given entity and the new created classes;
4. align the identified types, if a correct alignment is possible, to a set of given types from DBpedia.

In the task we will evaluate the extraction of all strings describing a type and the alignment to any of the subset of *DOLCE+DnS Ultra Lite classes* [4].

As an example, given the sentence:

Brian Banner is a fictional villain from the Marvel Comics Universe created by Bill Mantlo and Mike Mignola and first appearing in print in late 1985.

and the input target entity *Brian Banner*, task 2 requires to recognize any possible type for it. Correct answers include[26]:

Recognized string for the type	Generated Type	subClassOf
fictional villain	`oke:FictionalVillain`	`dul:Personification`
villain	`oke:Villain`	`dul:Person`

Again, the results are provided in NIF format, including the offsets of recognized string describing the type. Initial experiments of our tool with the provided Gold Standard showed precision and recall higher than to 67 % for task 2.

The evaluation of this task includes the following two aspects:

- *Ability to recognize strings that describe the type of a target entity* - since strings describing types often include adjectives as modifiers (in the example above, "fictional" is a modifier for villain), in the provided Gold Standard[27] all possible options are included; the system result is considered correct if at least one of the possibility is returned.
- *Ability to align the identified type with a reference ontology* - which for this evaluation is the subset of DOLCE+DnS Ultra Lite classes.

Precision, recall and F1 for these subtasks of task 2 are calculated by using GERBIL, as already stated in Sect. 3.

4 Results

Two datasets have been used for the evaluation of the challengers' systems. Each dataset included 100 entities extracted from Wikipedia. Dataset for task 1

---

[26] Prefix `oke:` stands for http://www.ontologydesignpatterns.org/data/oke-challenge/task-2/ and `dul:` stands for http://www.ontologydesignpatterns.org/ont/dul/DUL.owl#.

[27] https://github.com/anuzzolese/oke-challenge/tree/master/GoldStandard_sampleData.ata.

Table 1. Distribution of entities for task 1.

dul	Count
\<http://www.ontologydesignpatterns.org/ont/dul/DUL.owl#Person\>	167
\<http://www.ontologydesignpatterns.org/ont/dul/DUL.owl#Organization\>	108
\<http://www.ontologydesignpatterns.org/ont/dul/DUL.owl#Place\>	96
\<http://www.ontologydesignpatterns.org/ont/dul/DUL.owl#Role\>	56

Table 2. Distribution of entities for task 2.

dul	Count
\<http://www.ontologydesignpatterns.org/ont/dul/DUL.owl#InformationEntity\>	32
\<http://www.ontologydesignpatterns.org/ont/dul/DUL.owl#PhysicalObject\>	30
\<http://www.ontologydesignpatterns.org/ont/dul/DUL.owl#Person\>	29
\<http://www.ontologydesignpatterns.org/ont/dul/DUL.owl#Description\>	12
\<http://www.ontologydesignpatterns.org/ont/dul/DUL.owl#Personification\>	11
\<http://www.ontologydesignpatterns.org/ont/dul/DUL.owl#Organization\>	10
\<http://www.ontologydesignpatterns.org/ont/dul/DUL.owl#Situation\>	10
\<http://www.ontologydesignpatterns.org/ont/dul/DUL.owl#Organism\>	9
\<http://www.ontologydesignpatterns.org/ont/dul/DUL.owl#Collection\>	7
\<http://www.ontologydesignpatterns.org/ont/dul/DUL.owl#Abstract\>	6
\<http://www.ontologydesignpatterns.org/ont/dul/DUL.owl#Relation\>	3
\<http://www.ontologydesignpatterns.org/ont/dul/DUL.owl#Role\>	2
\<http://www.ontologydesignpatterns.org/ont/dul/DUL.owl#TimeInterval\>	2
\<http://www.ontologydesignpatterns.org/ont/dul/DUL.owl#Process\>	1

Table 3. Results on task 1.

Annotator	Micro F1	Micro precision	Micro recall	Macro F1	Macro precision	Macro recall
Adel	0.6075	0.6938	0.5403	0.6039	0.685	0.54
Fox	0.4988	0.6639	0.4099	0.4807	0.6329	0.4138
FRED	0.3473	0.4667	0.2766	0.2278	0.3061	0.1814

included entities extracted from biographies of Nobel prize winners that covered as many as possible the DOLCE types indicated in the guidelines for such a task. The overall number of triples of dataset for task 1 is 6432 whereas that for task 2 is 3686. Table 1 shows the distribution of entities extracted for task 1.

For task 2 entities have been extracted in order to distribute as much as possible entities to type on DOLCE types indicated in the guidelines for such a task. Table 2 shows the distribution of entities extracted for task 2.

Both datasets can be downloaded from the main pages of the challenge[28].

---

[28] https://github.com/anuzzolese/oke-challenge/tree/master/evaluation-data.

Table 4. Results on task 2.

Annotator	Micro F1	Micro precision	Micro recall	Macro F1	Macro precision	Macro recall
CETUS	0.4735	0.4455	0.5203	0.4478	0.4182	0.5328
OAK@Sheffield	0.4416	0.5155	0.39	0.3939	0.3965	0.3981
FRED	0.3043	0.2893	0.3211	0.2746	0.2569	0.3173

Tables 3 and 4 show the results of six different metrics calculated by GERBIL on the two tasks on the challengers' systems.

On one hand FRED has the strength to be flexible (it was the only submitted system used for two tasks without specific tuning); on the other hand it suffers from precision with respect to the other competitors. We are already working on this direction (constantly updating, improving and extending FRED) with the goal to obtain a holistic framework that can perform efficiently a huge set of machine reading and semantic web tasks while at the same time remaining flexible and fast.

5   Conclusions

In this paper we have shown how we have employed FRED, a machine reader that we have developed within our lab, to solve the first two tasks of the Open Knowledge Extraction (OKE) Challenge at the European Semantic Web Conference (ESWC) 2015. Our method uses Discourse Representation Theory, Linguistic Frames, Combinatory Categorial Grammar and is provided with several well known base ontologies and lexical resources. FRED is a novel approach and to the best of our knowledge we have not found yet a machine reader that computes similar tasks of it and that can be compared. Its novelty is therefore guaranteed. As future direction we would like to keep improving FRED and transform it in a framework that can be released with some sort of license.

Acknowledgement. The research leading to these results has received funding from the European Union Horizons 2020 the Framework Programme for Research and Innovation (2014–2020) under grant agreement 643808 Project MARIO Managing active and healthy aging with use of caring service robots.

References

1. Bizer, C., Heath, T., Berners-Lee, T.: Linked data - the story so far. Int. J. Semant. Web Inf. Syst. **5**(3), 1–22 (2009)
2. Bos, J.: Wide-coverage semantic analysis with boxer. In: Bos, J., Delmonte, R. (eds.) Semantics in Text Processing, pp. 277–286. College Publications, London (2008)
3. Ferragina, P., Scaiella, U.: Tagme: on-the-fly annotation of short text fragments (by wikipedia entities). In: Proceedings of the 19th ACM International Conference on Information and Knowledge Management, CIKM 2010, pp. 1625–1628. ACM, New York (2010)

4. Gangemi, A.: What's in a Schema?. Cambridge University Press, Cambridge (2010)
5. Gangemi, A., Draicchio, F., Presutti, V., Nuzzolese, A.G., Recupero, D.R.: A machine reader for the semantic web. In: Blomqvist, E., Groza, T. (eds.) International Semantic Web Conference (Posters & Demos). CEUR Workshop Proceedings, vol. 1035, pp. 149–152. CEUR-WS.org (2013)
6. Gangemi, A., Nuzzolese, A.G., Presutti, V., Draicchio, F., Musetti, A., Ciancarini, P.: Automatic typing of DBpedia entities. In: Cudré-Mauroux, P., et al. (eds.) ISWC 2012, Part I. LNCS, vol. 7649, pp. 65–81. Springer, Heidelberg (2012)
7. Gangemi, A., Presutti, V.: Ontology design patterns. In: Staab, S., Studer, R. (eds.) Handbook on Ontologies, 2nd edn. Springer, New York (2009)
8. Gangemi, A., Presutti, V., Recupero, D.R.: Frame-based detection of opinion holders and topics: a model and a tool. IEEE Comp. Int. Mag. 9(1), 20–30 (2014)
9. Iorio, A.D., Nuzzolese, A.G., Peroni, S.: Towards the automatic identification of the nature of citations. In: Castro, A.G., Lange, C., Lord, P.W., Stevens, R. (eds.) SePublica. CEUR Workshop Proceedings, vol. 994, pp. 63–74. CEUR-WS.org (2013)
10. Kamp, H.: A theory of truth and semantic representation. In: Groenendijk, J.A.G., Janssen, T.M.V., Stokhof, M.B.J. (eds.) Formal Methods in the Study of Language, vol. 1, pp. 277–322. Mathematisch Centrum (1981)
11. Musetti, A., Nuzzolese, A.G., Draicchio, F., Presutti, V., Blomqvist, E., Gangemi, A., Ciancarini, P.: Aemoo: exploratory search based on knowledge patterns over the semantic web. In: Semantic Web Challenge (2012)
12. Nuzzolese, A.G., Gangemi, A., Presutti, V.: Gathering lexical linked data and knowledge patterns from FrameNet. In: Proceedings of the 6th International Conference on Knowledge Capture (K-CAP), Banff, Alberta, Canada, pp. 41–48 (2011)
13. Peroni, S., Gangemi, A., Vitali, F.: Dealing with markup semantics. In: Proceedings of the 7th International Conference on Semantic Systems, pp. 111–118. ACM (2011)
14. Presutti, V., Consoli, S., Nuzzolese, A.G., Recupero, D.R., Gangemi, A., Bannour, I., Zargayouna, H.: Uncovering the semantics of wikipedia wikilinks. In: 19th International Conference on Knowledge Engineering and Knowledge Management (EKAW 2014) (2014)
15. Presutti, V., Draicchio, F., Gangemi, A.: Knowledge extraction based on discourse representation theory and linguistic frames. In: ten Teije, A., Völker, J., Handschuh, S., Stuckenschmidt, H., d'Acquin, M., Nikolov, A., Aussenac-Gilles, N., Hernandez, N. (eds.) EKAW 2012. LNCS, vol. 7603, pp. 114–129. Springer, Heidelberg (2012)
16. Recupero, D.R., Consoli, S., Gangemi, A., Nuzzolese, A.G., Spampinato, D.: A semantic web based core engine to efficiently perform sentiment analysis. In: Presutti, V., Blomqvist, E., Troncy, R., Sack, H., Papadakis, I., Tordai, A. (eds.) ESWC Satellite Events 2014. LNCS, vol. 8798, pp. 245–248. Springer, Heidelberg (2014)
17. Recupero, D.R., Presutti, V., Consoli, S., Gangemi, A., Nuzzolese, A.G.: Sentilo: Frame-based sentiment analysis. Cogn. Comput. 7, 211–225 (2014)

Exploiting Linked Open Data to Uncover Entity Types

Jie Gao[(⊠)] and Suvodeep Mazumdar

OAK Group, Department of Computer Science, University of Sheffield,
Sheffield, UK
{j.gao,s.mazumdar}@sheffield.ac.uk

Abstract. Extracting structured information from text plays a crucial role in automatic knowledge acquisition and is at the core of any knowledge representation and reasoning system. Traditional methods rely on hand-crafted rules and are restricted by the performance of various linguistic pre-processing tools. More recent approaches rely on supervised learning of relations trained on labelled examples, which can be manually created or sometimes automatically generated (referred as distant supervision). We propose a supervised method for entity typing and alignment. We argue that a rich feature space can improve extraction accuracy and we propose to exploit Linked Open Data (LOD) for feature enrichment. Our approach is tested on task-2 of the Open Knowledge Extraction challenge, including automatic entity typing and alignment. Our approach demonstrate that by combining evidences derived from LOD (e.g. DBpedia) and conventional lexical resources (e.g. WordNet) (i) improves the accuracy of the supervised induction method and (ii) enables easy matching with the Dolce+DnS Ultra Lite ontology classes.

1 Introduction

A vast amount of knowledge is made available in the form of text; text is easily understandable by humans, but not by machines: applications can access knowledge if it is made available in a structured form. Information Extraction techniques serve the purpose of extracting facts from text and represent them in a structured form. FreeBase[1] and DBpedia[2] are famous examples of an effort to produce large scale world knowledge in a structured form. The structured facts are quite useful in tasks like question answering [8,20], facilitating both understanding the question and finding the answer. For example, in order to answer the question *"Which personification in Marvel Comics Universe was created by Bill Mantlo and Mike Mignola?"*, the knowledge of relations include (?x *created-by* "Bill Mantlo") (?x *created-by* "Mike Mignola") (?y *is-a* ?y) (?y *type-of* "personification"). A wider application of relation data can be seen in the Wikipedia infoboxes and more recently in Google Knowledge Graph initiative [19]. The relation data comes from large knowledge bases, which can be

---

[1] https://www.freebase.com/.

[2] http://wiki.dbpedia.org/About.

© Springer International Publishing Switzerland 2015
F. Gandon et al. (Eds.): SemWebEval 2015, CCIS 548, pp. 51–62, 2015.
DOI: 10.1007/978-3-319-25518-7_5

represented using different formalisms. Resource Description Framework (RDF) is the industry standard, which is designed to provide a common data model to represent structured information on the Web. Services like DBpedia draw on Wikipedia info-boxes to create such large databases [12], which now has 3 billion RDF triples, 580 million of which are extracted from English Wikipedia.

Open Information Extraction (Open IE) systems aim to extract information without being constrained by pre-specified vocabularies. State-of-the-art Open IE systems, e.g. ReVerb [7] and NELL [5], have witnessed remarkable success. Compared with schema-driven IE, Open IE can usually gain broader coverage thanks to a lightweight logical schema, though the lack of proper schema or unique identifiers cause a fair amount of ambiguity in the extracted facts and further hinder the data linking across multiple data sources.

This paper is in response to Open Knowledge Extraction (OKE) Challenge[3] in order to fill the gap between Open IE and existing centralised knowledge bases. We present a tool[4] for (i) identifying the type of the given entity (known a priori) in the given definition context; (ii) create a owl:Class statement for defining each of them as a new class in the target knowledge base, (iii) create a rdf:type statement between the given entity and the new created classes, and (iv) align the identified types with Dolce+DnS Ultra Lite (DUL) ontology classes[5], if a correct alignment is available, to a set of given types. Our approach consists of three main steps: (i) learning (in a supervised fashion) a model to recognize the word(s) in the sentence that express the type for the given entity (ii) predicting one or multiple types for all recognized (in previous step) surface forms expressing types; (iii) aligning all identified types to a given ontology. Each component will be explained in detail in Sect. 3. Evaluation results and conclusions are presented in Sects. 4 and 5 respectively.

2   Related Work

Named Entity Recognition. Named Entity Recognition (NER) is closely related to type extraction that aims to locate and classify atomic elements in text into predefined categories such as the names of persons or biological species, organizations, locations, etc. Three broad categories of machine learning paradigm in NER [16] include supervised, semi-supervised and unsupervised techniques. Feature engineering plays a crucial role in NER and has been well studied for many years. However, the difference is that NER systems do not label nominal (e.g., identify *"fictional villain"* as a type of *"Personification"*) or associate nominal phrases to entities.

Relation Extraction. Current methodologies in building a relation extractor generally fall into three categories: pattern-based [10], supervised machine learning, semi- and un-supervised approaches respectively. A number of popular

---

[3] https://github.com/anuzzolese/oke-challenge.

[4] Source code can be found at https://github.com/jerrygaoLondon/oke-extractor.

[5] http://stlab.istc.cnr.it/stlab/WikipediaOntology/.

methods has recently emerged in the third category include bootstrapping (i.e., using seeds)[1], distant supervision [15] and unsupervised learning [14] from the web. Different from most of relation extraction tasks that need the presence of two entities, our goal is to identify the hypernym (i.e.,*instance-Of*) relation between a given entity and noun phrases.

Ontology Matching. Our approach in type alignment is inspired from current practice and research in the field of ontology matching [17]. In this paper, we explored the combination of the context-based techniques by the use of formal resource (i.e., linked data) in semantic level and the content-based matching by the use of terminological techniques including string metrics for lexical similarity and WordNet for word relation matching, with respect to the schema level alignment for the matching between identified entity types and DUL ontology classes.

Interlinking Open Data. Emergence of Linked Data (LD) has raised increasing attention in the pressing needs for interlinking vast amounts of open data sources [2]. On the one hand, linked data can be leveraged as an external source of information for ontology matching, with respect to the challenge of "matching with background knowledge" [9]. On the other hand, interlinking methods derived from ontology matching can facilitate the achievement of the promise of Semantic Web: the Web of interlinked data. Motivated by both the LD based alignment method [11] and state-of-the-art interlinking methods (e.g., Silk [4], RDF-AI [18]), particular attention is paid in our approach to evaluate the role of LD in type extraction and alignment.

3   Methodology

Our approach can be represented as three main phases: (i) *training*, (ii) *prediction*, (iii) *type annotation and alignment* as illustrated in following architecture diagram (Fig. 1). The gold standard data contains *definition sentences*, i.e. each sentence expresses the type of a certain given entity[6]. We pre-process the gold standard data, we perform feature extraction and feature enrichment and we learn a classifier to recognize the portion(s) of the sentence expressing the entity type (we learn hyperonym patterns). All type candidates are fed to the type annotator which annotates each surface form as a new *owl:Class* with generated URIs in the format of NIF 2.0[7]. The well-formed new owl classes are then associated (by *rdf:type*) with the target entity in the sentence. In the final phase, the type alignment component performs semantic integration based on domain ontology and DUL ontology by combining linked data discovering (LDD), terminological similarity computation (TSS) and semantic similarity computation (SSC).

---

[6] We use the training data encoded in NIF format provided by the challenge organisers in this experiment. The NLP Interchange Format (NIF) is an RDF/OWL-based format that aims to achieve interoperability between Natural Language Processing (NLP) tools, language resources and annotations.

[7] http://persistence.uni-leipzig.org/nlp2rdf/.

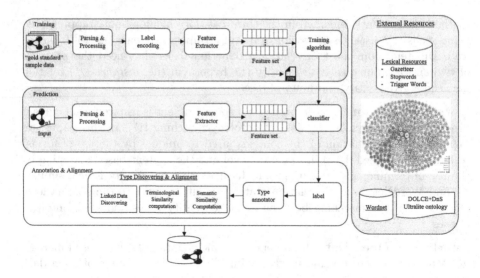

Fig. 1. Architecture of type induction and alignment

Aligned DUL classes will be associated with identified type by *rdfs:subClassOf*[8]. The rationale of each component implementation is discussed in detail below.

3.1 Type Induction

Type induction is treated as a classical machine learning task in this experiment. First, the training set is loaded, parsed and mapped from the underlying RDF model to object-oriented(OO) data models. Parsing and processing NIF2RDF data is implemented on top of a general RDF library written in python (RDFLib)[9], which facilitates the parsing and serialisation of linked data in various formats. We implement a simple solution for this task that maps RDF model into an in-memory OO data model including *"TaskContext"*, *"ContextEntity"* and *"EntityClass"* respectively. Managing RDF data in an OO paradigm enables a quicker and more convenient data access model shared across multiple components.

Next, Context data (e.g., sentences, pre-labelled entities and types) are transformed and encoded in token-based data models $W = w_1, w_2, ..., w_n$, which treats each token (or word) as atomic unit (called hereafter data point). Each data point $w_i \in W$ represents a token (or word) with its feature set, its class label and its unique identifier. Each data point from the sentence is considered as a learning instance which is labelled with corresponding class labels. Following the approach of [13], we adopt a two-class IO labelling scheme, where each data point is either in-type (labelled as "I") or out-of-type (labelled as "O").

---

[8] The *rdfs* stands for the namespace of RDF Schema (http://www.w3.org/2000/01/rdf-schema#).

[9] RDFLib: https://pypi.python.org/pypi/rdflib.

Feature Extraction. In the feature extraction phase we construct the feature set for each data point. We collect the following features:

1. Word-level features: For each data point which is not a stopword[10] we produce: "WORD_POS": word PoS category; "IS_TITLE": true if the word is a titlecased string, "ALL_CAPITAL": true if all cased characters in word are uppercase, "IS_WORD_ROOT_BE": true if the lemma of current word is 'be'; "IS_PUNCT_COMMA": true if current word is a comma punctuation; "WORD_WITH_DIGITS": true if current word contains digits; "LAST_2_LETTERS": last two characters of current word.

2. Named-entity: We include the feature "IS_ENTITY" to indicate whether current word is entity or not.

3. Gazetteer and trigger word features: Trigger words are a list of terms that might be useful for relation extraction. For example, trigger words like *"Mr"*, *"Miss"* and *"Dr"* for Person, *"city"* and *"street"* for location, *"Ltd"* and *"Co."* for Organisations, are obviously useful to recognise the instance-of relations. We also hand-picked a list of trigger words (e.g., *"name"*, *"form"*, *"class"*, *"category"*, *"variety"*, *"style"*, *"model"* and *"substance"*) that can indicate the type relations. WordNet can be employed to extract trigger words, e.g., look for synonyms. Gazetteer features can be a list of useful geo or geopolitical words e.g., country name list and other sub-entities such like person first name, person surname. We used the ANNIE Gazetteer[11] from GATE platform[12] in our experiment. A list of gazetteer based features used include "TYPE_INDICATOR": true if current word is matched with an item in type trigger words; "IS_STOPWORD": true if current word is stop word; "IS_ORGKEY": true if current word is matched with an item in organisation entity trigger words; "IS_LOCKEY": true if current word is matched with an item in location entity trigger words; "IS_COUNTRY": true if current word is country entity; "IS_COUNTRYADJ": true if current word is country adjective; "IS_PERSONNAME": true if current word is person name trigger words (e.g., firstname, surname); "IS_PERSONTITLE": true if current word is person title; "IS_JOBTITLE": true if current word is job title entity; "IS_FACKEY": true if current word is facility entity trigger words.

4. Neighborhood features: We include surrounding words and their corresponding features; this provides contextual evidence useful to discover hypernym pattern between identified entities and the target word expressing the type. Position information is encoded in the feature names and examples of such feature set are "PREV_2_WORD_WITH_DIGITS", "NEXT_1_WORD_IS_STOPWORD", "PREV_1_WORD_POS", "PREV_3_WORD_IS_COUNTRY" and so forth. In our experiment, features are extracted from a 8×3 sliding window.

---

[10] The SMART stop-word list built by Chris Buckley and Gerard Salton, which can be obtained from goo.gl/rBQNbO.

[11] https://gate.ac.uk/sale/tao/splitch13.html.

[12] https://gate.ac.uk/.

5. semantic distance: The"SEMANTIC_DISTANCE" is a numerical value which quantifies the "similarity of meaning" between the target token t_1, i.e. the word(s) potentially expressing the types, and the target entity t_2, i.e. the one for which the type is being expressed. The value is computed by looking at all possible types that we can gather for t_1 and t_2 from LOD (specifically DBpedia). Formally, the semantic distance is computed as:

$$sem\_dist(t_1, t_{2j}) = max[sim(S_n(t_1), S_n(t_{2j}))], t_{2j} \in rdf : type(E), n > 0 \qquad (1)$$

t_1 is the target token and t_{2j} is the one of linked data types (rdf:type) associated with entity (E). As entity is disambiguated by Dbpedia URI in the dataset, we can acquire that disambiguated type information by SPARQL query. S_n is the synset of a word where several meanings of the word can be looked up. $sim()$ is the maximum semantic similarity determined by the function of the path distance between words in hierarchical structure in Wordnet. Our assumption is based on the fact that existing resources like WordNet and DBpedia are a rich and reliable source of hyponymy/hypernymy relationships between entities, which are assumed to be able to provide very informative and potentially strong indications about instance-of relation between entity and target token. Even though type information is usually multi-word terms, our intuition is to identify head noun in multi-word type surface form. This is based on the assumption that terminological heads usually carry key conceptual semantics [6]. We implemented the sem_dict() based on NLTK WordNet[13] library and python SPARQLWrapper[14] for rdf type and label query. The semantic similarity is computed by the WordNet *path_similarity* function which is based on the shortest path connecting the word senses in the is-a (hyernym/hypnonym) taxonomy.

Model Selection. We experimented with three state-the-art classifiers, including Naïve Bayes, Maximum Entropy Markov Model (MEMM) and Support Vector Machine Model provided in NLTK's classify package[15]. Based on the same feature set and 100 iterations, our experiment indicates that even if Naïve Bayes classifier and SVM is much fast in training, MEMM give us the optimum performance for our class induction task. Moreover, as a discriminative classifier, more features make MEMM model more accurate.

Type Annotation. In order to identify all possible type surface forms for a certain entity, we combined the approach of head noun extraction and the PoS based grammar matching for compound words combining the modifiers and a head noun. For the above example, the continuing tokens *"American lightweight boxer"* can be picked out with type tag "I" after processed with type classifier, while *"lightweight boxer"* and *"boxer"* are also good candidate entity types. A set

---

[13] http://www.nltk.org/howto/wordnet.html.

[14] SPARQLWrapper is a python based wrapper around a SPARQL service, access via http://rdflib.github.io/sparqlwrapper/.

[15] http://www.nltk.org/howto/classify.html.

Table 1. A simplified version of PoS grammar patterns matching multiple type surface forms

<JJ |VBG|VBD>+ <NN|NNP|NNS>+   <NN|NNP|NNS>+ <JJ |VBD|VBG>* <NN|NNP|NNS>+

of PoS patterns grammars (Table 1) are applied iteratively in our experiment. Note that + and * are regular expression cardinality operators. PoS-tagging was achieved with the NLTK standard treebank POS tagger[16].

3.2   Type Alignment

The motivation of class alignment method in our experiment is to investigate how LOD datasets (typically DBpedia) can facilitate the alignment of heterogeneous type information. Our alignment method is based on the heuristics that the linked data resource is typed and linked by their dereferenceable URIs. For example (in Fig. 2), to identify whether a football club is type of "dul:Agent"[17], we can ask this question based on LOD knowledge base (typically DBpedia in our case), which can be constructed in the following SPARQL query.

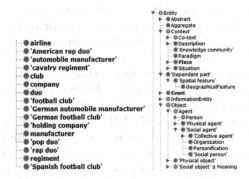

Fig. 2. Parts of extracted entity class and DUL classes

```
ASK {
    ?instance dbpedia-owl:type ?entity.
    <http://dbpedia.org/resource/Football_Club> dbpedia-owl:wikiPageRedirects ?entity.
    ?instance a ?type.
    FILTER(?type = dul:Agent)
}
```

In the task of DUL ontology alignment, early experiments show that there are 9 % (9 out of 99 entities) DBpedia entities in the gold standard dataset are classified with DUL classes. By using dereferenceable type URI with a more

---

[16] http://www.nltk.org/book/ch05.html.

[17] The *dul* stands for the prefix for http://www.ontologydesignpatterns.org/ont/dul/ DUL.owl.

Table 2. Parts of DUL classes and keywords

DUL Classes	Keywords & synonyms
dul:Activity	activity, task
d0:Characteristic	characteristic, feature
d0:CognitiveEntity	Attitudes, cognitive, ideologies, mind
dul:Goal	Goal, aim, achievement
d0:Location	Place, space
dul:Organism	Organism, animal, plant
dul:Personification	personification, fictional, imaginary
dul:Situation	situation, condition, circumstance, state

complex SPARQL query[18], we found that about 30 % (60 out of total 201) types can be directly matched with DUL classes pre-classified in DBpedia. If counting all the multi-word types containing the matched head nouns, there are 117 types (58.2 % of total) that can be aligned with DUL classes via DBpedia. A typical example as above, if "Club" is directly matched with "dul:Agent" via query, "Football Club" containing "Club" as the head noun can be further aligned with "dul:Agent".

Our alignment process can be divided into three steps: linked data discovery, terminological similarity computation and semantic similarity computation. Linked Data Discovery (LDD) is essentially the semantic query based on existing structural knowledge in DBpedia. We combine multiple classification schemes from DBpedia about the entity and extracted classes to determine best matched DUL classes. Entity based query is achieved by the DBpedia URI and the corresponding DUL classes about extracted entity types can be retrieved by automatically generated dereferencing URI following the practice in DBpedia [3]. Multi-word type terms that contain the matched head noun type in the same context will be aligned with the same DUL class. For many cases that no DUL classes can be found by LDD, we compute terminological similarity by Levenshtein distance normalised by the length of the longest sequence. The threshold is set to 0.9. The schema level matching is based on the lexicon expansion on both target class and DUL classes to be aligned. Target class is expanded by type labels extracted from both entity and dereferencable type from DBpedia. Meanwhile, DUL classes are expanded with keywords and synonyms. Table 2 illustrates the parts of DUL classes and keywords.

In the final step of our method, for the classes that cannot be aligned by string similarity, we adopt the semantic similarity computation approach that relies on semantic taxonomy in WordNet to determine hypernym relationship between expanded target type and expanded DUL classes labels. For multi-word terms, we compute the similarity based on head noun. Where either or both of the words had more than one synset in WordNet, we compute all the combinations

---

[18] The complete SPARQL query can be found in the projects source code repository.

to find the synsets pair of maximal similarity. The similarity threshold (i.e.,path distance) is set to 0.1.

4   Evaluation

4.1   Type Induction

For the experiment of type induction task, the gold-standard corpus was used which contains 99 sentences of entity definition context. The gold-standard corpus is split into 70 % for training and 30 % for testing. The performance of entity type extraction is computed in by Precision (P), Recall (R), and F-measure (F1 score) (as follows).

$$P = \frac{\#TruePositive}{\#TruePositive + \#FalsePositive} \qquad (2)$$

$$R = \frac{\#TruePositive}{\#TruePositive + \#FalseNegative} \qquad (3)$$

$$F_1 = \frac{2PR}{P + R} \qquad (4)$$

As shown in Table 3, the MEMM classifier trained with features not derived from LD source is used as baseline for performance comparison. By add the LD based feature "SEMANTIC_DISTANCE" to train MEMM model achieve overall 5.19 increase of F-score, with 1.02 and 6.38 increase in precision and recall.

Table 3. Results of evaluation of class induction method

	P(%)	R(%)	F1(%)
MEMM without LD features	84.23	47.10	60.27
MEMM with LD features	85.25	53.48	65.46

4.2   Type Alignment

Type alignment evaluation is implemented as follows.

$$P = \frac{\#correctIdentifiedAlignments}{\#identifiedAlignments} \qquad (5)$$

$$R = \frac{\#correctIdentifiedAlignments}{\#goldStandardData} \qquad (6)$$

$$F_1 = \frac{2PR}{P + R} \qquad (7)$$

In (5) and (6), the "#correctIdentifiedAlignments" is computed by combining string matching and subsumption reasoning. Specifically, if automatically aligned DUL types cannot be matched with labelled data (i.e., gold standards), we check

Table 4. Results of evaluation of type alignment method

	P(%)	R(%)	F1(%)
Linked Data Discovering (LDD)	35.48	22.2	27.33
Terminological Similarity Computation (TSC)	75.44	43.43	55.13
Semantic Similarity Computation (SSC)	38.38	38.38	38.38
TSC + SSC	57.58	57.58	57.58
LDD+TSC+SSC	34.34	34.34	34.34

whether the DUL type is the subclass of the labelled DUL type or vice versa. In other words, if at least one gold standards alignment can be matched lexically or semantically, the result is recognised as correct. We compared three different alignment strategies and a combination of two or three of them in Table 4.

From the evaluation results, even if LDD has good coverage 63 % (62 out of 99) for alignment suggestions, the performance of the LDD method has a low overall F-measure. TSC method achieved higher performance than LDD and SSC, which has further gained 2.45 % improvement with optimal result by combining with SSC.

4.3   Competition Result

The overall performance evaluated in official competition[19] is presented in Table 5.

Table 5. Official competition results of OKE Task 2

Annotator	Micro F1	Micro precision	Micro recall	Macro F1	Macro precision	Macro recall
CETUS	0.4735	0.4455	0.5203	0.4478	0.4182	0.5328
OAK@Sheffield	0.4416	0.5155	0.39	0.3939	0.3965	0.3981
FRED	0.3043	0.2893	0.3211	0.2746	0.2569	0.3173

5   Conclusion

Linked Open Data opens up a promising opportunity for machine learning in terms of feature learning from large scale and ever-growing graph-based knowledge sources. In this paper, we present a hybrid approach for automatic entity typing and type alignment. We experimented three different strategies in type alignment. The evaluation result suggests that LOD can complement extremely rich semantic information compared with WordNet, particularly for complex

---

[19] https://github.com/anuzzolese/oke-challenge.

multiword schema terms. Even though the type alignment directly suggested by LOD suffers low quality, the corresponding concept hierarchies from the multiple community-driven classification schemes can contribute very effective semantic evidences for facilitating alignment task with respect to the similarity and relatedness measurement.

Acknowledgments. Part of this research has been sponsored by the EPSRC funded project LODIE: Linked Open Data for IE, EP/J019488/1.

References

1. Agichtein, E., Gravano, L.: Snowball: extracting relations from large plain-text collections. In: Proceedings of the Fifth ACM Conference on Digital Libraries. DL 2000, pp. 85–94. ACM, New York, NY, USA (2000). http://doi.acm.org/10.1145/336597.336644
2. Bizer, C., Heath, T., Ayers, D., Raimond, Y.: Interlinking open data on the web. Media **79**(1), 31–35 (2007). http://people.kmi.open.ac.uk/tom/papers/bizer-heath-eswc2007-interlinking-open-data.pdf
3. Bizer, C., Lehmann, J., Kobilarov, G., Auer, S., Becker, C., Cyganiak, R., Hellmann, S.: Dbpedia-a crystallization point for the web of data. Web Seman. Sci. Serv. Agents World Wide Web **7**(3), 154–165 (2009)
4. Bizer, C., Volz, J., Kobilarov, G., Gaedke, M.: Silk - a link discovery framework for the web of data. In: 18th International World Wide Web Conference, April 2009. http://www2009.eprints.org/227/
5. Carlson, A., Betteridge, J., Kisiel, B., Settles, B., Hruschka, E.R., Mitchell, T.M.: Toward an architecture for never-ending language learning. In: AAAI (2010)
6. Daille, B., Habert, B., Jacquemin, C., Royauté, J.: Empirical observation of term variations and principles for their description. Terminology **3**(2), 197–257 (1996)
7. Fader, A., Soderland, S., Etzioni, O.: Identifying relations for open information extraction. In: Proceedings of the Conference on Empirical Methods in Natural Language Processing. EMNLP 2011, pp. 1535–1545. Association for Computational Linguistics, Stroudsburg, PA, USA (2011). http://dl.acm.org/citation.cfm?id=2145432.2145596
8. Fader, A., Zettlemoyer, L., Etzioni, O.: Open question answering over curated and extracted knowledge bases. In: Proceedings of the 20th ACM SIGKDD International Conference on Knowledge Discovery and Data Mining. pp. 1156–1165. KDD 2014. ACM, New York, NY, USA (2014). http://doi.acm.org/10.1145/2623330.2623677
9. Giunchiglia, F., Shvaiko, P., Yatskevich, M.: Discovering missing background knowledge in ontology matching. In: Proceedings of the 2006 Conference on ECAI 2006: 17th European Conference on Artificial Intelligence August 29 - September 1, 2006, Riva Del Garda, Italy. pp. 382–386. IOS Press, Amsterdam, The Netherlands (2006). http://dl.acm.org/citation.cfm?id=1567016.1567101
10. Hearst, M.A.: Automatic acquisition of hyponyms from large text corpora (1992)
11. Kachroudi, M., Moussa, E.B., Zghal, S., Ben, S.: Ldoa results for oaei 2011. Ontology Matching, p. 148 (2011)
12. Lehmann, J., Isele, R., Jakob, M., Jentzsch, A., Kontokostas, D., Mendes, P.N., Hellmann, S., Morsey, M., van Kleef, P., Auer, S., Bizer, C.: DBpedia - a large-scale, multilingual knowledge base extracted from wikipedia. Seman. Web J. **5**, 1–29 (2014)

13. Li, Y., Bontcheva, K., Cunningham, H.: Adapting svm for data sparseness and imbalance: a case study in information extraction. Nat. Lang. Eng. **15**(02), 241–271 (2009)
14. Min, B., Shi, S., Grishman, R., Lin, C.Y.: Ensemble semantics for large-scale unsupervised relation extraction. In: Proceedings of the 2012 Joint Conference on Empirical Methods in Natural Language Processing and Computational Natural Language Learning, pp. 1027–1037. Association for Computational Linguistics (2012)
15. Mintz, M., Bills, S., Snow, R., Jurafsky, D.: Distant supervision for relation extraction without labeled data. In: Proceedings of the Joint Conference of the 47th Annual Meeting of the ACL and the 4th International Joint Conference on Natural Language Processing of the AFNLP, ACL 2009, vol. 2, pp. 1003–1011. Association for Computational Linguistics, Stroudsburg, PA, USA (2009). http://dl.acm.org/citation.cfm?id=1690219.1690287
16. Nadeau, D., Sekine, S.: A survey of named entity recognition and classification. Lingvisticae Investigationes **30**(1), 3–26 (2007). http://dx.doi.org/10.1075/li.30.1.03nad
17. Otero-Cerdeira, L., Rodríguez-Martínez, F.J., Gómez-Rodríguez, A.: Ontology matching: a literature review. Expert Syst. Appl. **42**(2), 949–971 (2015). http://www.sciencedirect.com/science/article/pii/S0957417414005144
18. Scharffe, F., Liu, Y., Zhou, C.: Rdf-ai: an architecture for rdf datasets matching, fusion and interlink. In: Proceedings of IJCAI 2009 Workshop on Identity, Reference, and Knowledge Representation (IR-KR), Pasadena (CA US) (2009)
19. Singhal, A.: Introducing the knowledge graph: things, not strings. Official Google Blog, May 2012
20. Yao, X., Van Durme, B.: Information extraction over structured data: question answering with freebase. In: Proceedings of the 52nd Annual Meeting of the Association for Computational Linguistics, vol. 1 (Long Papers), pp. 956–966. Association for Computational Linguistics (2014). http://aclweb.org/anthology/P14-1090

Semantic Publishing Challenge
(SemPub2015)

Semantic Publishing Challenge – Assessing the Quality of Scientific Output by Information Extraction and Interlinking

Angelo Di Iorio[1], Christoph Lange[2], Anastasia Dimou[3],
and Sahar Vahdati[4(✉)]

[1] Università di Bologna, Bologna, Italy
`diiorio@cs.unibo.it`
[2] University of Bonn and Fraunhofer IAIS, Bonn, Germany
`math.semantic.web@gmail.com`
[3] Ghent University – iMinds – Multimedia Lab, Ghent, Belgium
`anastasia.dimou@ugent.be`
[4] University of Bonn, Bonn, Germany
`vahdati@uni-bonn.de`

Abstract. The Semantic Publishing Challenge series aims at investigating novel approaches for improving scholarly publishing using Linked Data technology. In 2014 we had bootstrapped this effort with a focus on extracting information from non-semantic publications – computer science workshop proceedings volumes and their papers – to assess their quality. The objective of this second edition was to improve information extraction but also to interlink the 2014 dataset with related ones in the LOD Cloud, thus paving the way for sophisticated end-user services.

1 Introduction: Semantic Publishing Today

The widely held assumption that 'scholarly communication by means of semantically-enhanced media-rich digital publishing is likely to have a greater impact than [print or PDF]' [1] is slowly coming true, pushed by regular events such as the workshop series on getting 'Beyond the PDF', semantic publishing and linked science[1]. Semantic technology is increasingly supporting researchers in disseminating, exploiting and evaluating their results using open formats. Concrete technical solutions investigated by the semantic publishing community include:

- machine-comprehensible representations of scientific methods, models, experiments and research data,
- links from papers to such data,
- alternative publication channels (e.g. social networks and micro-publications),

---

[1] See https://www.force11.org/meetings/beyond-pdf-2, http://sepublica.info, and http://linkedscience.org/category/workshop/.

© Springer International Publishing Switzerland 2015
F. Gandon et al. (Eds.): SemWebEval 2015, CCIS 548, pp. 65–80, 2015.
DOI: 10.1007/978-3-319-25518-7_6

- alternative metrics for scientific quality and impact, e.g., taking into account the scientist's social network, user-generated micro-content such as discussion post, and recommendations.

Sharing scientific data and building new research on them will lead to data value chains increasingly covering the whole process of scientific research and communication. The Semantic Publishing Challenges aim at supporting the buildup of such data value chains, initially by extracting information from non-semantic publications and interlinking this information with existing datasets. Our prime use case is the computation of novel quality metrics based on such information.

Section 2 presents the definition of this year's Challenge, Sect. 3 explains the evaluation procedure, Sects. 4 to 6 explain the definitions and outcomes of the three tasks in detail, and Sect. 7 discusses overall lessons learnt.

2   Definition of the Challenge

In 2014, we had found it challenging to define a challenge about semantic publishing [10]. Existing datasets focused on basic bibliographical metadata or on research data specific to one scientific domain; we did not consider them suitable to enable advanced applications such as a comprehensive assessment of the quality of scientific output. We had thus designed the first Challenge to produce, by information extraction and in an objectively measurable way, an initial data collection that would be useful for future challenges and that the community can experiment on. As the two information extraction tasks had received few submissions, and as the community had asked for a more exciting task w.r.t. the future of scholarly publishing, we added an open task with a subjective evaluation.

In 2015, we left **Task 1** of 3 largely unchanged: answering queries related to the quality of workshops by computing metrics from data extracted from their proceedings, also considering information about persons and events. The 2014 results had been encouraging, and we intended to give the 2014 participants an incentive to participate once more with improved versions of their tools. As in 2014, **Task 2** focused on extracting contextual information from the full text of papers: citations, authors' affiliations, funding agencies, etc. In contrast to 2014, we now used the same data source as for Task 1 (the CEUR-WS.org open access computer science workshop proceedings), to foster synergies between the two tasks and to encourage participants to compete in both tasks. Based on the data obtained as a result of the 2014 Task 1, we defined the objective of **Task 3** to interlink the CEUR-WS.org linked data with other relevant linked datasets.

3   Common Evaluation Procedures

The evaluation for all tasks followed a common procedure similar to the other Semantic Web Evaluation Challenges:[2]

---

[2] As no one participated in Task 3, our work on this task ended with step 3.

1. For each task, we initially published a *training dataset* (TD) on which the participants could test and train their extraction and interlinking tools.
2. For the information extraction tasks, we specified the basic structure of the RDF extracted from the TD source data, without prescribing a vocabulary.
3. We provided natural language queries and their expected results on TD.
4. A few days before the submission deadline, we published an *evaluation dataset* (ED), a superset of TD, which was the input for the final evaluation.
5. We asked the participants to submit their linked data resulting from extraction or interlinking (under an open license to permit reuse), SPARQL implementations of the queries, as well as their extraction tools, as we reserved the right to inspect them.
6. We awarded prizes for the best-performing (w.r.t. the F1 score computed from precision/recall) and for the most innovative approach (determined by the chairs[3]).
7. Both before and after the submission we maintained transparency. Prospective participants were invited to ask questions, e.g. about the expected query results, which we answered publicly. After the evaluation, we made the scores and the gold standard (see below) available to the participants.

The given queries contained placeholders, e.g. 'all authors of the paper titled *T*'. For training, we specified the results expected after substituting certain values from TD for the variables. We evaluated by substituting further values, mostly values that were only available in ED. We defined easy as well as challenging queries, all weighted equally, to help participants get started, without sacrificing our ability to clearly distinguish the best-performing approach. A collection of PHP scripts[4] helped to automate the evaluation: they compared a CSV form of the results of the participants' SPARQL queries over their data against a gold standard of expected results, and compiled a report with measures and a list of false positives and false negatives (see Figs. 1 and 2).

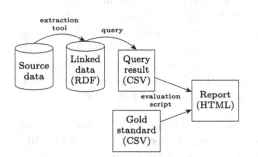

Fig. 1. Precision/recall evaluation

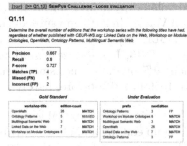

Fig. 2. Report for one query

---

[3] Anastasia Dimou, a co-author of one Task 1 submission [5], did not vote in this task.
[4] https://github.com/angelobo/SemPubEvaluator.

4   Task 1: Extraction and Assessment of Workshop Proceedings Information

4.1   Motivation and Objectives

Common questions related to the quality of a scientific workshop or conference include whether a researcher should submit a paper to it or accept an invitation to its program committee, whether a publisher should publish its proceedings, or whether a company should sponsor it [2]. Moreover, knowing the quality of an event helps to assess the quality of the papers accepted there. In the 2014 Challenge, we had designed Task 1 to extract from selected CEUR-WS.org workshop proceedings volumes RDF that would enable the computation of certain indicators for the workshops' quality [10]. The second objective of this effort was to bootstrap the publication of *all* CEUR-WS.org workshops - more than 1,400 at the time of this writing - as linked data. As discussed above in Sect. 2, we reused the 2014 queries, with two exceptions. As only one of the three 2014 submissions had addressed the two Task 1 queries that required metadata extraction from the PDF full text of the papers (cf. [7]), and as Task 2 focused on full-text extraction anyway, we replaced these queries (Q1.19 and Q1.20) by similar queries that only relied on information available from HTML sources.

4.2   Data Source

The input dataset for Task 1 consists of HTML documents at different levels of encoding quality and semantics.

- one HTML 4 index page linking to *all* workshop proceedings volumes (http://ceur-ws.org/; invalid, somewhat messy but still uniformly structured)
- the HTML tables of contents of selected volumes. Their format is largely uniform but has gained more explicit structural semantics over time, while old volumes remained unchanged. Microformat annotations were introduced with Vol-559 in 2010 and subsequently extended, to enable automatic indexing by DBLP [18]. RDFa (in addition to microformats) was introduced with Vol-994 in 2013, but its use is optional, and therefore it has been used in less than 10 % of all volumes since then. Valid HTML5 has been mandatory since Vol-1059 in 2013; before, hardly any volume was completely valid.

Challenges in processing tables of contents include the lack of standards for marking up editors' affiliations, invited talks, and further cases described in [10].

The training and evaluation datasets TD1 and ED1, available at https://github.com/ceurws/lod/wiki/Task1, balance different document formats. To enable reasonable quality assessment, TD1 already comprised certain complete workshop series, including, e.g., Linked Data on the Web, and, for some conferences, e.g., WWW 2012, all of its workshops that published with CEUR-WS.org. In ED1, some more workshop series and conferences were completed (Table 1).

Table 1. Task 1 data sources

	Training dataset (TD1)	Evaluation dataset (ED1)
Proceedings volumes	98	148 (98 + 50)
... including metadata of	1,700+ papers	2,400+ papers
Volumes using RDFa	6	12 (6 + 6)
... using microformats only	68	106 (68 + 38)

4.3 Queries

The queries were roughly ordered by increasing difficulty. Most queries from Q1.5 onward correspond to quality indicators discussed in Sect. 4.1; Q1.1-Q1.4 were intended to help the participants get started. Further background about Q1.1-Q1.18, which we reused from 2014, can be found in [10].

Q1.1 List the full names of all **editors of the proceedings of workshop** W.

Q1.2 Count the **number of papers in workshop** W.

Q1.3 List the full names of all **authors who have (co-)authored a paper** in workshop W.

Q1.4 Compute the **average length of a paper** (in pages) in workshop W.

Q1.5 (publication turnaround) Find out whether the proceedings of workshop W were published on CEUR-WS.org before the workshop took place.

Q1.6 (previous editions of a workshop) Identify all editions that the workshop series titled T has published with CEUR-WS.org.

Q1.7 (chairs over the history of a workshop) Identify the full names of those chairs of the workshop series titled T that have so far been a chair in every edition of the workshop published with CEUR-WS.org.

Q1.8 (all workshops of a conference) Identify all CEUR-WS.org proceedings volumes in which workshops of conference C in year Y were published.

Q1.9 Identify those papers of workshop W that were **(co-)authored by at least one chair** of the workshop.

Q1.10 List the full names of all **authors of invited papers** in workshop W.

Q1.11 Determine the **number of editions** that the workshop series titled T has had, regardless of whether published with CEUR-WS.org.

Q1.12 (change of workshop title) Determine the title (without year) that workshop W had in its first edition.

Q1.13 (workshops that have died) Of the workshops of conference C in year Y, identify those that did not publish with CEUR-WS.org in the following year (and that therefore probably no longer took place).

Q1.14 (papers of a workshop published jointly with others) Identify the papers of the workshop titled T (which was published in a joint volume V with other workshops).

Q1.15 (editors of one workshop published jointly with others) List the full names of all editors of the proceedings of the workshop titled T (which was published in a joint volume V with other workshops).

Q1.16 Of the workshops that had editions at conference C both in year Y and $Y+1$, identify the **workshop(s) with the biggest percentage of growth** in their number of papers.

Q1.17 (change of conference affiliation) Return the acronyms of those workshops of conference C in year Y whose previous edition was co-located with a different conference series.

Q1.18 (change of workshop date) Of the workshop series titled T, identify those editions that took place more than two months later/earlier than the previous edition published with CEUR-WS.org.

Q1.19 (institutional diversity and internationality of chairs) Identify the affiliations and countries of all editors of the proceedings of workshop W.

Q1.20 (continuity of authors) Identify the full names of those authors of papers in the workshop series titled T that have so far (co-)authored a paper in every edition of the workshop published with CEUR-WS.org.

Q1.5 (partly), Q1.12, Q1.13, Q1.16 and Q1.17 relied on the main index.

As Task 1 also aimed at producing linked data that we could eventually publish at CEUR-WS.org, the participants were additionally asked to follow a uniform URI scheme: http://ceur-ws.org/Vol-NNN/ for volumes, and http://ceur-ws.org/Vol-NNN/#paperM for a paper having the filename paperM.pdf.

4.4   Accepted Submissions and Winners

We received and accepted four submissions that met the requirements.

Milicka/Burget [11], the only new team, took advantage of the facts that, despite changes in *markup*, the visual *layout* of the proceedings volumes has hardly changed over 20 years, and that *within* one volume non-standard layout/-formatting choices are applied consistently. They do not rely on the microformat markup at all. The generic part of their data model covers a page's box layout and the segments of these boxes, which get tagged after text analysis. Further domain-specific analysis yields a logical tree structure, which is finally mapped to the desired output vocabulary. This submission won both awards: for the *most innovative approach* and for the *best performance*.

The three teams that had participated in 2014 evolved their submissions. The following overview focuses on new functionality; otherwise, we refer to the 2014 overview [10]. Kolchin et al. [8] (2014: [7]) enriched their knowledge representation and optimised precision by adding post-processing steps including name disambiguation. Heyvaert et al. [5] (2014: [4]) simplified their HTML→RDF mapping definitions thanks to improvements of the RML mapping language, and optimised precision and recall by running systematic tests over the output to reduce failure due to, e.g., malformed literals. Ronzano et al. [14] (2014: [13]) consulted additional external datasets and web services to support information extraction (e.g. the EU Open Data Portal for names of institutions) and improved their heuristics for validating, sanitising and normalising the data extracted. Their original submission performs poorly because they forgot the trailing slash of the volume URIs. We fixed this mistake to improve comparability.

Table 2. Task 1 evaluation results

Authors	Overall average precision	Overall average recall	Ov. avg. F1	Queries attempted	Average precision on these	Average recall on these	Avg. F1
Milicka/Burget [11]	0.774	0.591	0.64	1–20	0.774	0.591	0.64
Kolchin et al. [8]	0.658	0.531	0.565	1–18	0.731	0.591	0.628
Heyvaert et al. [5]	0.254	0.248	0.244	1–18, 20	0.268	0.261	0.257
Ronzano et al. [14]	0.028	0.046	0.034	1–12,	0.039	0.066	0.048
…with fixed URIs	0.375	0.290	0.302	14–15	0.536	0.414	0.432

Table 3. Task 1 comparison to 2014 (Q1–Q18)

2015	Average precision	Average recall	Avg. F1	2014	Average precision	Average recall	Avg. F1
Milicka/Burget [11]	0.805	0.603	0.657	n/a			
Kolchin et al. [8]	0.731	0.591	0.628	[7]	0.678	0.628	0.644
Heyvaert et al. [5]	0.283	0.276	0.271	[4]	0.153	0.103	0.117
Ronzano et al. [14]	0.031	0.051	0.037				
…with fixed URIs	0.417	0.322	0.336	[13]	0.372	0.348	0.319

4.5   Lessons Learnt

The four Task 1 submissions followed different technical approaches. Two solutions were solely developed to address this Challenge [8,14], whereas Heyvaert et al. and Milicka/Burget defined task-specific mappings in an otherwise generic framework [5,11]. The performance *ranking* of the three tools evolved from 2014 has not changed (cf. Table 2), but their performance has improved (cf. Table 3) - except for Kolchin et al., who improved precision but not recall. Disregarding the two queries that were new in 2015, the tool by Kolchin et al., which had won the best performance award in 2014, performs almost as well as Milicka's/Burget's.

In 2014, we had made first experiments with rolling out the tool by Kolchin et al. at CEUR-WS.org[5], but will now also evaluate Milicka's/Burget's tool. Its reliance on the layout (which hardly ever changes) rather than the underlying markup (which improves every few years) promises low maintenance costs.

---

[5] Licensing issues slowed down progress: from Vol-1265 the metadata are open under CC0, whereas for older volumes CEUR-WS.org does not have the editors' explicit permission to republish derivatives such as extracted RDF. Opinions diverge on the copyrightability of metadata [3]; DBLP actually republishes CEUR-WS.org metadata under ODC-BY. Still, CEUR-WS.org decided not to publish old metadata under their domain; instead, *we* will publish them as an outcome of this Challenge.

5   Task 2: Extracting Contextual Information from the PDF Full Text of the Papers

5.1   Motivation and Objectives

Task 2 was designed to test the ability to extract data from the full text of the papers. It follows last year's Task 2, which focused on extracting information about citations. The rationale was that the network of citations of a paper - including papers citing it or cited by that paper - is an important dimension to assess its relevance and to contextualise it within a research area.

This year we included further *contextual information*. Scientific papers are not isolated units. Factors that directly or indirectly contribute to the origin and development of a paper include citations, the institutions the authors are affiliated to, funding agencies, and the venue where a paper was presented. Participants had to make such information explicit and exploit it to answer queries providing a deeper understanding of the context in which papers were written.

The dataset's *format* is another difference from 2014. Instead of XML sources, we used PDF this year, taken from CEUR-WS.org. PDF is still the predominant format for publishing scientific papers, despite being designed for printing. The internal structure of a PDF paper does not correspond to the logical structure of its content, rather to a sequence of layouting and formatting commands. The challenge for participants was to recover the logical structure, to extract contextual information, and to represent it as semantic assertions.

5.2   Data Source

The construction of the input datasets was driven by the idea of covering a wide spectrum of cases. The papers were selected from 21 different workshops published with CEUR-WS.org. As these workshops had defined their own rules for submissions, the dataset included papers in the LNCS and ACM formats.

Even if all papers had used the same style, their internal structures differed nevertheless. For instance, some papers used numbered citations, others used the APA or other styles. Data about authors and affiliations used heterogeneous structures, too. Furthermore, the papers used different content structures and different forms to express acknowledgements and to refer to entities in the full text (for instance, when mentioning funding, grants, projects, etc.).

The datasets TD2 (training) and ED2 (evaluation) are available at https:// github.com/ceurws/lod/wiki/Task2, as a list of PDF files grouped by proceedings volume. Table 4 reports some statistics about these datasets. TD2 is a *randomly* chosen subset of papers from ED2. The final evaluation was performed on a randomly chosen subset of ED2 too. To cover all queries and balance results, we clustered input papers around each query and selected some of them from each cluster. Each cluster was composed of papers containing enough information to answer each query, and structuring that information in different ways.

Table 4. Task 2 data sources

	Training dataset (TD2)	Evaluation dataset (ED2)
Workshops	12	21 (12 + 9)
Papers	103 (28 ACM + 75 LNCS)	185 (103 + 22 ACM + 60 LNCS)

5.3 Queries

Our ten queries are not meant to be exhaustive but to cover a large spectrum of information. The first two collect information about authors' affiliations:

Q2.1 Identify the **affiliations** of the authors of paper X
Q2.2 Identify the **papers presented at workshop** X and written by researchers affiliated to an **organisation located in country** Y

Affiliations can be associated to authors in different ways: listed right after the author names, placed in footnotes, or placed in a dedicated space of the paper, and so on. The correct identification of affiliation and authors is tricky and opens complex issues of content normalisation and homonymity management. We adopted a simplified approach: participants were required to extract all information available in the input dataset and to normalise content.

Citations are key components of the context of a paper. Three queries deal with extracting data from bibliographies and filtering them by venue and year:

Q2.3 Identify all **works cited** by paper X
Q2.4 Identify all **works cited** by paper X and published **after year** Y.
Q2.5 Identify all **journal papers cited** by paper X

As in 2014, we some queries covered research funding. Such information is useful to investigate how funding was connected to, or even influenced, the research reported in a paper. Awareness of funding might influence the credibility and authoritativeness of a scientific work. The following two queries could be answered by parsing acknowledgements or other dedicated sections:

Q2.6 Identify the **grant(s)** that supported the research presented in paper X (or part of it)
Q2.7 Identify the **funding agencies** that funded the research presented in paper X (or part of it)

Research papers often result from large projects. Knowing them can help to better understand the scope and goal of a given work. The following query related to projects is distinct from the previous ones as these projects are peculiar and clearly identified in the papers (usually in the acknowledgements or in footnotes):

Q2.8 Identify the **EU project(s)** that supported the research presented in paper X (or part of it).

The last two queries were meant to test entity recognition from the papers' textual content. We focused on *ontologies*, as most papers in the dataset were about Semantic Web and formal reasoning and we expected ontologies to be clearly identifiable. For simplicity, we limited the search to the abstracts:

Q2.9 Identify **ontologies mentioned** in the abstract of paper X

Q2.10 Identify **ontologies introduced** in paper X (according to the abstract)

Note that we differentiated two queries: identifying all ontologies mentioned in the abstract vs. those introduced for the first time in the paper (again, search was limited to the abstract). We expected participants to analyse the text and to interpret the verbs used by the authors. Nonetheless the last five queries still proved difficult and only a few were answered correctly (see below for details).

5.4   Accepted Submissions and Winner

We received six submissions for Task 2:

Sateli/Witte [15] proposed a rule-based approach. They composed two logical components in a pipeline: a syntactic processor to identify the basic layout units and to cluster them into logical units, and a semantic processor to identify entities in text by pattern search. The framework is based on GATE and includes an RDF mapper that transforms the extracted data into RDF triples. The mapper's high flexibility contributed to this submission winning the *most innovative approach award*.

Tkaczyk/Bolikowski [19] won the *best performing tool award* for their CER-MINE framework: a Java application extracting metadata from scientific papers by supervised and unsupervised machine learning. The tool was successfully used for the Challenge with a few modifications, including the implementation of an RDF export. It performed extremely well in extracting affiliations and citations.

Klampfl/Kern [6] also used supervised and unsupervised machine learning. Their modular framework identifies and clusters building blocks of the PDF layout. Trained classifiers helped to detect the role of each block (authorship data, affiliations, etc.). The authors built an ontology of computer science concepts and exploited it for the automatic annotation of funding, grant and project data.

Ronzano et al. [14] extended their Task 1 framework to extract data from PDF. Their pipeline includes text processing and entity recognition modules and employs external services for mining PDF articles, and to increase the precision of the citation, author and affiliation extraction.

Integrating multiple techniques and services is also a key aspect of MACJa, the system presented by Nuzzolese et al. [12]. Mainly written in Python and Java, it extracts the textual content of PDF papers using PDFMiner and runs multiple analyses on that content. Named Entity Recognition (NER) techniques help to identify authors and affiliations; CrossRef APIs are queried to extract data from citations; NLP techniques, pattern matching and alignment to lexical resources are finally exploited for detecting ontologies, grants and funding agencies.

Kovriguina et al. [9] presented a simple but efficient architecture, implemented in Python and sharing code with their Task 1 submission [8]. Their approach is mainly based on templates and regular expressions and relies on some external services for improving the quality of the results (e.g., DBLP for checking authors and citations). An external module extracts the plain text from PDFs. This text is matched against a set of regular expressions to extract the relevant parts; the serialisation in RDF follows a custom ontology derived from BIBO.

Table 5 summarises the results of the performance evaluation.

Table 5. Task 2 evaluation results

Authors	Precision	Recall	F1 score
Tkaczyk/Bolikowski [19]	0.369	0.417	0.381
Klampfl/Kern [6]	0.388	0.285	0.292
Nuzzolese et al. [12]	0.274	0.251	0.257
Sateli/Witte [15]	0.3	0.252	0.247
Kovriguina et al. [9]	0.289	0.3	0.265
Ronzano et al. [14]	0.316	0.401	0.332

5.5   Lessons Learnt

We see two main reasons for the unexpectedly low performance:

The Complexity of the Task. When designing the task, we decided to explore a larger amount of contextual information to identify the most interesting issues in this area. In retrospect, this choice led us to defining a difficult task, which instead could have been structured differently. The queries are logically divided in two groups: queries Q2.1–Q2.5 required participants to identify logical units in PDFs; the others required additional content processing. As these two blocks required different skills, we could have separated them in two tasks. Queries within one group, however, were perceived as too heterogeneous. For next year, we are considering fewer types of queries with more cases each.

The Evaluation. As we considered only some papers for the final evaluation (randomly selected among those in the evaluation dataset) some participants were penalised: their tool could have worked well on other values, which were not taken into account. Some low scores also depended on imperfections in the output format. Since the evaluation was fully automated – though the content under evaluation was normalised and minor differences were not considered errors – these imperfections impacted results negatively.

6 Task 3: Interlinking

6.1 Motivation and Objectives

Task 3 was newly designed to assess the ability to identify same entities across different datasets of the same domain, thus establishing links between these datasets. Participants had to make such links explicit and exploit them to answer comprehensive queries about events and persons. The CEUR-WS.org data in itself provide incomplete information about conferences and persons. This information can be complemented by interlinking the dataset with others to broaden the context and to allow for more reliable conclusions about the quality of scientific events and the qualification of researchers.

6.2 Data Source

The input for Task 3 consists of datasets in different RDF serialisations and different levels of encoding quality and semantics. For each dataset, we made an RDF dump and an endpoint or Triple Pattern Fragments [20] available. The complete training dataset TD3, available at https://github.com/ceurws/lod/wiki/Task3, comprises multiple individual datasets accessible in different ways:

CEUR-WS.org. This dataset includes the workshop proceedings volumes up to Vol-1322; it was produced in January 2015 by Maxim Kolchin using his extraction tool, which had won Task 1 of the 2014 Challenge [7].
  RDF dump https://github.com/ceurws/lod/blob/master/data/ceur-ws.ttl
  Triple Pattern Fragments http://data.linkeddatafragments.org/ceur-ws
COLINDA. The Conference Linked Data[6] dataset exposes metadata about scientific events (conferences and workshops) announced at EventSeer and WikiCfP[7] from 2002. COLINDA includes information about the title, description, date and venue of events. It is interlinked with DBLP (see below), Semantic Web Dog Food (see below), GeoNames and DBpedia[8].
  RDF dump https://github.com/ceurws/lod/blob/master/data/colinda.nt
  Endpoint http://data.colinda.org/endpoint.html
  Triple Pattern Fragments http://data.linkeddatafragments.org/colinda
DBLP. The DBLP computer science bibliography [18] is the prime reference for open bibliographic information on computer science publications. It currently indexes over 2.6 million publications by more than 1.4 million authors, in more than 25,000 journal volumes, 24,000 conferences or workshops, and 17,000 monographs. We used the DBLP++ dataset[9].
  RDF dump http://dblp.l3s.de/dblp-2015-02-14.sql.gz
  Endpoint http://dblp.l3s.de/d2r/sparql
  Triple Pattern Fragments http://data.linkeddatafragments.org/dblp

---

[6] http://www.colinda.org/.
[7] See http://eventseer.net/ and http://www.wikicfp.com/.
[8] See http://www.geonames.org/ and http://dbpedia.org/.
[9] http://dblp.l3s.de/dblp++.php.

Lancet. The Semantic Lancet Triplestore dataset[10] contains metadata about papers published in the Journal of Web Semantics by Elsevier. For each paper, the dataset reports bibliographic metadata, abstract and citations.
RDF dump https://github.com/ceurws/lod/blob/master/data/lancet.ttl
Endpoint http://data.linkeddatafragments.org/lancet
Triple Pattern Fragments http://data.linkeddatafragments.org/lancet
SWDF. The Semantic Web Dog Food[11] metadata covers around 5,000 papers, 11,000 people, 3,200 organisations, 45 conferences and 230 workshops.
RDF dump http://data.semanticweb.org/dumps/
Triple Pattern Fragments http://data.linkeddatafragments.org/dogfood
Springer LD. This dataset[12] contains metadata of around 1,200 conference series and 8,000 proceedings volumes published by Springer in the Lecture Notes in Computer Science (LNCS), Lecture Notes in Business Information Processing (LNBIP), Communications in Computer and Information Science (CCIS), Advances in Information and Communication Technology (IFIP-AICT), and Lecture Notes of the Institute for Computer Sciences, Social Informatics and Telecommunications Engineering (LNICST) series.
RDF dump https://github.com/ceurws/lod/blob/master/data/springer.nt
Endpoint http://lod.springer.com/sparql
Triple Pattern Fragments http://data.linkeddatafragments.org/springer

6.3 Queries

The list of queries follows, ordered by increasing difficulty:

Q3.1 (Same entities within the CEUR-WS.org dataset) Identify and interlink same entities that appear with different URIs within the CEUR-WS.org dataset. Same persons (authors and/or editors) or same events (conferences) might have been assigned different URIs.

Q3.2 (Same entities across different datasets) Identify all different instances of the same entity in different datasets. Same entities (persons, articles, proceedings, events) might appear in different datasets with different URIs.

Q3.3 (Workshop call for papers) Link a CEUR-WS.org workshop W to its call for papers announced on EventSeer and/or WikiCfP.

Q3.4 (Workshop website) Link a workshop or conference X that appears in the CEUR-WS.org dataset to the workshop's or conference's website URL.

Q3.5 (Overall contribution to the conference) Identify all papers edited by an author A of a CEUR-WS.org paper P presented at workshop W co-located with conference C, and who was also author of a main track paper at the same conference C.

Q3.6 (Overall activity in a year) Identify, for an author A of a CEUR-WS.org paper P, all his/her activity in year Y.

---

[10] http://www.semanticlancet.eu/.
[11] http://data.semanticweb.org/.
[12] http://lod.springer.com/.

Q3.7 (Full series of workshops) Identify the full series of workshop W regard-less of whether individual editions published with CEUR-WS.org.

Q3.8 (Other co-authors) Identify people who co-authored with author A of a paper P published by CEUR-WS.org but did not co-author any CEUR-WS.org papers published in year Y with him/her.

6.4   Lessons Learnt

For Task 3, we did not receive any submissions, even though participants of the other two tasks had expressed interest. For the next challenge we are considering interlinking tasks that focus on directly extending the information extraction tasks. This way, we expect to lower the entrance barrier for participants of the information extraction tasks to also address interlinking.

7   Overall Lessons Learnt for Future Challenges

As a result of the 2014 Semantic Publishing Challenge, we had obtained an RDF dataset about the CEUR-WS.org workshops. This dataset served as the foundation to build the 2015 Challenge on. We designed all three tasks around the same dataset. This was a good choice in our opinion, as participants could extend their existing tools to perform multiple tasks, and it also opens new perspectives for future collaboration: participants' work could be extended and integrated in a shared effort for producing LOD useful for the whole community.

On the other hand, the evaluation process presented some weaknesses. One participant, for instance, suggested to use an evaluation dataset disjoint from the training dataset to avoid over-training; we should also consider a larger set of instance queries and provide users with intermediate feedback so that they can progressively refine their tools towards providing more precise results.

The definition of the tasks presented some issues this year as well. It was difficult, in particular, to define tasks that were appealing and with balanced difficulty. In retrospect, some tasks were probably too wide and difficult.

Next year, we plan to further increase the reusability of the extracted data, e.g., by asking for an explicit representation of licensing information, but primarily we want to put more emphasis on interlinking. For example, by linking publications to related social websites as SlideShare or Twitter, we will be able to more appropriately assess the impact of a scientific event within the community.

Acknowledgements. We thank our reviewers, our sponsors Springer and Mendeley, and our participants for their hard work, creative solutions and useful suggestions. This work has been partially funded by the European Commission under grant agreement no. 643410.

References

1. Allen, B.P., et al.: Improving future research communication and e-scholarship. FORCE11 Manifesto (2011). https://www.force11.org/about/manifesto
2. Bryl, V., et al.: What's in the proceedings? combining publisher's and researcher's perspectives. In: SePublica, vol. 1155 (2014). CEUR-WS.org
3. Coyle, K.: Metadata and Copyright. Libr. J. (2013). http://lj.libraryjournal.com/2013/02/opinion/peer-to-peer-review/metadataand-copyright-peer-to-peer-review
4. Dimou, A., Vander Sande, M., Colpaert, P., De Vocht, L., Verborgh, R., Mannens, E., Van de Walle, R.: Extraction and semantic annotation of workshop proceedings in HTML using RML. In: Presutti, V., et al. (eds.) SemWebEval 2014. CCIS, vol. 475, pp. 114–119. Springer, Heidelberg (2014)
5. Heyvaert, P., et al.: Semantically annotating CEUR-WS workshop proceedings with RML. In: Gandon, F., et al. (eds.) SemWebEval 2015. CCIS, vol. 548, pp. 165–176. Springer, Heidelberg (2015)
6. Klampfl, S., Kern, R.: Machine learning techniques for automatically extracting contextual information from scientific publications. In: Gandon, F., et al. (eds.) SemWebEval 2015. CCIS, vol. 548, pp. 105–116. Springer, Heidelberg (2015)
7. Kolchin, M., Kozlov, F.: A template-based information extraction from web sites with unstable markup. In: Presutti, V., et al. (eds.) SemWebEval 2014. CCIS, vol. 475, pp. 89–94. Springer, Heidelberg (2014)
8. Kolchin, M., et al.: CEUR-WS-LOD: conversion of CEUR-WS workshops to linked data. In: Gandon, F., et al. (eds.) SemWebEval 2015. CCIS, vol. 548, pp. 142–152. Springer, Heidelberg (2015)
9. Kovriguina, L., et al.: Metadata extraction from conference proceedings using template-based approach. In: Gandon, F., et al. (eds.) SemWebEval 2015. CCIS, vol. 548, pp. 153–164. Springer, Heidelberg (2015)
10. Lange, C., Di Iorio, A.: Semantic publishing challenge – assessing the quality of scientific output. In: Presutti, V., et al. (eds.) SemWebEval 2014. CCIS, vol. 475, pp. 61–76. Springer, Heidelberg (2014)
11. Milicka, M., Burget, R.: Information extraction from web sources based on multi-aspect content analysis. In: Gandon, F., et al. (eds.) SemWebEval 2015. CCIS, vol. 548, pp. 81–92. Springer, Heidelberg (2015)
12. Nuzzolese, A.G., Peroni, S., Recupero, D.R.: MACJa: metadata and citations jailbreaker. In: Gandon, F., et al. (eds.) SemWebEval 2015. CCIS, vol. 548, pp. 117–128. Springer, Heidelberg (2015)
13. Ronzano, F., del Bosque, G.C., Saggion, H.: Semantify CEUR-WS proceedings: towards the automatic generation of highly descriptive scholarly publishing linked datasets. In: Presutti, V., et al. (eds.) SemWebEval 2014. CCIS, vol. 475, pp. 83–88. Springer, Heidelberg (2014)
14. Ronzano, F., et al.: On the automated generation of scholarly publishing linked datasets: the case of CEUR-WS proceedings. In: Gandon, F., et al. (eds.) SemWebEval 2015. CCIS, vol. 548, pp. 177–188. Springer, Heidelberg (2015)
15. Sateli, B., Witte, R.: Automatic construction of a semantic knowledge base from CEUR workshop proceedings. In: Gandon, F., et al. (eds.) SemWebEval 2015. CCIS, vol. 548, pp. 129–141. Springer, Heidelberg (2015)
16. Presutti, V., et al. (eds.): SemWebEval 2014. CCIS, vol. 475. Springer, Heidelberg (2014)
17. Gandon, F., et al. (eds.) SemWebEval 2015. CCIS, vol. 548. Springer, Heidelberg (2015)

18. The DBLP Computer Science Bibliography. http://dblp.uni-trier.de
19. Tkaczyk, D., Bolikowski, L.: Extracting contextual information from scientific literature using CERMINE system. In: Gandon, F., et al. (eds.) SemWebEval 2015. CCIS, vol. 548, pp. 93–104. Springer, Heidelberg (2015)
20. Verborgh, R., et al.: Low-cost queryable linked data through triple pattern fragments. In: ISWC Posters and Demonstrations, vol. 1272 (2014). CEUR-WS.org

Information Extraction from Web Sources
Based on Multi-aspect Content Analysis

Martin Milicka[✉] and Radek Burget

Faculty of Information Technology, IT4Innovations Centre of Excellence,
Brno University of Technology, Bozetechova 2, 612 66 Brno, Czech Republic
{imilicka,burgetr}@fit.vutbr.cz

Abstract. Information extraction from web pages is often recognized as
a difficult task mainly due to the loose structure and insufficient semantic annotation of their HTML code. Since the web pages are primarily
created for being viewed by human readers, their authors usually do not
pay much attention to the structure and even validity of the HTML code
itself. The CEUR Workshop Proceedings pages are a good illustration
of this. Their code varies from an invalid HTML markup to fully valid
and semantically annotated documents while preserving a kind of unified
visual presentation of the contents. In this paper, as a contribution to the
ESWC 2015 Semantic Publishing Challenge, we present an information
extraction approach based on analyzing the rendered pages rather than
their code. The documents are represented by an RDF-based model that
allows to combine the results of different page analysis methods such
as layout analysis and the visual and textual feature classification. This
allows to specify a set of generic rules for extracting a particular information from the page independently on its code.

Keywords: Document modeling · Information extraction · Page
segmentation · Content classification · Ontology · RDF

1 Introduction

The documents available on the web present a large and ever growing source
of information. However, extracting information from the HTML documents
remains a challenging tasks mainly because of the high variability of the markup,
loose structure of the documents and very rare use of any kind of semantic
annotations that could be used for recognizing a particular information in the
document.

The research in this area includes many different approaches including a
direct HTML code analysis by different methods [7,8], DOM analysis [6], page
layout [2] or other visual feature analysis [10]. As the research results show, the
web documents are too variable for the a simple and straightforward solution.
The document processing cannot be based only on single aspect such as the text
content, visual features or document structure because each approach is suitable

© Springer International Publishing Switzerland 2015
F. Gandon et al. (Eds.): SemWebEval 2015, CCIS 548, pp. 81–92, 2015.
DOI: 10.1007/978-3-319-25518-7_7

for a different kind of documents. Therefore, we propose an approach that can combine multiple aspects of the document.

The documents may be described on different levels of abstraction starting with the code through the rendered page layout and visual features of the contents to a logical structure as it is expected to be interpreted by a human reader. We propose an ontology-based document model that is able to capture all the mentioned kinds of information. For each level of the description, we use a specific ontology. The highest abstraction level represents the target domain of the extracted information.

In this paper, we apply this approach to the processing of the CEUR Workshop proceedings as a part of the ESWC 2015 Semantic Publishing Challenge. We employ a combination of algorithms such as page segmentation or content classification for building the proposed model from source documents. Based on a combination of different features, we propose the way of extracting the logical structure of the document. This structure is finally transformed to the specific domain ontology. This approach allows to abstract from the HTML implementation details and increase the robustness of the extraction.

2   System Architecture

The presented information extraction system is based on our recently developed FITLayout[1] framework [9] – a generic framework for web page segmentation and its further analysis. The complete architecture overview is shown in Fig. 1. Implementation details specific for the Semantic Publishing Challenge 2015 are described later in Sect. 4.

Unlike most existing information extraction systems, our system does not analyze the HTML or CSS code of the input documents directly. Instead, it operates on the rendered page trying to use the same information as the user who is actually browsing. This allows to abstract from the HTML-related problems such as irregular code structure, invalid markup, etc.

The individual documents (CEUR pages) are processed independently on each other. The processing consists of several steps. The results of each step are stored to an internal RDF repository; each step adds more information to the model of the processed document. First, source pages are rendered using a built-in rendering engine that provides the information about the layout and visual features of the individual pieces of the contents. Additionally, basic text analysis steps are applied on the document in order to recognize important entities in the text such as dates, times, capitalized sequences or personal names. Subsequently, the obtained model is analyzed and the desired information such as editors, paper titles, authors, etc. is recognized using a set of quite simple rules based on the actual presentation of the individual content parts. Based on the recognized parts of the contained information, we build a *logical structure* of the document that represents the semantic relationships. Finally, this structure is transformed to the resulting linked data set.

---

[1] http://www.fit.vutbr.cz/~burgetr/FITLayout/.

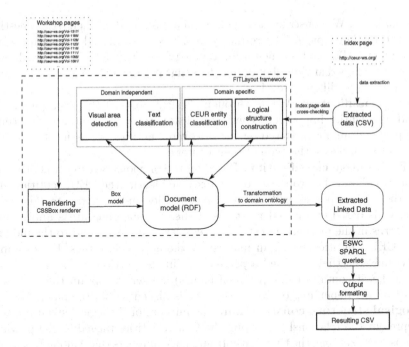

Fig. 1. Extraction system architecture

2.1   Page Rendering

The rendering engine processes the input HTML and the linked CSS files and produces the information about the content layout in the page. The layout is represented by a *box model* generally defined in the CSS specification [1]. This model describes the positions of the individual pieces of content in the resulting page and their further visual properties (fonts, colors, etc.) Each box corresponds to a rectangular area in the rendered page. The boxes are organized in a hierarchical structure called a *box tree* that roughly corresponds to the source DOM structure.

The obtained box tree is transformed to RDF data using the FITLayout box model ontology described in Sect. 3.1. In the subsequent steps of the model building, more information is added to the page model as the result of the individual analysis methods.

2.2   Model Building

The model building phase consists of four analysis steps. The first two of them are domain-independent; they are not specific for the SemPub2015 task. The other two steps are specific for the target domain. The details of the individual steps are described later in Sect. 4.

1. **Visual area detection.** We identify all the boxes in the box tree that are visually distinguishable in the resulting pages. These boxes form the basic

visual areas. We construct a tree of visual areas based on their visual nesting in the rendered page. The resulting area tree is described using the corresponding FITLayout segmentation ontology (see Sect. 3.2). Later, each area may be assigned any number of text *tags* that represent the expected meaning of the area at different levels.

2. **Text classification.** We go through the leaf areas of the visual area tree and we identify important generic entities in the text such as dates, times or personal numbers. Based on the discovered entities, we assign tags to the areas that indicate the type of their content.

3. **CEUR entity classification.** Based on the previous two steps, i.e. the layout model and the properties of the text, we identify the CEUR entities such as the workshop title, editor names, paper titles and authors, etc. Their discovery is based on mutual positions of the corresponding areas and regular patterns in the presentation styles. The areas that correspond to the individual CEUR entities are again marked by the appropriate tags. For example, a visual area that obtained a *persons* tag in the previous text classification step (i.e. it contains some personal names) is likely to obtain the *editors* or *authors* tag depending on where the area is placed within the page.

4. **Logical structure construction.** The purpose of the logical structure is to represent the relationships among the CEUR entities tagged in the previous steps. For example, the title, authors and page numbers that belong to a single paper, papers that belong to a single section, etc. In a domain-dependent way, we transform the tagged area tree to the logical structure tree where the logical nodes correspond to particular text strings (e.g. the names themselves) and the parent-child relationships correspond to the semantic subordination of the entities (e.g. the title, authors and pages are child nodes of a paper node). Each node is marked with a single tag that specifies its semantic.

The whole process corresponds to the transition from the rendered page model (the box tree) through the page layout model (the visual area tree) to its semantic interpretation (the logical area tree). In the next step, the resulting logical model can be transformed to the target domain ontology.

2.3   Output Dataset Generation

The resulting logical structure tree that is obtained from the model building phase and stored in the intrenal RDF repository contains the complete information extracted from the source page together with its structure. The output dataset generation only consists of transforming the data represented using the FITLayout internal visual area ontology to the target domain ontology described in Sect. 3.5. This is implemented as a single SPARQL query[2] on the internal RDF repository.

---

[2] https://github.com/FitLayout/ToolsEswc/blob/master/sparql/logicalTree2domain.sparql.

3 Ontological Model

The ontological model describes the processed document at multiple levels of abstraction. We have defined five abstraction levels of document description where each higher level adds specific knowledge to the previous one. Each level of description is characterized by its ontology. The hierarchy of levels is shown in Fig. 2. We can see that all the levels can be divided in two groups: domain-independent and domain-specific. The tagging level in the middle joins the two parts together.

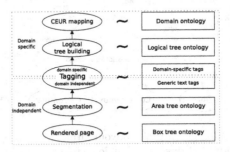

Fig. 2. Ontological model

3.1 Rendered Page Level

At the level of the rendered page, the ontology-based model corresponds to the document box model where its rendering is based on the source data presented in the HTML document and visual features defined by Cascading Style Sheets (CSS).

The schema of the presented *Box model ontology* is on Fig. 3(A). Every class is based on the *Rectangle* class which defines characteristic size, position and visual features. A *Box* denotes a base displayed document element. It follows the definition from the CSS formatting model [1]. The boxes may be nested, which creates a hierarchical structure similar to the Document Object Model (DOM). The *Page* class represents the whole rendered page. The *belongsTo* property denotes the relationship between the Page and some rectangular objects (boxes) that create the contents of the page. The *Box* can be further specialized into the *ContainerBox* or *ContentBox* classes where the *ContainerBox* may contain other boxes (allows nesting). The *ContentBox* represents a Box that contains a connections of content objects like images, textual information or common objects like Flash, video, etc.

3.2 Segmentation Level

Page segmentation generally detects the visually distinguished segments in the rendered page (we call them *visual areas* in this paper). There exist many page segmentation algorithms; one of the most popular ones is called VIPS [4].

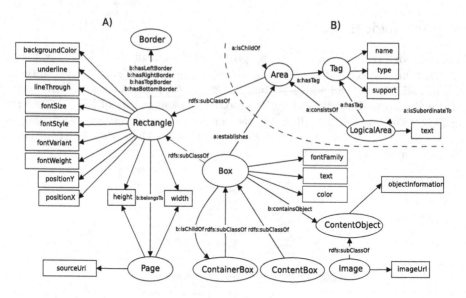

Fig. 3. (A) Box tree ontology (http://fitlayout.github.io/ontology/render.owl#) (B) Area based ontology (http://fitlayout.github.io/ontology/segmentation.owl#)

The segmentation model extends the Box model by a possibility of representing the visual areas. In the Fig. 3(B) we can see a part of segmentation ontology design. The basic *Area* class is defined as a specialization of the *Rectangle* class from the Box model ontology. It represents the visual areas detected during the page segmentation. A visual area is usually created by a collection of boxes contained in this visual segment. Visual areas may be nested and create a hierarchy based on their visual nesting similarly to boxes.

3.3   Tagging Level

The tags are represented by the *Tag* class (in Fig. 3(B)); multiple tags may be assigned to a single visual area. Each tag is represented by its *name* and *type* where the type represents a set of tags with the same purpose (e.g. the tags obtained from text classification) and the name corresponds to the actual tag value.

In Sect. 4, we give an overview of the tags used for the given domain. Some of them are domain-independent (Table 1), some are domain-dependent (Table 2).

3.4   Logical Tree Level

The logical structure represents the actual interpretation of the tagged visual areas in the target domain. Each logical area corresponds to a semantic entity identified as a text string contained in some visual areas (e.g. an author name). It is represented by the *LogicalArea* class in (Fig. 3). Each logical area has a single tag assigned that denotes its meaning in the target domain (e.g. a paper title).

The logical areas are organized to a hierarchical structure again (using the *isSubordinateTo* property). However, unlike the visual areas, where the hierarchy represents the visual nesting, for logical areas, the hierarchy corresponds to the logical relationships among the entities – e.g. a paper and its title or page numbers.

The resulting logical area tree provides a generic representation of the extracted information and its structure and it can be directly mapped to the target domain ontology.

3.5 Domain Level

The domain ontology defines the entities and their properties in the target domain. It is used for the resulting data set produced by our extraction tool. For the the CEUR proceedings domain, we use a combination of existing ontologies shown in Fig. 4 that is greatly inspired by [8] with some simplifications.

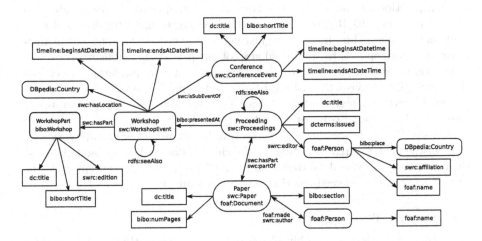

Fig. 4. Domain ontology – ESWC proceedings

4 System Implementation

The FITLayout framework used as a base for our system implements a variety of general tasks such as page rendering, page segmentation and text feature analysis. Moreover, it allows to implement custom extensions and add them to the page processing chain. For the purpose of the CEUR proceedings processing, we have implemented several domain-specific extensions that include the CEUR entity recognition and a custom logical structure builder specific for this particular task[3].

We made several experiments with using the microformats available in some of the CEUR volume pages for training a visual feature classifier that would

---

[3] https://github.com/FitLayout/ToolsEswc.

be later used for the remaining volumes. However, the presentation style of the individual volumes is quite variable in terms of the used fonts, layout or information ordering. Therefore, we have decided to process the individual pages independently. In the final version of our tools, we do not use any kind of classifier training (apart from the pre-trained Stanford NER classifier used for recognizing the personal names as described in Sect. 4.2). Instead of this, we just gather statistic about the frequently used presentation patterns and styles used in the currently processed page and we assume the most frequent one to be consistently used in the page as described in Sect. 4.3. The microformats are not used at all in the end because their availability is not guaranteed.

In the following sections, we explain the most important details of the whole information extraction process.

4.1   Layout Analysis

The FITLayout framework assumes a usage of a page segmentation method for the construction of the visual area tree. However, due to the relatively simple layout of the CEUR proceedings, we decided not to use a full-featured page segmentation algorithm. Instead, we just use a basic visual area recognition algorithm that corresponds to the initial step of our previously published page segmentation algorithm [3]. From the box tree obtained from rendering, we choose the boxes that are visually distinguishable in the page: they directly represent a piece of text or image content or they have some visible visual separator: a separating background color or a border around the box.

For the CEUR proceedings, the resulting layout model is usually very flat: Most of the content areas are directly the child nodes of the root node because there is usually no visual nesting used in the layout. The only exception is the title of some of the proceedings that is visually framed.

4.2   Generic Text Tagging

Area tagging is used to roughly classify the visual areas that contain certain kind of information. The FITLayout framework provides a set of general purpose taggers that assign tags of the `FitLayout.TextTag` type to the visual areas by a simple analysis of the contained text mainly using regular expressions. Table 1 describes the text tags we have used for the given task and the way of their assignment to the visual areas.

The used regular expressions are quite general (especially for the paper titles), and the used generic NER classifier is not 100 % accurate neither. Therefore, the tag assignment obtained in this phase provides just a rough and approximate classification of the areas. Further refining is performed in the following CEUR entity recognition phase.

4.3   CEUR Entity Recognition

The CEUR entity recognition consists of assigning another set of tags to the discovered visual areas. These tags correspond to the individual types of information

Table 1. Tags added during the text feature analysis (tag type `FitLayout.TextTag`)

Tag	Meaning	Way of recognition
dates	A date in recognizable format	Regular expressions and specific keywords (months)
pages	Page span specification	Regular expression
persons	Personal names	Stanford NER classifier [5]
title	Paper title	Regular expression

that we want to extract from the source document. The complete list of the assigned tags (with the type `ESWC`) and their meaning is in Table 2.

Table 2. Tags used for the CEUR entity annotation (tag type `ESWC`)

Tag	Meaning	Tag	Meaning
vtitle	Volume title	*subtitle*	Volume subtitle (proceedings)
vcountry	Workshop location (country)	*title*	Paper title
veditor	Editor name	*authors*	Paper author(s)
vdate	Date(s) of the workshop	*pages*	Paper pages

The transition from the general *text tags* listed in Table 1 to the *semantic tags* listed in Table 2 corresponds to the disambiguation and refining of the rough text classification. We assume that some text tags may be missing or may have been assigned incorrectly. Some tags are ambiguous, e.g. the *persons* tag may indicate author or editor names depending on context.

For assigning the semantic tags, our refining algorithms take into account the following aspects:

– *Common visual presentation rules* – there exist some commonly used rules for visual formatting of the presented information in a document. E.g. a title or subtitle is written in larger font or at least bolder than a normal text.
– *Regularity in presentation style* – we assume that all the information of the same meaning (e.g. all paper titles) is presented with the same visual style (fonts, colors, etc.) in a single proceedings page.
– *Regularity in layout* – some proceedings put author names before the paper title, some put them below or on the same line. However, this layout is again consistent through the whole proceedings page.
– *Locality of the information* – information of the same kind is presented in one area of the page. We can identify an area containing editors, papers, etc. The order of these area remains the same in all the proceedings pages.
– *Textual hints* – some key phrases such as "Edited by" or "Table of Contents" are commonly used in most of the proceedings. When they are found in the page, they can be used to refine the expected area where a particular information is located within the page.

Our algorithm works in the following steps:

1. We discover the position of the workshop title and the repeating layout and style patterns that (together with the assigned text tags from Table 1) correspond to the published papers and their authors and similarly for editors and their affiliations.
2. Based on the discovered patterns, we guess approximate areas in the rendered page that are likely to contain a particular information: the workshop title, subtitle (proceedings information), editors, papers and submission details. If the text hints such as "Edited by" are present in the pages, the expected area bounds are adjusted appropriately.
3. In these areas, we find the most frequent font style used for each type of information (e.g. author names) and the most frequent layout pattern (authors before or after the title, etc.) Then, we assign the appropriate semantic tags from Table 2 to all the visual areas using the same font style that correspond to the discovered layout pattern. This solves the possible inaccuracy of the text tag assignment.

The workshop title is discovered by its font size (it's always written with the largest font size used in the page). The editor area is guessed by searching personal names between the workshop title and the papers (the "Table of contents" text may be used as a hint when present) and the subtitle is located between the title and the editors.

As the result, we obtain a refined tagging of the visual areas that indicates their semantics.

4.4 Logical Structure Construction

The last logical structure construction phase has two main goals:

- Extract the text data from the tagged visual areas. The area may contain multiple kinds of information (e.g. several author names, several editors or some additional text that should be omitted).
- Put together the information that belongs to a single entity: the name and affiliation of a single editor or the title, authors and pages of a single paper.

These goals correspond to the construction of a tree of *logical areas* as defined in Sect. 3.4. The text extraction corresponds to the identification of the logical areas and the relationships among the areas (denoted using the *a:isChildOf* property) are used for creating a tree of logical areas where the child nodes specify the properties of its parent node.

We have implemented a custom logical tree builder that goes through the visual area tree and creates the logical areas organized in subtrees depending on the assigned semantic tags. For this, some more text processing is usually required: splitting the author area to several author names by separators, completing the editor affiliations by matching the different kinds of symbols and bullets and extracting the data such as workshop date from longer text lines.

The countries in the editor affiliations are recognized by a simple matching with a fixed list of countries and their DBPedia resource IRIs (a CSV extracted from DBPedia).

The workshop and conference acronym extraction is based on a simple text parser that recognizes all the acronyms and the ordinals in the text. In order to distinguish between the workshop and the conference acronyms, we try to locate the particular keywords (e.g. "colocated with") in the subtitle and we also compare the sets of acronyms found in the title and the subtitle since the conference acronym is very rarely present in the main title.

Some information such as the paper IRIs must be obtained from the underlying code from the `id` or `href` attributes. Therefore, in our stored rendered page model, we maintain the information about the source DOM nodes that produce the given box displayed in the page.

The resulting logical structure description is added to the FITLayout internal RDF repository and it can be directly transformed to the output linked data set by mapping to the target ontology.

4.5 CEUR Index Page Processing

The CEUR proceedings index page is a specific source of information. We use this page for locating the related workshops (the *see also*) information, the date of publication. We also use the volume title from the index page in the final output because the title in the individual pages is slightly different in some cases.

Since the index page is just a single HTML document with a specific style and quite a regular structure, we have just used a simple "old school" Unix `awk` script for extracting this data directly from the HTML code. This script produces a CSV output that is used by the logical tree builder to complete the logical structure.

5 Conclusions

In this paper, we have presented a web information extraction approach based on a complex modelling of different aspects of the processed document. Our system analyzes the rendered document and in multiple steps, it guesses and later disambiguates the semantics of the individual text parts by combining the page segmentation and text classification methods with specific extraction rules based on visual presentation of the content. This approach allows to avoid HTML-related implementation details. The extraction task is specified on quite a high level of abstraction that ensures the tolerance of the method to different variations in the processed documents.

Acknowledgments. This work was supported by the BUT FIT grant FIT-S-14-2299 and the IT4Innovations Centre of Excellence CZ.1.05/1.1.00/02.0070.

References

1. Bos, B., Lie, H.W., Lilley, C., Jacobs, I.: Cascading style sheets, level 2, CSS2 specification. The World Wide Web Consortium (1998)
2. Burget, R.: Layout based information extraction from HTML documents. In: ICDAR 2007, pp. 624–629. IEEE Computer Society (2007)
3. Burget, R., Rudolfová, I.: Web page element classification based on visual features. In: 1st Asian Conference on Intelligent Information and Database Systems ACIIDS 2009, pp. 67–72. IEEE Computer Society (2009)
4. Cai, D., Yu, S., Wen, J.R., Ma, W.Y.: VIPS: a Vision-based page segmentation algorithm. Microsoft Research (2003)
5. Finkel, J.R., Grenager, T., Manning, C.: Incorporating non-local information into information extraction systems by gibbs sampling. In: Proceedings of the 43rd Annual Meeting on Association for Computational Linguistics, ACL 2005, pp. 363–370 (2005)
6. Hong, J.L., Siew, E.G., Egerton, S.: Information extraction for search engines using fast heuristic techniques. Data Knowl. Eng. **69**(2), 169–196 (2010). http://dx.doi.org/10.1016/j.datak.2009.10.002
7. Hong, T.W., Clark, K.L.: Using grammatical inference to automate information extraction from the web. In: Siebes, A., De Raedt, L. (eds.) PKDD 2001. LNCS (LNAI), vol. 2168, pp. 216–227. Springer, Heidelberg (2001)
8. Kolchin, M., Kozlov, F.: A template-based information extraction from web sites with unstable markup. In: Presutti, V., et al. (eds.) SemWebEval 2014. CCIS, vol. 475, pp. 89–94. Springer, Heidelberg (2014). http://dx.doi.org/10.1007/978-3-319-12024-9_11
9. Milicka, M., Burget, R.: Multi-aspect document content analysis using ontological modelling. In: Proceedings of 9th Workshop on Intelligent and Knowledge Oriented Technologies (WIKT 2014), pp. 9–12. Vydavatelstvo STU (2014)
10. You, Y., Xu, G., Cao, J., Zhang, Y., Huang, G.: Leveraging visual features and hierarchical dependencies for conference information extraction. In: Ishikawa, Y., Li, J., Wang, W., Zhang, R., Zhang, W. (eds.) APWeb 2013. LNCS, vol. 7808, pp. 404–416. Springer, Heidelberg (2013). http://dx.doi.org/10.1007/978-3-642-37401-2_41

Extracting Contextual Information from Scientific Literature Using CERMINE System

Dominika Tkaczyk[✉] and Łukasz Bolikowski

Interdisciplinary Centre for Mathematical and Computational Modelling,
University of Warsaw, Warsaw, Poland
{d.tkaczyk,l.bolikowski}@icm.edu.pl

Abstract. CERMINE is a comprehensive open source system for extracting structured metadata and references from born-digital scientific literature. Among other information, the system is able to extract information related to the context the article was written in, such as the authors and their affiliations, the relations between them or references to other articles. Extracted information is presented in a structured, machine-readable form. CERMINE is based on a modular workflow, whose loosely coupled architecture allows for individual components evaluation and adjustment, enables effortless improvements and replacements of independent parts of the algorithm and facilitates future architecture expanding. The implementation of the workflow is based mostly on supervised and unsupervised machine-learning techniques, which simplifies the procedure of adapting the system to new document layouts and styles. In this paper we outline the overall workflow architecture, describe key aspects of the system implementation, provide details about training and adjusting of individual algorithms, and finally report how CERMINE was used for extracting contextual information from scientific articles in PDF format in the context of ESWC 2015 Semantic Publishing Challenge. CERMINE system is available under an open-source licence and can be accessed at http://cermine. ceon.pl.

1 Introduction

Academic literature is a very important communication channel in the scientific world. Keeping track of the latest scientific findings and achievements, typically published in journals or conference proceedings, is a crucial aspect of the research work. Unfortunately, studying scientific literature, and in particular being up-to-date with the latest positions, is difficult and extremely time-consuming. The main reason for this is huge and constantly growing volume of scientific literature, and also the fact, that publications are mostly available in the form of unstructured text.

Semantic publishing addresses these issues by the enhancement of scholarly data with metadata and interlinking, allowing the machines to better understand the structure, meaning and relations of published information. Machine-readable

© Springer International Publishing Switzerland 2015
F. Gandon et al. (Eds.): SemWebEval 2015, CCIS 548, pp. 93–104, 2015.
DOI: 10.1007/978-3-319-25518-7_8

metadata describing scholarly communication, for example metadata related to citations, authors, organizations, research centres, projects or datasets, facilitates solving tasks like building citation and author networks, providing useful tools for intelligent search, detecting similar and related documents and authors, the assessment of the achievements of individual authors and entire organizations, identifying people and teams with a given research profile, and many more.

Unfortunately, in practice good quality metadata is not always available, sometimes it is missing, full of errors or fragmentary. In such cases there is a need to automatically extract the metadata directly from source documents, often stored in PDF format. Such automatic analysis of PDF documents is challenging, mainly due to the vast diversity of possible layouts and styles used in articles. In different documents the same type of information can be displayed in different places using a variety of formatting styles and fonts. For instance, a random subset of 125,000 documents from PubMed Central [5] contains publications from nearly 500 different publishers, many of which use original layouts and styles in their articles. What is more, PDF format does not preserve the information related to the document's structure, such as words and paragraphs, lists and enumerations, or the reading order of the text. This information has to be reverse engineered based on the text content and the way the text is displayed in the source file.

These problems are addressed by CERMINE [13] — a comprehensive, open-source tool for automatic metadata extraction from born-digital scientific literature. CERMINE's extraction algorithm performs a thorough analysis of the input scientific publication in PDF format and extracts:

- a rich set of the document's metadata, including the title, authors, their affiliations, emails, abstract, keywords, year of publication, etc.,
- a list of bibliographic references along with their metadata.

Designed as a universal solution, CERMINE is able to handle a vast variety of publication layouts reasonably well, instead of being perfect in processing a limited number of document layouts only. This was achieved by employing supervised and unsupervised machine-learning algorithms trained on large and diverse datasets. It also resulted in increased maintainability of the system, as well as its ability to adapt to previously unseen document layouts.

CERMINE is based on a modular workflow composed of a number of steps with carefully defined input and output. By virtue of such workflow architecture individual steps can be maintained separately, making it easy to perform evaluation or training, improve or replace one step implementation without changing other parts of the workflow. CERMINE web service, as well as the source code, can be accessed online at http://cermine.ceon.pl [14].

The system is participating in ESWC 2015 Semantic Publishing Challenge. Its task is to mine PDF articles from CEUR workshop proceedings in order to extract the information related to the context in which the papers were written.

This article describes the overall extraction workflow architecture and key steps implementations, provides details about the training of machine-learning based algorithms, and finally reports how CERMINE was used for information extraction in the context of ESWC 2015 Semantic Publishing Challenge.

2   System Overview

CERMINE accepts a scientific publication in PDF format on the input. The extraction algorithm inspects the entire content of the document and produces two kinds of output in NLM JATS format [3]: the document's metadata and bibliography.

CERMINE's web service can be accessed at http://cermine.ceon.pl. The code is available on GitHub at https://github.com/CeON/CERMINE. The system provides also a REST service that allows for executing the extraction process by machines. It can be accessed using cURL tool:

```
$ curl -X POST --header "Content-Type: application/binary" -v \
  --data-binary @article.pdf http://cermine.ceon.pl/extract.do
```

2.1   Models and Formats

CERMINE's input document format is PDF, currently the most popular format for storing the sources of scientific publications. A PDF file contains by design the text of the document in the form of a list of chunks of various length specifying the position, size, and other geometric features of the text, as well as the information related to the fonts and graphics. Unfortunately, the format does not preserve any information related to the logical structure of the text, such as words, lines, paragraphs, enumerations, sections, section titles or even the reading order of text chunks.

The inner model of the document used during CERMINE's analysis is a hierarchical structure that holds the entire text content of the article, while also preserving the information related to the way elements are displayed in the corresponding PDF file. In this representation an article is a list of pages, each page contains a list of zones, each zone contains a list of lines, each line contains a list of words, and finally each word contains a list of characters. Each structure element can be described by its text content and bounding box (a rectangle enclosing the element). The structure contains also the natural reading order for the elements on each structure level and labels describing the role of the zones. The model can be serialized using XML TrueViz format.

The original output format of the extraction process is NLM JATS [3]. JATS (Journal Article Tag Suite) defines a rich set of XML elements and attributes for describing scientific publications. Documents in JATS format can store a wide range of structured metadata of the document, hierarchical full text and the bibliography in the form of a list of references along with their metadata.

Recently added functionality, essential for the semantic publishing challenge, is exporting information extracted from a set of articles as LOD dataset in RDF format. Currently exported dataset contains only the relevant subset of extracted metadata.

2.2   System Architecture

CERMINE's extraction workflow (Fig. 1) is composed of the following stages:

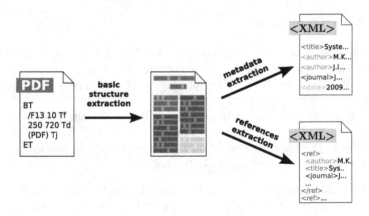

Fig. 1. CERMINE's extraction workflow architecture. At the beginning the geometric structure is extracted from the input PDF file. Then metadata and bibliography are extracted in two parallel paths.

[A] **Basic structure extraction** stage — analysing the input PDF file in order to construct its geometric hierarchical representation by executing the following steps:

    [A1] **Character extraction** — extracting individual characters with their coordinates and dimensions from the input PDF using iText library [2].

    [A2] **Page segmentation** — constructing the document's geometric hierarchical structure containing pages, zones, lines, words and characters, using enhanced Docstrum algorithm [11].

    [A3] **Reading order resolving** — determining the reading order for all structure elements using bottom-up heuristic-based algorithm.

    [A4] **Initial zone classification** — classifying the document's zones into categories: *metadata*, *body*, *references* and *other* using Support Vector Machines classifier.

[B] **Metadata extraction** stage — extracting a rich set of document's metadata from zones labelled as *metadata* by executing the following steps:

    [B1] **Metadata zone classification** — classifying the document's zones into specific metadata classes using Support Vector Machines classifier.

    [B2] **Metadata extraction** — extracting atomic metadata information from labelled zones using a list of simple rules.

    [B3] **Affiliation parsing** — identifying organization, address and country in affiliation strings using Conditional Random Fields classifier.

[C] **Bibliography extraction** stage — extracting a list of parsed citations from zones labelled as *references* by executing the following steps:

    [D1] **Reference extraction** — dividing the content of *references* zones into individual reference strings using K-Means clustering.

    [D2] **Reference parsing** — extracting metadata information from references strings using Conditional Random Fields token classifier.

3   Metadata Extraction Algorithms

This section provides details about the implementations of key steps of the workflow. More information about the system implementation can be found in [13].

3.1   Geometric Structure Extraction

Structure extraction is the initial phase of the entire workflow. Its goal is to create a hierarchical structure of the document preserving the entire text content of the input document and also features related to the way the text is displayed in the PDF file.

Geometric structure extraction is composed of three steps:

1. Character extraction — extracting individual characters from the input PDF document.
2. Page segmentation — joining individual characters into words, lines and zones.
3. Reading order determination — calculating the reading order for all structure levels.

The purpose of character extraction is to extract individual characters from the PDF stream along with their positions on the page, widths and heights. The implementation is based on open-source iText [2] library. We use iText to iterate over PDF's text-showing operators. During the iteration we extract text strings along with their size and position on the page. Next, extracted strings are split into characters and their individual widths and positions are calculated.

The goal of page segmentation is to create a geometric hierarchical structure storing the document's content, consisting of pages, zones, lines, words and characters. Page segmentation is implemented with the use of a modified bottom-up Docstrum algorithm [11]. In this approach, the histograms of nearest-neighbor pairs of individual characters are analyzed in order to estimate the text orientation angle and also within-line and between-line spacings. This allows to determine text lines and finally group lines into zones.

A PDF file contains by design a stream of strings that undergoes extraction and segmentation process. As a result we obtain pages containing characters grouped into zones, lines and words, all of which have a form of unsorted bag of items. The aim of setting the reading order is to determine the right sequence in which all the structure elements should be read. The algorithm is based on a bottom-up strategy: first characters are sorted within words and words within lines horizontally, then lines are sorted vertically within zones, and finally we sort zones using heuristics taken from [4], making use of an observation that the natural reading order descends from top to bottom, if successive zones are aligned vertically, otherwise it traverses from left to right.

3.2   Content Classification

The goal of content classification is to label each zone with a functional class. The classification is done in two stages: initial classification assigns general categories (*metadata, references, body, other*), while the goal of metadata classification is to classify all metadata zones into specific metadata classes (*abstract, bib info, type, title, affiliation, author, correspondence, dates, editor, keywords*). Content classification is a crucial stage of the entire analysis and, along with page segmentation have the biggest impact on the extraction results.

Both classifiers use Support Vector Machines and their implementation is based on LibSVM library [7]. The classifiers differ in SVM parameters, but in both cases the best parameters were found by performing a grid-search using a set of 100 documents from PubMed Central Open Access Subset (PMC) and maximizing mean F1 score obtained during a 5-fold cross validation.

In order to perform zone classification, each zone is transformed into a vector of feature values, which are to a great extent the same for both classifiers. The initial and metadata classifiers use 83 and 62 features, respectively:

- geometrical — based on attributes such as the dimensions and coordinates, distance to the nearest zone, free space below and above the zone, etc.,
- lexical — based upon keywords characteristic for different parts of narration, that is: affiliation, acknowledgment, abstract, references, article type, etc.,
- sequential — based on sequence-related information, eg. class of the previous zone, presence of the same text blocks on the surrounding pages, etc.,
- formatting — eg. font size in the current and adjacent zones, the amount of blank space inside zones etc.,
- heuristics — eg. uppercase word count, percentage of numbers in a text block, if each line starts with enumeration-like tokens, etc.

3.3   Author and Affiliation Extraction

As a result of classifying the document's fragments, we usually obtain a few regions labelled as *author* or *affiliation*. In this step we extract individual author names and affiliations and determine relations between them.

In general the implementation is based on heuristics and regular expressions, but the details depend on the article's layout. There are two main styles used in different layouts: (1) author names are grouped together in a form of a list, and affiliations are also placed together below the author's list, at the bottom of the first page or even just before the bibliography section (an example is shown in Fig. 2), and (2) each author is placed in a separate zone along with its affiliation and email address (an example is shown in Fig. 3).

In the case of a layout of the first type (Fig. 2), at the beginning authors' lists are split using a predefined lists of separators. Then we detect affiliation indexes based on predefined lists of symbols and also geometric features. Detected indexes are then used to split affiliation lists and assign affiliations to authors.

In the case of a layout of the second type (Fig. 3), each author is already assigned to its affiliation by being placed in the same zone. It is therefore enough to detect author name, affiliation and email address. We assume the first line of such a zone is the author name, email is detected based on regular expressions,

Fig. 2. An example fragment of a page from a scientific publication with authors and affiliations zones. In this case the relations author-affiliation (coded with colors) can be determined with the use of upper indexes.

Efficient blocking method for a large scale citation matching

Mateusz Fedoryszak
Interdisciplinary Centre for Mathematical and
Computational Modelling
University of Warsaw
m.fedoryszak@icm.edu.pl

Łukasz Bolikowski
Interdisciplinary Centre for Mathematical and
Computational Modelling
University of Warsaw
l.bolikowski@icm.edu.pl

Fig. 3. An example fragment of a page from a scientific publication with authors and affiliations zones. In this case the relations author-affiliation can be determined using the distance and other geometric features of the text.

and the rest is treated as the affiliation string. In the future we plan to implement this step using a supervised token classifier.

3.4   Affiliation Parsing

The goal of affiliation parsing is to recognize affiliation string fragments related to institution, address and country. Additionally, country names are decorated with their ISO codes. Figure 4 shows an example of a parsed affiliation string.

Interdisciplinary Centre for Mathematical and
Computational Modelling, University of Warsaw,
ul. Pawińskiego 5A blok D, 02-106 Warsaw, Poland

Fig. 4. An example of a parsed affiliation string. Colors mark fragments related to institution, address and country.

Affiliation parser uses Conditional Random Fields classifier and is built on top of GRMM and MALLET packages [10]. First affiliation string is tokenized, then each token is classified as *institution, address, country* or *other*, and finally neighbouring tokens with the same label are concatenated. The main feature used by token classifier is the classified word itself. Additional features are all binary: whether the token is a number, whether it is all uppercase/lowercase word, whether it is a lowercase word that starts with an uppercase letter, whether the token is contained by dictionaries of countries or words commonly appearing in institutions or addresses. Additionally, the token's feature vector contains not only features of the token itself, but also features of two preceding and two following tokens.

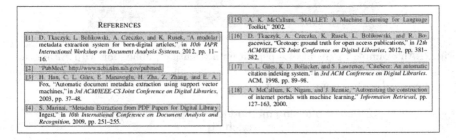

Fig. 5. A fragment of the references section of an article. Marked lines are the first lines of their references. After detecting these lines, the references section content can be easily split to form consecutive references strings.

3.5 References Extraction

References zones detected by content classifiers contain a list of reference strings, each of which can span over one or more text lines. The goal of reference strings extraction is to split the content of those zones into individual reference strings. This step utilizes unsupervised machine-learning techniques, which allows to omit time-consuming training set preparation and learning phases, while achieving very good extraction results.

Every bibliographic reference is displayed in the PDF document as a sequence of one or more text lines. Each text line in a reference zone belongs to exactly one reference string, some of them are first lines of their reference, others are inner or last ones. The sequence of all text lines belonging to bibliography section can be represented by the following regular expression:

```
[fontsize=\small]
(
   <first line of a reference>
   (
     <inner line of a reference>*
     <last line of a reference>
   )?
)*
```

In order to group text lines into consecutive references, first we determine which lines are first lines of their references. A set of such lines is presented in Fig. 5. To achieve this, we transform all lines to feature vectors and cluster them into two sets. We make use of a simple observation that the first line from all references blocks is also the first line of its reference. Thus the cluster containing this first line is assumed to contain all first lines. After recognizing all first lines it is easy to concatenate lines to form consecutive reference strings.

For clustering lines we use KMeans algorithm with Euclidean distance metric. As initial centroids we set the first line's feature vector and a vector with the largest distance to the first one. We use 5 features based on line relative length, line indentation, space between the line and the previous one, and the text content of the line (if the line starts with an enumeration pattern, if the previous line ends with a dot).

3.6   Reference Parsing

Reference strings extracted from references zones contain important reference metadata. In this step metadata is extracted from reference strings and the result is the list of document's parsed bibliographic references. The information we extract from the strings include: *author* (author's fullname), *title*, *source* (journal or conference name), *volume, issue, pages, year* and *DOI*. An example of a parsed reference is shown in Fig. 6.

[9] L. O'Gorman. The document spectrum for page layout analysis. IEEE Transactions on Pattern Analysis and Machine Intelligence, 15(11):1162–1173, 1993.

Fig. 6. An example of a bibliographic reference with various metadata information highlighted using different colors, these are in order: *author, title, journal, volume, issue, pages* and *year*.

First the reference strings are tokenized. The tokens are then transformed into vectors of features and classified by a supervised classifier. Finally the neighbouring tokens with the same label are concatenated, the labels are mapped into final metadata classes and the resulting reference metadata record is formed.

The heart of the implementation is the classifier that assigns labels to reference string tokens. For better performance, the classifier uses slightly more detailed set of labels than the target ones: *first_name* (author's first name or initial), *surname* (author's surname), *title, source* (journal or conference name), *volume, issue, page_first* (the lower bound of pages range), *page_last* (the upper bound of pages range), *year* and *text* (for separators and other tokens without a specific label). The token classifier employs Conditional Random Fields and is built on top of GRMM and MALLET packages [10].

The basic features are the tokens themselves. We use 42 additional features to describe the tokens:

– Some of them are based on the presence of a particular character class, eg. digits or lowercase/uppercase letters.

– Others check whether the token is a particular character (eg. a dot, a square bracket, a comma or a dash), or a particular word.
– Finally, we use features checking if the token is contained by the dictionary built from the dataset, eg. a dictionary of cities or words commonly appearing in the journal title.

It is worth to notice that the token's label depends not only on its feature vector, but also on surrounding tokens. To reflect this in the classifier, the token's feature vector contains not only features of the token itself, but also features of two preceding and two following tokens.

After token classification fragments labelled as *first_name* and *surname* are joined together based on their order to form consecutive author names, and similarly fragments labelled as *page_first* and *page_last* are joined together to form pages range. Additionally, in the case of *title* or *source* labels, the neighbouring tokens with the same label are concatenated.

Since the dataset used for training the token classifier does not contain enough references with DOI, the classifier is not responsible for extracting this information. DOI is recognized separately by matching a regular expression against the citation string.

Finally, the type of the reference (journal paper, conference proceedings or technical report) is detected by searching for specific keywords in the reference string.

4   Semantic Publishing Challenge of ESWC 2015

CERMINE system participated in Task 2 of Semantic Publishing Challenge of ESWC 2015 conference. The system is able to extract data sufficient for answering queries related to affiliations and citations (the first 5 queries out of 10 total, Q2.1 — Q2.5).

Solving queries Q2.1 (Affiliations in a paper) and Q2.2 (Papers from a country) relies on the following system features: document title extraction, authors and affiliations extraction, establishing relations author — affiliations, detecting country in the affiliation string.

Solving queries Q2.3 (Cited Works), Q2.4 (Recent Cited Works) and Q2.5 (Cited Journal Papers) relies on the following system features: extracting citations from a document, detecting DOI, title and year in the citation string, recognizing the type of a citation.

The following changes were made to the system in order to prepare it for the challenge:

– An additional step for generating the LOD dataset in RDF format was added to the original extraction workflow.
– The metadata classifier was retrained on a slightly extended set of documents, with the addition of documents of ACM layout.
– Heuristics for extracting authors and affiliations from hybrid zones (the second type described in Sect. 3.3, shown in Fig. 3) were added.

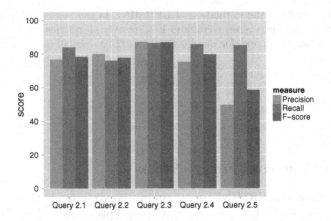

Fig. 7. The results of the evaluation of CERMINE in the SemPub Challenge. The figure shows mean precision, recall and F-score values for queries Q2.1 — Q2.5.

- Extracting DOI from reference strings based on regular expressions was implemented.
- Additional step for recognizing the type of the reference was added.

Originally both zone classifiers were trained with the use of a set of 2,551 documents randomly chosen from GROTOAP2 dataset [12]. Since GROTOAP2 was built using PMC resources, the dataset does not contain documents of ACM layout. For the purpose of the challenge, additional set of 165 ACM documents was manually chosen from computer science conferences and manually labelled. The combined set of 2,716 documents was used to retrain the metadata classifier.

Affiliation dataset used for affiliation parser training contains 8,267 parsed affiliations from PMC resources. For reference parser training we used Cite-Seer [8], Cora-ref [9] and PMC resources combined together into a set of 4,000 references.

The LOD dataset generated by the workflow contains currently only the information needed to answer the challenge queries. More precisely, the dataset contains the following resources: volumes, documents, authors, affiliations (representing the relations between the document, author and organization), countries and citations. For all properties we use Dublin Core [1] and vCard [6] ontologies.

During the challenge 5 queries for each query type (50 single queries in total) were executed on the generated LOD dataset and the results were compared with the gold standard. The comparison was done after some normalization of the output and partial matches were also taken into account. For each query precision and recall were measured.

Figure 7 shows the mean scores of CERMINE for each query type Q2.1 — Q2.5. Since the generated LOD dataset did not contain any information supporting solving queries Q2.6 — Q2.10, all the scores for these queries were equal to 0. Table 1 shows the average precision, recall and F-score achieved by CERMINE over all queries, as well as only over the supported queries Q2.1 — Q2.5.

Table 1. The results of the evaluation of CERMINE in the SemPubl Challenge. The table lists the average precision, recall and F-score over all queries, as well as only for the first 5 queries. The scores for queries Q2.6 — Q2.10 were all equal to 0.

Queries	Q2.1 — Q2.10	Q2.1 — Q2.5
Precision	36.9 %	73.8 %
Recall	41.7 %	83.4 %
F-score	38.1 %	76.2 %

5   Conclusions and Future Work

The article presents CERMINE — a system for extracting both metadata and bibliography from scientific articles in a born-digital form. CERMINE is very useful for digital libraries and similar environments whenever they have to deal with documents with metadata information missing, fragmentary or not reliable. The modular architecture makes CERMINE flexible and easily maintainable.

CERMINE was designed as a universal solution, and therefore is able to handle a vast variety of potential publication layouts reasonably well, instead of being perfect in processing a limited number of document layouts only. This was achieved by employing supervised and unsupervised machine-learning algorithms trained on large, diverse datasets.

The system is open source and available online at http://cermine.ceon.pl.

References

1. Dublin Core. http://dublincore.org/
2. iText. http://itextpdf.com/
3. NLM. http://dtd.nlm.nih.gov/archiving/
4. PdfMiner. http://www.unixuser.org/~euske/python/pdfminer/
5. PubMed. http://www.ncbi.nlm.nih.gov/pubmed
6. vCard. http://www.w3.org/TR/vcard-rdf/
7. Chang, C., Lin, C.: LIBSVM: a library for support vector machines. ACM TIST **2**(3), 27 (2011)
8. Giles, C.L., Bollacker, K.D., Lawrence, S.: Citeseer: An automatic citation indexing system. In: Proceedings of the 3rd ACM International Conference on Digital Libraries, pp. 89–98 (1998)
9. McCallum, A., Nigam, K., Rennie, J.: Automating the construction of internet portals with machine learning. Inf. Retrieval **3**, 127–163 (2000)
10. McCallum, A.K.: MALLET: A Machine Learning for Language Toolkit (2002)
11. O'Gorman, L.: The document spectrum for page layout analysis. IEEE Trans. Pattern Anal. Mach. Intell. **15**(11), 1162–1173 (1993)
12. Tkaczyk, D., Szostek, P., Bolikowski, Ł.: GROTOAP2 - the methodology of creating a large ground truth dataset of scientific articles. D-Lib Magazine (2014)
13. Tkaczyk, D., Szostek, P., Fedoryszak, M., Dendek, P.J., Bolikowski, Ł.: CERMINE: automatic extraction of structured metadata from scientific literature. Int. J. Doc. Anal. Recogn. (IJDAR), 1–19 (2015). http://dx.doi.org/10.1007/s10032-015-0249-8. doi:10.1007/s10032-015-0249-8
14. Tkaczyk, D., et al.: Cermine: Cermine 1.6 (2015). http://dx.doi.org/10.5281/zenodo.17594

Machine Learning Techniques for Automatically Extracting Contextual Information from Scientific Publications

Stefan Klampfl[(✉)] and Roman Kern

Know-Center GmbH, Inffeldgasse 13, 8010 Graz, Austria
{sklampfl,rkern}@know-center.at

Abstract. Scholarly publishing increasingly requires automated systems that semantically enrich documents in order to support management and quality assessment of scientific output. However, contextual information, such as the authors' affiliations, references, and funding agencies, is typically hidden within PDF files. To access this information we have developed a processing pipeline that analyses the structure of a PDF document incorporating a diverse set of machine learning techniques. First, unsupervised learning is used to extract contiguous text blocks from the raw character stream as the basic logical units of the article. Next, supervised learning is employed to classify blocks into different meta-data categories, including authors and affiliations. Then, a set of heuristics are applied to detect the reference section at the end of the paper and segment it into individual reference strings. Sequence classification is then utilised to categorise the tokens of individual references to obtain information such as the journal and the year of the reference. Finally, we make use of named entity recognition techniques to extract references to research grants, funding agencies, and EU projects. Our system is modular in nature. Some parts rely on models learnt on training data, and the overall performance scales with the quality of these data sets.

Keywords: PDF extraction · Machine learning · Named entity recognition

1 Introduction

The constant growth of the volume of scholarly publications makes it increasingly difficult to manage collections of scientific literature and to assess the quality of scientific output. It poses the need for automated processing systems that semantically enrich documents with information that support these tasks. One important aspect of scientific publications is that they are not isolated units, but originate in a specific *context*. In fact, several factors contribute to the development of a paper, for example, the authors' affiliations, funding information, or the venue or journal where a paper was presented or published. Also the list

© Springer International Publishing Switzerland 2015
F. Gandon et al. (Eds.): SemWebEval 2015, CCIS 548, pp. 105–116, 2015.
DOI: 10.1007/978-3-319-25518-7_9

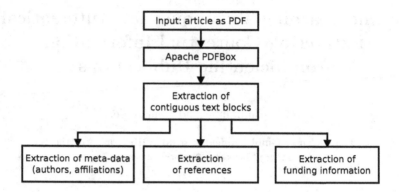

Fig. 1. Overview of the overall architecture of our system, most of which builds on our previous work. Given a scientific article in PDF, the raw character stream obtained via PDFBox is clustered into contiguous text blocks [6], which serve as the basis for the following stages: the extraction of author and affiliation meta-data [4], the extraction of references [7], and the extraction of funding information [8].

of referenced papers constitutes important contextual information to take into account in order to assess its credibility and relevance.

To that end, the Semantic Publishing Challenge 2015[1] (SemPub 2015) asked participants to automatically annotate these elements within a set of input documents. This paper describes our contribution to Task 2 of this challenge, which focuses on the extraction of contextual information from scientific publications given as PDF files. PDF is the most common format for scholarly articles, however, it is optimised for presentation, but lacks structural information. It only contains information about individual characters and their position on the page, and this information might additionally be noisy. Intelligent and flexible algorithms are required that extract words with correct boundaries in the right order and group these words to lines and contiguous text blocks, which might then be classified to contain a specific type of information. Furthermore, these algorithms have to deal with the large variety of layouts of scholarly articles.

We have developed a system that exploits the flexibility of a variety of supervised and unsupervised machine learning techniques to deal with these challenges. It builds upon the open-source Apache PDFBox[2] library and processes a given PDF file in a number of individual processing modules (see Fig. 1). First, it uses unsupervised learning (clustering) to analyse the physical layout of a scientific article by extracting contiguous text blocks, which we consider as the basic building blocks of a PDF document (Sect. 2). Next, these text blocks on the first page of the article are classified into different meta-data categories, including authors and affiliations, using supervised learning (Sect. 3). Then, heuristics are applied to detect the reference section at the end of the paper and to segment it into individual reference strings. The tokens of these reference strings are

---

[1] https://github.com/ceurws/lod/wiki/SemPub2015.
[2] http://pdfbox.apache.org/.

further categorised using sequence classification to obtain information such as the journal and the year of the reference (Sect. 4). Finally, we use basic named entity recognition techniques to extract information about research grants, funding agencies, and EU projects (Sect. 5). Parts of our system have already been described in [4–8]. A demonstration of the system can be accessed online[3], and the source code is available under an open source license[4].

2 Unsupervised Extraction of Contiguous Text Blocks as Basic Units of a PDF

Before we can extract contextual information from a scholarly article we have to process the low-level character stream of the PDF file to obtain logical units such as words or lines. The stream obtained through PDFBox consists of a list of characters, their bounding boxes (x and y position on the page, as well as their width and height), and information about their font. In our system, we consider contiguous text blocks as the basic building blocks of a PDF document. Each block consists of several lines, each of which is composed of a number of words, which themselves consist of multiple characters. The main challenge here is that the information provided by PDFBox might be unreliable: for example, height and width information might be slightly wrong, or information about the font of some characters might be missing. We therefore require algorithms which are flexible enough to deal at the same time with both this noisy data and the variety of layouts of scientific publications.

We use methods from unsupervised machine learning, in particular clustering, to iteratively combine individual characters to words, lines, and blocks of text in a bottom-up manner. We employ a sequence of alternating *Merge* and *Split* steps: Each *Merge* step is implemented by hierarchical agglomerative clustering (HAC) with Euclidean distance measure and Single Linkage. In the first *Merge* step individual characters are merged to words: pairs of characters with increasing distance to each other are combined into clusters, until a maximum distance threshold is reached. Since the resulting clusters of characters might now encompass multiple words, a *Split* step is incorporated in the form of standard k-means clustering on the horizontal distances between characters ($k = 2$). Ideally, this partitions the spaces between characters into spaces between words and spaces within words, yielding the final set of words. This *Split* step can also be understood as an outlier detection which removes too large inter-character distances from the words obtained in the *Merge* step.

Another pair of *Merge* and *Split* steps is used to combine words to lines and lines to blocks. First words are merged to lines by combining pairs of words with increasing Euclidean distance to each other. This typically yields lines spanning multiple columns, which is resolved in the *Split* step that separates word spaces within columns from inter-column spaces. Finally, lines are merged to blocks,

---

[3] http://code-annotator.know-center.at.
[4] https://svn.know-center.tugraz.at/opensource/projects/code/trunk.

again by first combining them until a maximum distance threshold is reached, and then by splitting the resulting clusters at large vertical distances.

PDFBox already uses its own mechanisms for detecting word, line, and paragraph boundaries for the conversion to plain text. These methods are based on simple heuristics depending on the relative position of neighbouring characters. However, we decided to build our own generic text block extractor and did not reuse existing approaches provided by PDF parsing libraries, mainly because we want to leave open the possibility to apply our system also to other input formats, for example the output of OCR software. Another reason for not using PDFBox for the extraction of text blocks is that it does not provide any geometric information about these compound objects. It might also be desirable to extend our block extractor by incorporating font information or special rules such as the splitting of words at superscripts or subscripts.

The result of this stage is a hierarchical data structure containing the geometrical information of blocks, lines, and words, as well as the reading order of blocks within the document [1]. Most importantly, this block structure effectively provides a segmentation of the text into single columns, a fact that is particularly helpful for extracting contextual information from references. We have presented a more detailed description of our algorithms as well as an evaluation of the block extraction in [6].

3   Supervised Classification of Author and Affiliation Meta-Data

Major factors that directly contribute to the origin and development of a paper are the research institutions the authors of a scientific article are affiliated to, the venue where a paper was presented or the journal in which it was published. These meta-data thus constitute an important aspect of the context in which the paper was written.

For the extraction of meta-data from scientific articles we employed supervised machine learning techniques which use labelled training examples to learn a classification scheme for the individual text elements of an article. This stage directly builds upon the output of the text block extraction stage and consists of two phases. We first classify the text blocks extracted from the first page of the article into multiple meta-data categories: apart from author related information (names, e-mail addresses, and affiliations) we also categorise the title (and optional subtitle) of the article, the name of the journal, conference, or venue, abstract and keywords. For author-related blocks we then re-apply the classification to the tokens of these blocks in order to obtain given names, surnames, and affiliations.

As a supervised learning mechanism we use Maximum Entropy (ME) [2] combined with Beam Search [10], which incorporates sequential information by taking into account the classification results of preceding instances in order to avoid unlikely label sequences. Both algorithms are included in the open-source library OpenNLP[5]. The features used for classification are derived from the layout, the

---

[5] http://opennlp.apache.org.

formatting, the words within and around a text block, and common name lists for detecting author names. Since the classification method is restricted to binary features, this information needs to be mapped to binary values.

We have called this the TeamBeam algorithm for extracting meta-data information. It has been described and evaluated in [4], where it was shown to achieve a satisfactory performance on a number of different datasets. Figure 2 shows a snapshot from a sample paper from the biomedical domain where title, author names, emails, and affiliations are correctly classified.

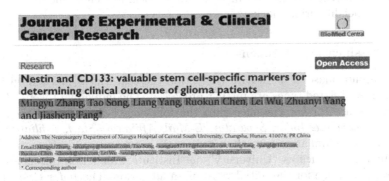

Fig. 2. Snapshot of a sample paper with text blocks on the first page classified into different meta-data categories, indicated by different colours, including journal, title, authors, and affiliations. The classification is further applied to the tokens of the author and affiliation block, yielding given names, surnames, and emails.

3.1 Classification of Text Blocks

In the first phase the text blocks are classified into the following labels: *Title, Subtitle, Journal, Abstract, Keywords, Author, E-Mail, Affiliation, Author-Mixed* and *Other*. Author related information might appear in separate text blocks, or different meta-data types might be combined in a single block (such as e-mail addresses and affiliations). In the latter case, this block would be labelled with *Author-Mixed*. The *Other* class is assigned to all blocks without any meta-data information.

The following features are generated for the text block classification:

- **Language model features** For each text block type, a language model is calculated by counting the frequency of words within this block type in the training set. This is used to generate features encoding the most probable block type for the words within the block.
- **Layout features** describe the position of a single block within a page: *isFirstBlock, isLastBlock, isLeftHalf, isRightHalf, isTopHalf, isBottomHalf, isRight, isLeft, isTop, isBottom, isCenter*.
- **Formatting features** encode font and text flow: *isBigFont, isBiggerFont, isSmallFont, isSmallerFont, isLeftAligned, isRightAligned. Big/Small* and *Bigger/Smaller* are set if the deviation of the font size from the average font size exceeds ±1 SD and ±1.5 SD, respectively.

- **Dictionary features** consist of features *containsGivenName* and *contains-Surname*, which are set depending on whether the block contains a word found in one of the common name lists: a list of 7,133 common first names taken from the GATE project[6], and a list of 88,799 most common surnames of the US Census[7].
- **Heuristic features** contains simple features such as *containsEMail*, *containsAtChar*, *containsDigits*, *containsPunctuation*, *containsDOI*, and *containsISSN*.
- **Term features** include all words within a block, as well as the first and last word of neighbouring blocks.

3.2   Classification of Tokens

In the second phase of meta-data extraction the text blocks labelled with one of the author related types are further processed. The individual tokens of these text blocks are further classified into the following labels: *GivenName*, *MiddleName*, *Surname*, *Index*, *Separator*, *E-Mail*, *Affiliation-Start*, *Affiliation*, and *Other*. Because affiliations are often written in a sequence and often start with a common word, such as "University" or "Institute", affiliation tokens are split into two parts, one for the initial word of an affiliation. The *Index* class is used for special characters linking authors to their affiliation and/or e-mail address, typically an asterisk or superscript numbers. Multiple index characters are separated by a token labelled as *Separator*, usually a comma.

The following features are generated for the token classification:

- **Language model features** reflect the relative frequencies of words: *isCommonWord* (>0.1), *isInfrequentWord* (<0.01), *isRareWord* (<0.001).
- **Layout features** encode the token's position: *isFirstInLine*, *isFirst*, *isLast*.
- **Formatting features** include the font size compared to the average font size (*isBigger*, *isSmaller*), as well as the number of characters within the token.
- **Dictionary features** are set if the token occurs in one of the common name lists (*containsGivenName*, *containsSurname*).
- **Heuristic features** are reused from the block classification, including a feature for initials (upper-case character followed by a dot).
- **Term features** include a normalized version of the token itself as a feature.

4   Detection, Segmentation, and Tokenisation of References

Another contextual dimension to take into account in order to assess the credibility and relevance of a paper is the network of related papers, for instance, those that cite or are cited by a given one, or those that address similar issues. Researchers often use this information to search for literature that is relevant

---

[6] http://gate.ac.uk.
[7] http://www.census.gov/genealogy/www/index.html.

References

1. Dell'Albani Paola: **Stem Cell Markers in Gliomas.** *Neurochem Res* in press.
2. Reifenberger G, Collins VP: **Pathology and molecular genetics of astrocytic gliomas.** *J Mol Med* 2004, 82:656-670.
3. Lassman Andrew B: **Molecular Biology of Gliomas.** *Current Neurology and Neuroscience Reports* 2004, 4:228-233.
4. Frederick L, Wang XY, Eley G, James CD: **Diversity and frequency of epidermal growth factor receptor mutations in human glioblastomas.** *Cancer Res* 2000, 60:1383-1387.
5. Ranuncolo SM, Varela M, Morandi A, Lastiri J, Christiansen S: **Prognostic value of Mdm2, p53 and p16 in patients with astrocytomas.** *Journal of Neuro-Oncology* 2004, 68:113-121.
6. Chakravarti AB, Delaney MA, Noll E, Black PM, Loeffler JS, Muzkansky A, Dyson NJ: **Prognostic and pathologic significance of quantitative protein expression profiling in human gliomas.** *Clin Cancer Res* 2001, 7:2387-2395.
7. Gritci A, Vescovi AL, Galli R: **Adult neural stem cells: plasticity and developmental potential.** *J Physiol Paris* 2002, 96(1-2):81-90.

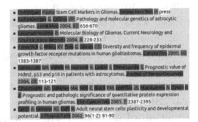

Fig. 3. Snapshot of the beginning of the reference section of a sample paper (left) and extracted reference strings with classified tokens (right). The extraction of references involves the detection of the reference section within the paper and the segmentation of individual reference strings (bullet points). Individual tokens of the reference strings are classified into different categories (indicated by different colours), including given names and surnames of authors, titles, journals, years, volumes, and pages.

for their own work or for a specific field of research. Here, we focus on the information contained in the reference section, a section scientific articles usually conclude with and which acknowledges relevant and related work in the form of a list of citations or references.

The automated extraction of this type of contextual information requires the detection of the reference section within a paper, the segmentation of individual reference strings, and the labelling of single tokens within each string as to which field they belong (e.g., author, title, year, journal). We use heuristics to detect and segment references within a scientific article, and supervised sequence classification to assign labels to the tokens within each reference string. This part of our system has been described in [7], where we have shown that the extension of ParsCit [3], an existing state-of-the-art reference extraction system, with additional formatting and layout information improves the extraction of references. In particular we are able to correctly segment references with an F1 of about 0.94 and detect most reference token types with an F1 of at least 0.9 on a dataset from PubMed[8]. Figure 3 shows samples of extracted references, including segmented reference strings and categorised tokens, from an example paper.

4.1   Reference Line Extraction

The first step is to detect the reference section within a scientific article and directly builds upon the output of the text block extraction stage. We look for a specific heading that indicates the beginning of the reference section, which is usually one of "References", "Bibliography", "References and Notes", "Literature cited", and common variations of those strings (e.g., upper-case variants). We iterate over all blocks in the reading order and use a regular expression to find the reference headers. Then we collect all lines until we encounter either another section heading, starting with "Acknowledgement", "Autobiographical", "Table", "Appendix", "Exhibit", "Annex", "Fig", or "Notes", or the end of the document.

---

[8] http://www.ncbi.nlm.nih.gov/pubmed/.

In addition, we incorporate layout information into the reference line extraction in three ways. First, column information is implicitly provided through the consideration of text blocks. Second, we ignored the content of decoration blocks (headers and footers consisting of page numbers, authors, or journal names), which we computed by associating blocks across neighbouring pages based on their content and geometrical position [6]. Finally, we ignored all lines following a vertical gap that is larger than the average gap size plus two times the standard deviation of gap sizes. This criterion has been introduced as the block of references is often followed by footnotes, copyright information or other types of text which is visually separated from the references by a bigger gap.

4.2   Reference Segmentation

After the reference lines of the article have been collected, the next step is the segmentation of these lines into individual reference strings. We distinguish three cases how reference strings can be marked: (1) with square or round brackets (e.g., "[1]" or "(1)"), (2) with naked numbers, and (3) strings are unmarked. For cases 1 and 2 the most common marker type is found via regular expressions, and the marker is also used to segment the references. For case 3 we incorporate layout information by looking for start lines which visually stick out from the rest of the lines, e.g., by a negative indentation. Our algorithm uses clustering to separate first lines from the rest of lines, assuming that the first lines will be the minority class.

We inspect each text block containing reference lines. If a block contains just a single line, this line is assumed to be an artefact of the PDF extraction process and is completely ignored. For blocks with more than two lines we cluster the lines using a simple version of the k-means clustering algorithm. The sole feature we use for this is the minimal x-coordinate of a line's bounding box. We set the number of clusters to 2 and initialize the two centroids with the minimal and maximal value of the feature. Then we assign each line to that centroid which is closer to the line's x-coordinate. We stop after a single iteration and update the centroids with the mean of the assigned features. At this stage all lines are assigned to one of the two clusters. Only if two conditions are met the layout based splitting is applied: The minimum cluster must contain fewer lines than the maximum cluster and the centroids differ by at least $0.05 * maxLineWidth$. If this is the case all lines from the minimum cluster are considered to be the first line of a new reference at which the reference lines are split into individual reference strings.

4.3   Reference Preprocessing

The task of the reference preprocessing step is to clean the text of the references before the token classification is applied. The preprocessing consists of two parts, dehyphenation and normalization.

In the first part we resolve hyphenations by removing hyphens "-" and concatenating the split word parts if they are the result of a proper English hyphenation. For each line that ends with a hyphen we apply hyphenation on the concatenated word using a list of hyphenation patterns taken from the T$_{\!E}$X distribution, and if the line split occurs at one of the proposed split points we resolve the hyphenation.

For normalization, we align the pages information to the form "<number>–<number>", even if there are multiple tokens or different dash characters.

4.4 Reference Token Classification

The final step is the categorisation of the individual tokens of the extracted and preprocessed reference strings. We used the following token types: *author-GivenName, authorSurname, authorOther, editor, title, date, publisher, issueTitle, bookTitle, pages, location, conference, source, volume, edition, issue, url, note,* and *other.* The class *authorOthers* is used for intermediate tokens in the author substring, such as "and".

At the core of the reference extraction process lies a supervised sequential machine learning algorithm. We use a conditional random field (CRF) [9], which has also been used in the original ParsCit system [3]. As implementation we use the freely available *crfsuite* software[9]. We use all the original features from the original ParsCit approach (see Sect. 2 in [3] for the complete list). In addition, we incorporate layout and formatting information by a set of binary features specifying whether the font of the tokens inside a sliding window from -2 to +2 tokens is equal to the font of the current token. Two fonts are considered equal if they share the same font name, the same font size, and the same binary attributes specifying whether they are bold or italic.

5 Extracting Funding Information Using Named Entity Recognition

Another major aspect in understanding the context in which a paper was written are the funding agencies, EU projects, and research grants that participated in funding a research and that obviously contributed to the development of a publication. These stakeholders are typically mentioned in the Acknowledgement section of a paper. In principle, we use basic techniques from Named Entity Recognition to extract this type of contextual information, however, our work is embedded within the larger goal of ontologically mapping the domain of computer science. We have recently made some initial steps in that direction [8].

For many domains ontologies already exist, which help to describe the content of scientific articles. This is in particular true for the biomedical domain; in other domains, such ontologies do not exist. In our recent work we found out that such ontologies are lacking for the domain of computer science [8]. Therefore we

---

[9] http://www.chokkan.org/software/crfsuite/.

devised an ontological structure, which describes the main concepts in computer science literature, including the information about grants and funding agencies. In addition, we modelled the relationship between the concepts, see Fig. 4.

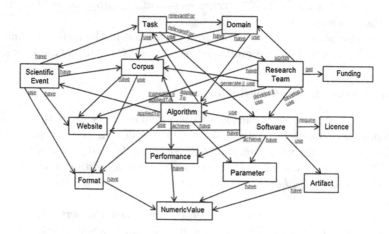

Fig. 4. Ontological description of the computer science domain, with the funding information being one of the concepts. The domain model contains categories (boxes) as well as linkage information in the form of relation categories (arrows).

Once the ontological structure had been finalised, we manually crafted a ground truth data set by annotating a selection of scientific articles. The final data set contained more than 5,000 manually curated entities and relations. This process shaped our understanding of the complexity of the task and possible ways to automatically infer these annotations.

Equipped with the understanding of what constitutes certain concepts in computer science literature, we realised a heuristics based automatic annotation scheme. In particular, for the funding information, we relied on a set of manually selected trigger phrases. We combined the information of the presence of one of the trigger phrases with the information of the noun phrases of the sentence, containing the trigger phrase. This first, basic approach already provided a performance of 0.79 precision and 0.70 recall in a preliminary evaluation.

Next, we applied machine learning for the automatic annotation of all concepts and relationship found in our ontological structure, including the information on grants and funding agencies. Therefore we utilised a general purpose information extraction pipeline, found in the CODE annotator[10]. This pipeline provides a flexible framework of different feature generation algorithms and highly configurable sequence classification algorithms. The framework itself is thereby not limited to the extraction of information from scientific articles alone, but can be applied on any textual resources. In the case of extracting funding

---

[10] http://code-annotator.know-center.at.

information, it has been sufficient to convert the human annotations into the format suitable as training data for our framework. In this scenario we had only 37 instances of funding information, of which 30 were unique. This is a very low number for a supervised machine learning scenario, even too low to conduct a cross-evaluation. As a point of reference, our framework was able to achieve 0.75 precision and 0.61 recall, when tested on the training data set. This is certainly not representative of the performance, which can be expected in a real world scenario.

6   Conclusion and Discussion

In this work we have presented a system for extracting contextual information from scientific publications that are given as PDF files. It utilises the flexibility of both unsupervised and supervised machine learning techniques (i) to form words, lines, and blocks out of the raw character stream of the PDF, (ii) to classify these blocks into different meta-data categories, such as authors and affiliations, and (iii) to detect and segment reference strings and to classify tokens of these reference strings into different categories such as authors, title, journal, or year of publication. The features for our algorithms are composed of layout information (e.g., the absolute and relative geometrical positioning of text blocks on a page), formatting information (e.g., the type, style, and size of fonts), and textual information. Furthermore, we used techniques from information extraction and named entity recognition to extract information about funding agencies, research grants, and EU projects.

One major problem with PDFBox and other low-level PDF parsing tools is that the information provided about individual characters in the PDF is inherently noisy, for example, height and width information might be wrong, or information about the font of some characters might be missing. This implicit noise affects every stage of our system and thus its overall performance.

Parts of our system rely on models being learnt based on training data; hence the overall performance of our system also scales with the quality and size of these data sets. Our system is flexible and modular in nature and allows a separate training of different stages on different training sets. In many cases we used a subset of the PubMed database as a training set, mainly because it provides a rigorous annotation of the complete content of each document, in particular, meta-data and references. The publications in this database are from a wide variety of journals the biomedical domain, which we consider as representative for the general domain of scientific articles. Still it might not perform well on a specific sub-domain, such as conference publications from computer science. This would have to be addressed by a different training set that is more representative for this type of publications, which to the best of our knowledge does not yet exist in a reasonable size.

In the future we plan to address the aforementioned limitations and further improve the performance of the individual components. In particular, we plan to replace the remaining heuristics and manual rules by more flexible machine learning algorithms. Following this approach should enable us in the future to extend the information that we harvest out of scientific articles even further.

Acknowledgements. The presented work was in part developed within the CODE project (grant no. 296150) and within the EEXCESS project (grant no. 600601) funded by the EU FP7, as well as the TEAM IAPP project (grant no. 251514) within the FP7 People Programme. The Know-Center is funded within the Austrian COMET Program Competence Centers for Excellent Technologies under the auspices of the Austrian Federal Ministry of Transport, Innovation and Technology, the Austrian Federal Ministry of Economy, Family and Youth and by the State of Styria. COMET is managed by the Austrian Research Promotion Agency FFG.

References

1. Aiello, M., Monz, C., Todoran, L., Worring, M.: Document understanding for a broad class of documents. Int. J. Doc. Anal. Recogn. **5**(1), 1–16 (2002)
2. Berger, A.L., Pietra, V.J.D., Pietra, S.A.D.: A maximum entropy approach to natural language processing. Comput. Linguist. **22**(1), 39–71 (1996)
3. Councill, I.G., Giles, C.L., Kan, M.Y.: ParsCit: an open-source CRF reference string parsing package. In: Calzolari, N., Choukri, K., Maegaard, B., Mariani, J., Odjik, J., Piperidis, S., Tapias, D. (eds.) Proceedings of LREC, vol. 2008, pp. 661–667. Citeseer, European Language Resources Association (ELRA) (2008)
4. Kern, R., Jack, K., Hristakeva, M., Granitzer, M.: TeamBeam - meta-data extraction from scientific literature. D-Lib Mag. **18**(7/8) (2012)
5. Kern, R., Klampfl, S.: Extraction of references using layout and formatting information from scientific articles. D-Lib Mag. **19**(9/10) (2013)
6. Klampfl, S., Granitzer, M., Jack, K., Kern, R.: Unsupervised document structure analysis of digital scientific articles. Int. J. Digit. Libr. **14**(3–4), 83–99 (2014)
7. Klampfl, S., Kern, R.: An unsupervised machine learning approach to body text and table of contents extraction from digital scientific articles. In: Aalberg, T., Papatheodorou, C., Dobreva, M., Tsakonas, G., Farrugia, C.J. (eds.) TPDL 2013. LNCS, vol. 8092, pp. 144–155. Springer, Heidelberg (2013)
8. Kröll, M., Klampfl, S., Kern, R.: Towards a marketplace for the scientific community: accessing knowledge from the computer science domain. D-Lib Mag. **20**(11/12) (2014)
9. Lafferty, J., McCallum, A., Pereira, F.: Conditional random fields: probabilistic models for segmenting and labeling sequence data. In: Proceedings of the International Conference on Machine Learning (ICML-2001), pp. 282–289 (2001)
10. Ratnaparkhi, A.: Maximum entropy models for natural langual ambiguity resolution. Ph.D. thesis (1998)

MACJa: Metadata and Citations Jailbreaker

Andrea Giovanni Nuzzolese[1,2(✉)], Silvio Peroni[1,2],
and Diego Reforgiato Recupero[1]

[1] Semantic Technology Laboratory, ISTC-CNR, Rome, Italy
{andrea.nuzzolese,diego.reforgiato}@istc.cnr.it
[2] Department of Computer Science and Engineering,
University of Bologna, Bologna, Italy
silvio.peroni@unibo.it

Abstract. This paper presents the *Metadata And Citations Jailbreaker*
(a.k.a. *MACJa* – IPA /'matsja/), i.e., a method for processing the
research papers available in CEUR-WS.org and stored as PDF files in
order to extract relevant semantic data and publish them in a RDF triplestore according to the *Semantic Publishing And Referencing (SPAR)
Ontologies*. In particular, the extraction of all the information needed
for addressing the queries of the Semantic Publishing Challenge 2015
(task 2) is guaranteed by MACJa by using techniques based on Natural
Language Processing (i.e., Combinatory Categorial Grammar, Discourse
Representation Theory, Linguistic Frames), Semantic Web technologies
and good Ontology Design practices (i.e., Content Analysis, Ontology Design Patterns, Discourse Referent Extraction and Linking, Topic
Extraction).

Keywords: MACJa · SPAR Ontologies · Semantic Publishing

1 Introduction

The knowledge management of scholarly products is an emerging research area
in the Semantic Web field known as Semantic Publishing [32]. The Semantic
Publishing is aimed at contributing to the realisation of the Web of Data by
providing access to semantic enhanced scholarly products in order to enable a
variety of tasks focused on the exploitation of scholarly data, such as knowledge
discovery, knowledge exploration and data integration. However, the most of
research outcomes are still locked up in flat PDF documents that do not provide
any machine-readable data and prevent publishing and accessing scholarly data
as Linked Data.

Hence, we propose the *Metadata And Citations Jailbreaker* (a.k.a. *MACJa –*
IPA /'matsja/) as a solution for addressing such a problem. MACJa is a method
and a tool for processing research papers available as PDF documents in order
to extract relevant semantic data and publish them as Linked Data. MACJa
uses the *Semantic Publishing And Referencing (SPAR) Ontologies* [25] as the
reference model for organising scholarly knowledge extracted from PDFs.

© Springer International Publishing Switzerland 2015
F. Gandon et al. (Eds.): SemWebEval 2015, CCIS 548, pp. 117–128, 2015.
DOI: 10.1007/978-3-319-25518-7_10

MACJa implements a novel solution for dealing with natural language and extracting relevant metadata from scholarly articles by hybridising techniques based on Natural Language Processing (i.e., Combinatory Categorial Grammar, Discourse Representation Theory, Linguistic Frames) with Semantic Web technologies and good Ontology Design practices (i.e., Content Analysis, Ontology Design Patterns, Discourse Referent Extraction and Linking, Topic Extraction). Additionally, MACJa employs FRED [12], a novel machine reader that is quickly spreading along the Semantic Web community and that we have developed, for some of the queries of the Semantic Publishing Challenge 2015 (task 2).

More in detail, the paper is organised as follows: Sect. 2 presents the related work; Sect. 3 presents materials and methods related to our project, while Sect. 4 introduces our contribution, i.e., MACJa. Finally, in Sect. 5 we conclude the paper introducing our results in the Semantic Web Challenge 2015 and sketching out some future works.

2   Related Work

The most literature about the extraction of metadata and citations from scholarly articles in the research area of Semantic Publishing has converged, during last years, into the *Jailbreaking the PDF* initiative [15]. This initiative is aimed at creating a formal flexible infrastructure to extract semantic information from PDF documents by combining existing solutions and tools for extracting data and annotations, and for identifying the argumentative discourse of scholarly papers.

Cermine [33] provides a Java library and a web service for extracting metadata and content from PDF files containing academic publications. It does not include any OCR phase, but it analyses only the PDF text stream found in the input document. The workflow inspects the entire content of the document and produces two kinds of output in NLM format [23]: the document's metadata and parsed bibliographic references.

PDFMiner [24] is a Python tool for extracting information from PDF documents, which focuses entirely on getting and analysing text data and allows to extract the outline of a paper and its tagged content, to reconstruct the original layout by grouping text chunks and to convert the PDF to an HTML.

PDFX [4] is a rule-based system designed to reconstruct the logical structure of scholarly articles stored in PDF, regardless of their formatting style. The system's output is an XML document that describes the input article's logical structure in terms of title, sections, tables, references, etc. and also links it to geometrical typesetting markers in the original PDF, such as paragraph and column breaks.

ParseCit+SectLabel [19] is an open source system to solve two related subtasks in logical structure discovery: (i) logical structure classification, and (ii) generic section classification. ParseCit uses the machine learning methodology of conditional random fields (CRF) [17] - i.e., a model that blends sequential labeling techniques with pointwise entropy-based classification. ParseCit+SectLabel is an open source system that extends ParsCit in order to provide logical structure discovery and classification of a scholarly article.

CiTalO [7] is an algorithm and a tool that allows inferring the rethorical function of citations linking scholarly articles. CiTalO relies on (i) FRED [29] for generating a logical representation (expressed as RDF/OWL) of a sentence containing a citation and on (ii) a set of rules for interpreting such a logical representation in order to map the rethorical function of a citation to the properties of the *Citation Typing Ontology (CiTO)* [26].

All the approaches described so far extract the high level structure of the PDF document and do not focus on the extraction of fine-grained information, as required by the Semantic Publishing Challenge 2015 (task 2).

Approaches that tried to solve the same problem of ours, such as [2,9], were presented at the Semantic Publishing challenge [18] held at the Extended Semantic Web Conference 2014, that consisted of similar tasks. Bertin and Atanassova [2] proposes an hybrid method for the extraction and characterization of citations in scientific papers by combining machine learning with rule-based techniques. The solution consists of extraction of metadata, bibliography parsing, section titles processing, and fine-grained semantic annotation on the sentence level of texts. Dimou et al. [9] presents a solution to extract and map data of workshop proceedings published from HTML to RDF. The solution exploits RML [10], which is an extension of the R2RML mapping language [6] for defining customized mapping rules from data expressed in heterogeneous formats to the RDF data model.

To the best of our knowledge none of the previosly mentioned works (except CiTalO to some extent) use Combinatory Categorial Grammar, Discourse Representation Theory or Linguistic Frames. Therefore, *MACJa* is the first method of its kind that is built on top of them and represents a novelty in this domain.

3   Metadata and Citations Jailbreaker

In this section we introduce the materials and methods used by our *Metadata And Citations Jailbreaker (MACJa)* project.

3.1   Materials and Ontologies

All the data that are extracted through the scripts introduced in Sect. 4 are stored according to the *Semantic Publishing and Referencing (SPAR) Ontologies* [25]. Such ontologies form a suite of orthogonal and complementary ontology modules for creating comprehensive machine-readable RDF metadata for all aspects of semantic publishing and referencing. In particular, they allow researchers to describe far more than simply bibliographic entities such as books and journal articles, by enabling RDF metadata to include information related to citations, bibliographic records, specific sections of documents, and various aspects of the scholarly publication process. In the context of the MACJa project, four of them are relevant for the data related to the questions of the challenge:

- the *FRBR-aligned Bibliographic Ontology* (*FaBiO*) [26] is an ontology for describing entities that are published or potentially publishable (e.g., journal articles, conference papers, books), and that contain or are referred to by bibliographic references;
- the *Citation Typing Ontology* (*CiTO*) [26] is an ontology that enables characterization of the nature or type of citations, both factually and rhetorically;
- the *Bibliographic Reference Ontology* (*BiRO*) [8] is an ontology that defines bibliographic references and their compilation into bibliographic lists;
- the *Publishing Roles Ontology* (*PRO*) [27] is an ontology for the characterisation of the roles of agents – people, corporate bodies and computational agents in the publication process. These agents can be authors, editors, reviewers, publishers or librarians;
- the *Funding, Research Administration and Projects Ontology* (*FRAPO*) is an ontology for describing the administrative information of research projects, e.g., grant applications, funding bodies, project partners, etc.

3.2 Methods

MACJa employs and integrates several tools and techniques. Natural Language Processing (NLP) techniques have been used to pre-process the text, to break it down in sections and sentences, and to extract specific sub-sections.

First of all, for extracting the plain text of the articles, we use the PDFMiner Python library, which is a tool for extracting information from PDF documents that focuses entirely on getting and analyzing text data. For gathering metadata of existing papers starting from their DOIs or from the full text of the bibliographic references that describe them, we use the CrossRef API (http://api.crossref.org) and FreeCite (http://freecite.library.brown.edu/).

Once we extracted the text, we have developed on top of the Stanford CoreNLP [20] and the Natural Language Toolkit (NLTK, http://www.nltk.org). CoreNLP and NLTK are two of the leading platforms for building programs to work with human language data and that includes several corpora and lexical resources, along with a suite of text processing libraries for classification, tokenization, stemming, tagging, parsing, and semantic reasoning.

One more tool that we have included in MACJa is FRED [29]. FRED automatically produces RDF/OWL ontologies and linked data from text. FRED was successfully applied in the past to several semantic web applications [7,11–14,28,30,31]. FRED formally represents, integrates, improves, and links the output of several NLP tools. The backbone deep semantic parsing is currently provided by Boxer [3], which uses a statistical parser (C&C) producing Combinatory Categorial Grammar trees, and thousands of heuristics that exploit existing lexical resources and gazetteers to generate representation structures according to Discourse Representation Theory (DRT) [16]. The basic NLP tasks performed by Boxer, and reused by FRED, include: (mostly) verbal event detection, semantic role labeling with VerbNet and FrameNet roles, first-order logic representation of predicate-argument structures, logical operators scoping (called boxing), modality detection, and tense representation. FRED produces

RDF/OWL ontologies having classes (and related taxonomies) depending on the lexicon used in the text. In order to provide a public identity to such classes, FRED exploits Word-Sense Disambiguation (WSD) to resolve classes into Word-Net or BabelNet [22]. FRED can use any WSD system, such as UKB [1] or Babelfy [21]. WSD also enables FRED to generate alignments to two top-level ontologies: WordNet supersenses and a subset of DOLCE+DnS Ultra Lite (DUL) classes.

Figure 1 shows a RDF graph produced by FRED for the example sentence "This work has been funded by the Federal Ministry of Education and Research, Germany (BMBF), within the SMART project". The example sentence has been taken from the acknowledgment section of one of the paper of the training set and gives some hints on the *patient* and *agent* roles for the instance of the verb *fund*. Patient would be the object funded whereas the agent would be the funding entity.

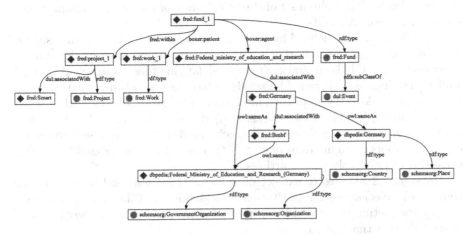

Fig. 1. RDF graph for the sentence "This work has been funded by the Federal Ministry of Education and Research, Germany (BMBF), within the SMART project".

4   Implementation Details

The workflow implemented in MACJa for extracting all the data of interest is actually organised as a sequential execution of several scripts and existing tools written in different languages – mainly Python and Java. The first script executed, called *text extractor* (based on PDFMiner), is responsible for extracting the full text of the article from PDF files. All the other scripts start from the outcome of the *text extractor* and return appropriate JSON objects that contain the data needed for answering all the queries of the challenge and reported below. Then, all these JSON objects are converted into RDF according to the SPAR Ontologies [25] and published on the MACJa triplestore, available at http://six.eelst.cs.unibo.it:8080 (dataset *macja*).

4.1   Queries Q2.1 and Q2.2: Affiliations

The main requirement of question 2.1 is to identify in a PDF article the information about the affiliations of the authors. Affiliations are complex pieces of information, as they contain data of different nature. For example, an affiliation string provides references to entities that can be typed as organisations, such as research units/laboratories (e.g., STLab) or institutions (e.g., National Research Council). Moreover, an affiliation string typically contains geographical information about the organisation that can be general (the city and the country where the organisation is based) or more detailed (addresses, postal codes, etc.). The first step performed by MACJa is the identification of the chunk of words that provides authors' names and their affiliations. MACJa uses a predefined set of heuristics for identifying authors and affiliation syntactically. The basic intuition is that these kinds of information typically occur in the front-matter of scholarly articles. Then, MACJa relies on Named Entity Recognition (NER) based on Stanford CoreNLP [20] plus a set of statistical rules for identifying organizations, sub-organizations and units.

The rules have been defined by recording frequent occurring patterns used for describing organisations in author's affiliations introduced in scholarly articles. Additionally, MACJa keeps track of extracted data in order to use already parsed affiliation strings as background knowledge. Once the data about affiliations have been extracted, MACJa maps each affiliation to its corresponding author (even in case of multiple affiliations), by using (i) the order in which affiliations and authors' names appear in a paper, (ii) special marker used in a source article for coupling authors and affiliations (e.g., †, ‡, *), and (iii) the background knowledge consisting of previously parsed articles.

Question 2.2 requires to extract data about affiliations and to identify the country where each research institution is located in. MACJa answers this question by completing the parsing step presented in Q2.1 with the recognition of Named Entities that identify countries.

4.2   Queries Q2.3, Q2.4 and Q2.5: Citations

The requirements needed for addressing questions 2.3, 2.4 and 2.5 are all related with the citation network of the papers. This citation network must include metadata of the cited papers, i.e., their titles and DOIs (when available), and the name of the venue where they have been published (only if it is a journal).

The process followed for extracting these data is implemented by means of several scripts (developed in Python), called in sequential order – where $script_1$ uses the text extracted by the *text extractor* as input, while the $script_i$ $(i > 1)$ uses the output of $script_{i-1}$ as input.

Extract-References.py. The script *extract-references.py* is responsible for the extraction of the text belonging to the reference section only starting from the full text of the paper obtained by running the text extractor described in Sect. 4.

Organise-References.py. The script *organise-references.py* extracts (by means of regular expressions) each of the reference and organises them in a JSON file which also includes information (i.e., IRI, URL and venue) about the paper containing the reference:

```
[
    {
        "paper": "http://ceur-ws.org/Vol-1155/#paper-05",
        "url": "http://ceur-ws.org/Vol-1155/paper-05.pdf",
        "venue": "http://ceur-ws.org/Vol-1155/",
        "ref": "Barabucci, G., Di Iorio, A., ... DOI:
            10.1145/2517978.2517990"
    }, ...
]
```

Enhance-References.py. For each JSON file generated, *enhance-references.py* tries to identify additional information (in particular URLs and DOIs) by parsing the text of each reference, and update the JSON accordingly by adding two additional fields, i.e., `doi` and `links`.

Gather-doi.py. The script *gather-doi.py* queries existing services to retrieve additional (and, sometimes, authoritative) information about each reference. For each reference, the script proceeds as follows. If a DOI has been identified previously, it tries to gather additional information about the reference (i.e., the title, the publication year, the type of publication and the name of the venue) by means of the CrossRef API. Otherwise, if we have no information about the DOI, the script tries to query CrossRef to retrieve the best entity that is similar to the actual text of the reference we have available. Thus, in case the entity retrieved has a similarity score (given by CrossRef) greater than a certain threshold (we set at *3* after some empirical tests), we use all the information of such entity in order to update the JSON.

In case none of the aforementioned approaches works as expected (e.g., if the paper denoted by the reference is in the CrossRef database or if it has no DOI associated, as in case of CEUR-WS papers), the script queries the FreeCite REST API for the identification of the various part of the reference (e.g., authors, date, title, venue). In addition, in order to assess whether the paper referenced is a journal article or not, we also check if the string identifying the venue contains the pattern "journal" or if such a venue is included in the lists of journal names (full and abbreviated) downloaded online from SCIMago Journal and Country Rank and Web of Science.

Despite of the approach that is followed, provenance information about the API which provided the data were added and stored in the update JSON file as follows:

```
"doi": {
        "value": "10.1145/2517978.2517990",
        "agent": "crossref" },
"container": {
        "value": "Proceedings of the 1st International Workshop...",
        "agent": "crossref" }, ...
```

Create-push.py. Finally, all the JSON produced by executing the aforementioned scripts are parsed by the script *create-push.py*. In particular, this script is responsible for the conversion of the information stored in JSON into RDF according to the SPAR ontologies (in particular CiTO and FaBiO). Once converted, the new RDF data are pushed to the triplestore and, if needed, aligned with the other RDF data that currently exist on the triplestore itself. This alignment guarantees that no multiple entities (referring to the same real world paper) are created on the triplestore if they are cited by different papers in the dataset.

4.3   Queries Q2.6, Q2.7 and Q2.8: Research Grants, Funding Agencies and EU Projects

The challenge's instructions state that the analysis of research grant, funding and EU projects must be restricted to those whose number or identifier is explicitly mentioned in the underlying paper. This means that it is not possible to look for other information in external data sources. For example, the EU system http://cordis.europa.eu/projects/home_en.html would have helped us a lot with the extraction of detailed information of EU projects. This requirement drove us to focus on the analysis of when a grant, funding agency or EU project can be mentioned in a given paper. The first consideration we had is that those information are often mentioned within the acknowledgement section of a paper and only in rare cases as footnote in other sections (usually in the first page, within the introduction). As an example, in the training set, only 7 papers out of 109 included information related to queries Q2.6, Q2.7 and Q2.8 as footnote in the first page. Also, 57 papers contained a dedicated acknowledgement section and 45 did not provide any data about it. This consideration helped us to limit the search for grants, funding agencies and EU projects to the acknowledgement section of a given paper or to footnotes present in the first page and containing identified keywords.

Query Q2.6: Research Grants. We have identified the possible type of patterns that are used for specifying a grant number. Therefore we have developed a set of regular expressions for grant identification, which include expressions such as *grant number, grant, under the, award*, etc. The extracted grant is also checked to be either a number or a mixture of letters and numbers that may contain dashes. The obtained result were then cleaned in order to remove punctuations, common expressions and words included into a stop-word list we came up with that helped us to remove some noise.

Query Q2.7: Funding Agencies. As a funding agency is usually explicitly mentioned (if present) using verb such as *fund, promote, support* we decided to apply FRED to each sentence of the acknowledgement section/footnote. We want to underline that FRED does not use any external ontology related to info about funding agencies but only lexical resources such as Verbnet or Wordnet.

Once we obtained the RDF graph from FRED for each sentence of the acknowledgement section of each processed paper, we looked for any of the verbs above, and, in particular, if any node had a *boxer:agent* or *vn.role:Agent* role property connected to the verb. That node would correspond to the agency itself. For instance, in the example sentence reported in Fig. 1, the reader may notice the presence of the instance node *fund_1*, verb of type *Fund*. The role *boxer:agent* in such an example reports the name of the mentioned funding agency. After we extracted the information tied to the agent role we augmented the result using some regular expressions in case of FRED's errors and in presence of compound expressions involving projects. The reason is that it may happen that a given paper is supported by a project and not an agency, and we would obtain that information from FRED's graph. With this step we removed such information from our result. A further step was needed to remove punctuations from our final results.

Query Q2.8: EU Projects. We analysed the possible forms to mention EU projects in a research paper. There several ways a EU project can be mentioned: either explicitly mentioned using verbs such as *support, fund, acknowledge*, or by referencing to it using the acronym or the EU call identifier. Therefore we decided to not use any NLP tool nor FRED and, in order to extract EU projects names, we identified a set of regular expressions that included terms such as *fp6, fp7, 7th programme, european project, etc.*. The extracted information were then cleaned to remove punctuations, common expressions and words included into a stop-word list we defined.

Grant.py. The script *grant.py* processes each paper in a specified folder. Processed papers are already text files extracted from the original PDF files using the *text extractor*. The script first identifies the acknowledgment section of the underlying paper and the footnotes contained in the first page. Then, it applies regular expressions and heuristics defined above and calls via *curl* FRED to get RDF graphs representation for finding funding agencies data. At the end it outputs triples according to Semantic Publishing Challenge 2015 (task 2) requirements. One more task of the grant.py script is to convert these triples in JSON format (it writes one JSON file for each processed paper) for the publication on the MACJa triplestore.

4.4   Queries Q2.9 and Q2.10: Related and New Ontologies

The query Q2.9 is about the identification of the ontologies explicitly mentioned in the abstract of a scholarly paper. We address this query by relying on FRED [29] for identifying all possible named entities that match the name of existing ontologies. This matching is performed by using an index that contains a list of existing ontologies. The index was built as a SOLr index by exploiting publicly available registries, i.e. Watson [5] and ontologydesignpatterns.org[1].

---

[1] http://www.ontologydesignpatterns.org.

The query Q2.10 is similar to the query Q2. However, in this case it is not possible to rely on pre-built index of existing ontologies. Hence, we use FRED in order to identify the named entities in the abstract that cannot be linked neither to DBpedia entites or to our pre-built index and that are typed by FRED as `fred:Ontology`, `fred:Vocabulary`, or `fred:Taxonomy`. These types are produced by FRED by applying the machine reading of the original natural language text. For example, given the sentence *"In this work we introduce the ontology Xyz."* FRED returns a graph containing the triple

`fred:Xyz rdf:type fred:Ontology`

This triple allows us to identify Xyz as an ontology. Our method marks as new ontologies only those entities that are explicitly mentioned as *ontologies*, *vocabularies* or *taxonomies* in the text, e.g., *the xyx ontology, xyx is a taxonomy*, ecc. This is a limitation that we want to solve in our future work.

5   Conclusions

We have presented MACJa, a framework for processing the research papers stored as PDF files. Its goal is to extract relevant semantic information and create a RDF triplestore according to the Semantic Publishing And Referencing (SPAR) Ontologies. MACJa employs Discourse Representation Theory, Combinational Categorial Grammar, Linguistic Frames, NLP, Semantic Web and good Ontology Design practices to achieve its goal. The information that MACJa can extract are limited to those identified within the Task 2 of the Semantic Publishing Challenge 2015 that was held during the Extended Semantic Web Conference 2015. According to the challenge evaluation dataset, we obtained 0.274 in precision, 0.251 in recall, and 0.257 in F-score.

As future direction we want to improve the scripts in order to increase precision and recall, and to extend MACJa so as to extract, collect and link other information present in research papers (not just papers from CEUR-WS.org) in order to come up with a triplestore useful for querying research data and to make available to the research community.

References

1. Agirre, E., Soroa, A.: Personalizing pagerank for word sense disambiguation. In: EACL, Athens, Greece, 2009. The Association for Computer Linguistics (2009)
2. Bertin, M., Atanassova, I.: Hybrid Approach for the Semantic Processing of Scientific Papers. In Semantic Publishing Challenge (2014)
3. Bos, J.: Wide-coverage semantic analysis with boxer. In: Bos, J., Delmonte, R. (eds.) Semantics in Text Processing, pp. 277–286. College Publications, London (2008)
4. Constantin, A., Steve, P., Andrei, V.: PDFX: fully-automated PDF-to-XML conversion of scientific literature. In: Proceedings of the 2013 ACM Symposium on Document Engineering, pp. 177–180. ACM, New York (2013). doi:10.1145/2494266.2494271

5. d'Aquin, M., Baldassare, C., Gridinoc, L., Sabou, M., Angeletou, S., Motta, E.: Watson: supporting next generation semantic web applications. In: Proceedings of WWW/Internet Conference 2007 (2007)
6. Das, S., Sundara, S., Cyganiak, R.: R2RML: RDB to RDF Mapping Language. W3C recommendation (2012). http://www.w3.org/TR/r2rml/
7. Di Iorio, A., Nuzzolese, A.G., Peroni, S.: Towards the automatic identification of the nature of citations. In: Castro, A.G., Lange, C., Lord, P.W., Stevens, R. (eds.) SePublica. CEUR Workshop Proceedings, vol. 994, pp. 63–74. CEUR-WS.org (2013)
8. Di Iorio, A., Nuzzolese, A.G., Peroni, S., Shotton, D., Vitali, F.: Describing bibliographic references in RDF. In: Castro, A.G., Lange, C., Lord, P., Stevens, R. (eds.) Proceedings of 4th Workshop on Semantic Publishing (SePublica 2014) (2014). http://ceur-ws.org/Vol-1155/paper-05.pdf
9. Dimou, A., Vander Sande, M., Colpaert, P., De Vocht, L., Verborgh, R., Mannens, E., Van de Walle, R.: Extraction and Semantic Annotation of Workshop Proceedings in HTML Using RML. In: Presutti, V., Stankovic, M., Cambria, E., Cantador, I., Di Iorio, A., Di Noia, T., Lange, C., Reforgiato Recupero, D., Tordai, A. (eds.) SemWebEval 2014. CCIS, vol. 475, pp. 114–119. Springer, Heidelberg (2014)
10. Dimou, A., Vander Sande, M., Colpaert, P., Mannens, E., Van De Walle, R.: Extending R2RML to a source-independent mapping language for RDF. In: Proceedings of the ISWC 2013 Posters & Demonstrations Track. CEUR-WS (2013)
11. Gangemi, A.: A comparison of knowledge extraction tools for the semantic web. In: Cimiano, P., Corcho, O., Presutti, V., Hollink, L., Rudolph, S. (eds.) ESWC 2013. LNCS, vol. 7882, pp. 351–366. Springer, Heidelberg (2013)
12. Gangemi, A., Draicchio, F., Presutti, V., Nuzzolese, A.G., Recupero, D.R.: A machine reader for the semantic web. In: Blomqvist, E., Groza, T. (eds.) International Semantic Web Conference (Posters & Demos). CEUR Workshop Proceedings, vol. 1035, pp. 149–152. CEUR-WS.org (2013)
13. Gangemi, A., Nuzzolese, A.G., Presutti, V., Draicchio, F., Musetti, A., Ciancarini, P.: Automatic typing of DBpedia entities. In: Cudré-Mauroux, P., et al. (eds.) ISWC 2012, Part I. LNCS, vol. 7649, pp. 65–81. Springer, Heidelberg (2012)
14. Gangemi, A., Presutti, V., Reforgiato Recupero, D.: Frame-based detection of opinion holders and topics: a model and a tool. IEEE Comp. Int. Mag. 9(1), 20–30 (2014)
15. Garcia, A., Murray-Rust, P., Burns, G.A., Stevens, R., Tkaczyk, D., McLaughlin, C., Belin, A., Di Iorio, A., García, L., Gruson-Daniel, C., Mounce, R., Nuzzolese, A.G., Peroni, S., Spinks, J., Villazon-Terrazas, B., Corcho, O., Giraldo, O.: Wabiszewski, M.: PDFJailbreak-a communal architecture for making biomedical PDFs semantic. In Proceedings of BioLINK SIG (2013)
16. Kamp, H.: A theory of truth and semantic representation. In: Groenendijk, J.A.G., Janssen, T.M.V., Stokhof, M.B.J. (eds.) Formal Methods in the Study of Language, vol. 1, pp. 277–322. Mathematisch Centrum (1981)
17. Lafferty, J., McCallum, A., Pereira, F.C.N.: Conditional random fields: probabilistic models for segmenting and labeling sequence data. In: Proceedings of the 18th International Conference on Machine Learning, pp. 282–289. Morgan Kaufmann, San Francisco (2001)
18. Lange, C., Di Iorio, A.: Semantic publishing challenge – assessing the quality of scientific output. In: Presutti, V., et al. (eds.) SemWebEval 2014. CCIS, vol. 475, pp. 61–76. Springer, Heidelberg (2014)

19. Luong, M.T., Dung Nguyen, T., Kan, M.Y.: Logical structure recovery in scholarly articles with rich document features. Int. J. Digit. Libr. Syst. (IJDLS) **1**(4), 1–23 (2010)
20. Manning, C.D., Surdeanu, M., Bauer, J., Finkel, J., Bethard, S.J., McClosky, D.: The Stanford CoreNLP natural language processing toolkit. In: Proceedings of 52nd Annual Meeting of the Association for Computational Linguistics: System Demonstrations, pp. 55–60 (2014)
21. Moro, A., Raganato, A., Navigli, R.: En-tity linking meets word sense disambiguation: a unified approach. Trans. Assoc. Comput. Linguist. **2**, 231–244 (2014)
22. Navigli, R., Ponzetto, S.P.: BabelNet: the automatic construction, evaluation and application of a wide-coverage multilingual semantic network. Artif. Intell. **193**, 217–250 (2012)
23. NLM. http://dtd.nlm.nih.gov/archiving/
24. PDFMiner: Python PDF parser and analyzer (2010)
25. Peroni, S.: Semantic Web Technologies and Legal Scholarly Publishing. Law, Governance and Technology Series 15. Springer, New York (2014). ISBN 978-3-319-04776-8
26. Peroni, S., Shotton, D.: FaBiO and CiTO: ontologies for describing bibliographic resources and citations. Web Semant. Sci. Serv. Agents World Wide Web **17**, 33–43 (2012). doi:10.1016/j.websem.2012.08.001
27. Peroni, S., Shotton, D., Vitali, F.: Scholarly publishing and linked data: describing roles, statuses, temporal and contextual extents. In: Sack, H., Pellegrini, T., (eds.) Proceedings of the 8th International Conference on Semantic Systems (i-Semantics 2012), pp. 9–16. ACM Press, New York (2012). doi:10.1145/2362499.2362502
28. Presutti, V., Consoli, S., Nuzzolese, A.G., Recupero, D.R., Gangemi, A., Bannour, I., Zargayouna, H.: Uncovering the semantics of wikipedia wikilinks. In: 19th International Conference on Knowledge Engineering and Knowledge Management (EKAW 2014) (2014)
29. Presutti, V., Draicchio, F., Gangemi, A.: Knowledge extraction based on discourse representation theory and linguistic frames. In: ten Teije, A., Völker, J., Handschuh, S., Stuckenschmidt, H., d'Acquin, M., Nikolov, A., Aussenac-Gilles, N., Hernandez, N. (eds.) EKAW 2012. LNCS, vol. 7603, pp. 114–129. Springer, Heidelberg (2012)
30. Recupero, D.R., Consoli, S., Gangemi, A., Nuzzolese, A.G., Spampinato, D.: A semantic web based core engine to efficiently perform sentiment analysis. In: Presutti, V., Blomqvist, E., Troncy, R., Sack, H., Papadakis, I., Tordai, A. (eds.) ESWC Satellite Events 2014. LNCS, vol. 8798, pp. 245–248. Springer, Heidelberg (2014)
31. Recupero, D.R., Presutti, V., Consoli, S., Gangemi, A., Nuzzolese, A.G.: Sentilo: frame-based sentiment analysis. Cogn. Comput. **7**, 211–225 (2014)
32. Shotton, D.: Semantic publishing: the coming revolution in scientific journal publishing. Learn. Publ. **22**(2), 85–94 (2009)
33. Tkaczyk, D., Szostek, P., Jan Dendek, P., Fedoryszak, M., Bolikowski, L.: CERMINE - automatic extraction of metadata and references from scientific literature. In: Proceedings of the 11th IAPR International Workshop on Document Analysis Systems, pp. 217–221 (2014)

Automatic Construction of a Semantic Knowledge Base from CEUR Workshop Proceedings

Bahar Sateli and René Witte[✉]

Semantic Software Lab, Department of Computer Science
and Software Engineering, Concordia University, Montréal, Canada
witte@semanticsoftware.info

Abstract. We present an automatic workflow that performs text segmentation and entity extraction from scientific literature to primarily address Task 2 of the Semantic Publishing Challenge 2015. The goal of Task 2 is to extract various information from full-text papers to represent the context in which a document is written, such as the affiliation of its authors and the corresponding funding bodies. Our proposed solution is composed of two subsystems: *(i)* A text mining pipeline, developed based on the GATE framework, which extracts structural and semantic entities, such as authors' information and references, and produces semantic (typed) annotations; and *(ii)* a flexible exporting module, the LOD-eXporter, which translates the document annotations into RDF triples according to custom mapping rules. Additionally, we leverage existing Named Entity Recognition (NER) tools to extract named entities from text and ground them to their corresponding resources on the Linked Open Data cloud, thus, briefly covering Task 3 objectives, which involves linking of detected entities to resources in existing open datasets. The output of our system is an RDF graph stored in a scalable TDB-based storage with a public SPARQL endpoint for the task's queries.

1 Introduction

Semantic Publishing is a new, thriving research domain, driven by a synergic community of semantic web researchers, computational linguists, librarians and publishing companies, all aiming towards a platform for the dissemination of scientific literature, accessible to both humans and machines. The vision is to develop tools and frameworks to enrich scholarly literature with metadata in order to facilitate retrieval, automatically exploiting and evaluating research artifacts, such as articles and datasets. The ever-increasing amount of available scientific literature, however, has rendered manual efforts of annotating documents ineffective. Consequently, researchers are in dire need of automatic systems that can detect various entities from scientific literature and make them available in open formats.

The *Semantic Publishing Challenge*, started in 2014, is a recent series of competitive efforts to produce linked open datasets from multi-format and multi-source

© Springer International Publishing Switzerland 2015
F. Gandon et al. (Eds.): SemWebEval 2015, CCIS 548, pp. 129–141, 2015.
DOI: 10.1007/978-3-319-25518-7_11

input documents. The 2015 edition of the challenge[1] targeted the automatic analysis of several computer science workshop proceedings to extract fine-grained bibliographical metadata from workshops' full-text papers. The dataset under study is composed of 183 workshop papers, published between 2007 and 2014 by CEUR-WS.org. The challenge is to automatically extract authors, affiliations, cited works, funding bodies and mentioned ontology names from the text and populate a knowledge base, in which all the detected entities are semantically described and inter-linked with each other, where applicable.

The generated knowledge base is finally evaluated against a set of 10 predefined queries for its correctness and completeness and exploited as a means of assessing the quality of scientific production in the respective workshops. The challenge queries are concerned with searching for entities, categorized as follows:

- Authors, their Affiliations (**Q2.1**) and the country where the affiliation is located in (**Q2.2**);
- References cited in a paper (**Q2.3**), their year of publication (**Q2.4**), and type (**Q2.5**);
- Research Grant numbers (**Q2.6**), names of Funding Agencies (**Q2.7**) and European Projects (**Q2.8**) supporting the research presented in the paper; and
- Names of existing (**Q2.9**) and new (**Q2.10**) Ontologies mentioned in a paper.

In this paper, we present our automatic workflow that performs text segmentation and entity detection to address Task 2 of the challenge. Our system is able to extract contextual information, such as the entities required to answer the challenge queries, from the full-text of the given papers, and make them available as a linked open dataset. Additionally, we briefly cover Task 3 objectives, by linking named entities that appear in the documents to their corresponding resources on the Linked Open Data (LOD) cloud, whenever possible. We leverage a combination of multiple techniques from the Natural Language Processing (NLP) and Semantic Web domains to automatically construct a semantic representation of the knowledge contained in a scientific document. We believe that such a rich representation can pave the way for a variety of advanced use cases, such as creating automatic literature reviews, facilitating information synthesis and literature-based knowledge discovery. Note that you can find supplementary material, such as the populated knowledge base and the text mining pipeline resources at http://www.semanticsoftware.info/sempub-challenge-2015.

2   Design

The ultimate goal of our approach is to automatically extract the entities needed to answer the challenge queries from the given dataset and store them in a knowledge base with semantic metadata. In our approach, we use text mining to detect the desired entities from a document's full-text. Given the lack of training

---

[1] Semantic Publishing Challenge 2015, https://github.com/ceurws/lod/wiki/SemPub 2015.

data for computer science literature, we decided to adopt a rule-based approach, as opposed to applying machine-learning techniques.

Figure 1 provides a high-level overview of our system. The NLP pipeline accepts a document as input, which goes through multiple processing phases, and produces semantic triples as output. The *Syntactic Processing* phase breaks down full-text of the document into smaller segments and pre-processes the text for further semantic analysis. The *Semantic Processing* phase takes the results of syntactic analysis and attempts to annotate various entities in text. Finally, the document's annotations will be translated into semantic triples according to a series of custom *mapping rules* and made persistent in a knowledge base. Throughout this section, we provide examples from the challenge training dataset to clarify our approach. Each example sentence will also bear a reference to its corresponding paper.

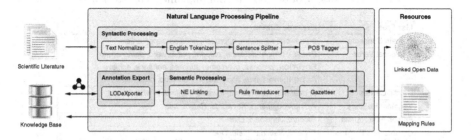

Fig. 1. Automatic workflow to transform scientific literature into a knowledge base

2.1 Syntactic Processing

The input of our text mining pipeline are documents (e.g., the dataset PDF files) containing the collected work of its authors in a descriptive format, as well as other additional content, like title, figures and references. In our pipeline, we first scrape the text of documents and normalize the output, such as, whitespace trimming and faulty character encoding replacement. As a prerequisite step, we then break down the content of the document into individual tokens,[2] sequences of tokens (e.g., n-grams) and sentences. Since our semantic processing components rely on specific characteristics of sentences, like their verbs, we also label each lexical item in a sentence with a Part-Of-Speech (POS) tag, like *adjective* or *pronoun*, as its grammatical category. The pre-processed text is subsequently passed onto the semantic processing subsystem for entity detection.

2.2 Semantic Processing

The semantic processing subsystem is responsible for detecting entities required for the challenge queries from text and generate typed annotations as output. Here, we provide a detailed description of each of our subsystem's components.

---

[2] Tokens are smallest, meaningful units of text, such as words, numbers or symbols.

Gazetteer. The *Gazetteer* component is essentially a dictionary with several lists of carefully curated words that are matched against the text to mark tokens for further processing. In addition to reusing GATE's gazetteer of person and location names for author and affiliation extraction, we curated a list for detection of segment headers (7 entries), as well as a list of general terms used in computer science (30 entries), discourse deictic cliches (8 entries), and verbs used in the scientific argumentation context (160 entries) for rhetorical analysis of documents. We curated these gazetteer lists – a subset of which is shown in Table 1 – from manual inspection of the training dataset documents and Teufel's AZ corpus[3] for rhetorical entities. The role of the Gazetteer component is to compare the text tokens against its dictionary entries and generate so-called *lookup* words subsequently utilized within our entity detection rules.

Table 1. A subset of our text mining pipeline's gazetteer lists

List Type	Example Entries
Domain Concepts	*framework, algorithm, approach, position paper, article*
Rhetorical Verbs	PRESENTATION: *describe, present, put forward, demonstrate*
	SOLUTION: *propose, overcome, address, enhance, achieve*
	ACTION: *investigate, apply, assess, develop, construct*
Deictic Cliches	*to deal with this problem, towards this end, in what follows*
Segment Headers	*Acknowledgments, Keywords, References*
Person First Names	*Richard, Jamshaid, Olaf*
Organization Prefixes	*Federal, National, Freie, Open*
Organization Base	*University, Universität, Department, Faculty, Institute*

Rule Transducers. The *Rule Transducers* are responsible for detecting the desired entities of the challenge. Transducers apply pattern-matching rules to classify the text tokens and sentences into one of several pre-defined classes (or none). The input to the transducers are sentences, word tokens with their POS and root form,[4] as well the lookup words marked by the Gazetteer component. Whenever a match is found in text, this component annotates the boundary of the matched sequence with a semantic type, such as Author or Title. We developed several rules for the following categories:

Text Segmentation. Based on segment headers detected by the Gazetteer component, we blindly annotate the span between each two headers (and Start-of-Document and End-of-Document) with the corresponding header as its class. For example, we annotate everything from the start of the document until the word "*Abstract*" as the document's Metadata_body.

---

[3] Argumentation Zoning (AZ) Corpus, http://www.cl.cam.ac.uk/~sht25/AZ_corpus. html.

[4] The root or *lemma* of a word is its canonical form without any inflectional endings.

Authors. The person name detection is based on the tokens marked by the Gazetteer component as first names. All first name tokens followed by an upper initial token are annotated as Persons in text. Subsequently, we extract each Person name in the document's Metadata_body (excluding the ones that appear within an organization name) as an Author annotation.

Affiliations. We designed several rules to capture various patterns of organization names, limited to academic institutions, from the document's metadata body. We also capture the geographical location of the organization from *(i)* the name of the institution, or *(ii)* the location name mentioned closest to the organization, in terms of its start offset in text. We retain the detected location name along with the affiliation annotation in order to answer query **Q2.2** of the challenge (see Sect. 1).

(1) *"University of **Trento, Italy**"*(Vol315_paper01)

(2) *"The Open University, **UK**"*(Vol523_deWaard)

Authors-Affiliations Relations. We developed a separate processing resource that implements multiple heuristics to extrapolate which Authors are employed by a detected Affiliation entity. If both Author and Affiliation mentions in text are indexed (e.g., with numbers or symbols), the matching is performed based on the indices. Otherwise, the processing resource merely infers such a relationship between each Author and its closest Affiliation annotation using their start offsets in text. Subsequently, the result of the matching process is stored as the *"employedBy"* feature of the Author annotation.

References. Detection of references titles, authors and publishing venue is one of the most challenging parts of document analysis, mostly due to inconsistencies in bibliographical styles used in the papers (e.g., see Vol-721[5] in the dataset). We tackled this problem by hand-crafting rules for multiple styles, including `abbrv` and `plain` classes used in the training set. We break down the References_body segment into smaller fragments: Similar to author names described above, we detect author names and paper title from each reference. We then annotate the tokens in between the paper title and the year of publication (or End-of-Line) as the publishing venue. References are eventually categorized into either *"journal"* or *"proceedings"* classes based on whether a journal citation (volume, number and pagination) is present, like the ones shown below:

(3) *"G. Tummarello, R. Cyganiak, M. Catasta, S. Danielczyk, R. Delbru, and S. Decker. Sig.ma: Live views on the web of data. **Journal** of Web Semantics, **8(4):355-364**, 2010"*(ldow2011_paper10)

(4) *"M. Hausenblas, "Exploiting linked data to build applications," IEEE Internet Computing, **vol. 13, no. 4, pp. 68-73**, 2009"*(ldow2011_paper12)

---

[5] Task 2 Dataset, https://github.com/ceurws/lod/wiki/Task2#data-source.

Ontologies. Ontology name detection is performed using the root form of word tokens. We capture three forms of ontology mentions: *(i)* concatenated or camel-case ontology names, *(ii)* upper initial ontology names, and *(iii)* acronyms or all-caps tokens mentioned in a sentence on a fixed window distance from the word "*ontology*".

(5) "*...two versions of an ontology of the hydrographical domain: **hydrOntology**.*"(Vol571_paper4)

(6) "*...the **Privacy Preference Ontology (PPO)** that enables users to create...*"(Idow2011_paper01)

(7) "*The **GoodRelations Ontology** is experiencing the first stages of...*"(Idow2011_paper12)

Contributions. An interesting subtask of the challenge is to find the new ontologies introduced in a paper. To this end, we attempt at finding sentences in the document's abstract that describe the Contributions of the authors. We first look for *deictic* phrases, such as "*in this paper*". Deictic phrases are expressions within an utterance that refer to parts of the discourse. For example, the word "*here*" in "*here, we describe a new methodology...*" refers to the article that the user is reading. In scientific literature, deictic phrases are often used in sentences that provide a high-level overview of what is presented in the paper, referred to as the *metadiscourse* elements, such as the following examples:

(8) "*In this paper we introduce the Publishing Workflow Ontology (PWO)...*"(Vol1302_paper01)

We designed hand-crafted rules to capture Contribution sentences that look at sequences of deictic phrases, metadiscourse mentions and the rhetorical function of the verbs mentioned in the sentence [1]. Note that we require an explicit reference to the agent (i.e., authors) or the discourse deixis in each sentence. Subsequently, each sentence containing a metadiscourse element followed by a noun phrase is annotated as a Contribution entity. Finally, the ontologies mentioned in the Abstract section within the boundary of a Contribution are extracted for **Q2.10** of the challenge (see Sect. 1).

Funding Agencies. Funding agency mentions in text are extracted from the Acknowledgement segment of each paper. The agency name is detected as either *(i)* one or more upper-initial word tokens, or *(ii)* an organization name. We plan to integrate a parsing component into our text mining pipeline, so that the funding agency name can be extracted from the noun phrase following the "*funded by*" verb phrase in the sentence's dependency tree.

(9) "*This work has been funded by the **SemanticHealthNet Network of Excellence**...*"(Vol1302_paper06)

(10) "*This work was partially supported by **European Commission**...*"(Vol1118_paper1)

NE Linking. Previously, we investigated how we can use generic Named Entity Recognition (NER) tools to extract topics from scientific literature in a domain-independent manner, as a means of modeling the knowledge in a paper [1]. In our text mining pipeline, we use external NER components to extract topics (named entities) of the document and link them to their corresponding resources on the LOD cloud [1].

2.3   Knowledge Base Construction

In order to generate a semantic representation of the detected entities described in the previous sections, we export all annotations into semantic triples using the W3C RDF[6] standard to construct a knowledge base. While the type of annotations, e.g. Affiliation, is determined by the Rule Transducers component, we still would like to have the flexibility to express the mapping of annotations to RDF triples and their inter-relations at run-time. This way, various representations of knowledge extracted from documents can be constructed based on the intended use case and customized without affecting the underlying syntactic and semantic processing components.

Reuse of Vocabularies. Conforming to the best practices of producing linked open datasets,[7] we decided to reuse existing open vocabularies to describe both the structural and semantic metadata that we extract from each document. In scientific literature mining, controlled vocabularies are used in form of *markup* languages, which are added to text (either manually or automatically) to annotate various entities of documents.

In order to tolerate the formatting variations of the datasets items (e.g., ACM vs. LNCS, double-column vs. single-column), we decided to remove all formatting from documents during processing and use the DoCO ontology [2] to describe various units of information, such as Sentences or Bibliography section, in the document. DoCO is an OWL 2 DL ontology that serves as a general-purpose vocabulary for describing documents in RDF. Additionally, it integrates DEO[8] and SALT [3] ontologies for annotation of rhetorical entities, such as Contributions, in a scholarly document. By linking to instances of the DoCO ontology, we can attach syntactic and semantic markup to the document, which can be later queried to answer the challenge queries, e.g., by annotating parts of the Abstract text that describe the authors' Contributions, so that we can detect new ontologies introduced in a paper (see **Q2.10** in Sect. 1).

Publication Ontology (PUBO). We developed the *PUBlication Ontology* (PUBO)[9] – a vocabulary for scientific literature constructs that describes a document's various segments (e.g., sentences) and their contained entities. Wherever possible, we reused existing Linked Open Vocabularies (LOV): To express the semantic types of entities, like Sentences and Contributions, we chose to link to DoCO[10] and SALT Rhetorical Ontology (SRO) for our experiments. We also added our own vocabulary to describe the relation between a source document and its contained entities, for example, to describe the topics that appear within the boundary of a rhetorical entity. Our ontology uses "pubo" as its namespace throughout this paper.

---

[6] Resource Description Framework (RDF), http://www.w3.org/RDF/.

[7] Best Practices for Publishing Linked Data, http://www.w3.org/TR/ld-bp/.

[8] Discourse Elements Ontology (DEO), http://purl.org/spar/deo.

[9] PUBlication Ontology, http://lod.semanticsoftware.info/pubo/pubo.rdf.

[10] Document Components Ontology (DoCO), http://purl.org/spar/doco.

LODeXporter. We designed the *LODeXporter*[11] component in our text mining workflow that accepts mapping rules as input and transforms the designated document's annotations into their equivalent RDF triples. For each annotation type that is to be exported, the mapping rules have an entry that describes: *(i)* the annotation type in the document and its corresponding semantic type, *(ii)* the annotation's features and their corresponding semantic type, and *(iii)* the relations between exported triples and the type of their relation. Given the mapping rules, the mapper component then iterates over the document's entities and exports each designated annotation as the subject of a triple, with a custom predicate and its attributes, such as its features, as the object. Table 2 shows some example mapping rules.

Table 2. Example mapping rules for transforming annotations to RDF triples

Mapping rule examples for Subjects		
Resource	*Type*	*Corresponding class in LOV*
Contribution	annotation type	http://salt.semanticauthoring.org/ontologies/sro#Contribution
Author	annotation type	http://xmlns.com/foaf/0.1/Person

Mapping rule examples for Properties		
Domain	*Range*	*Corresponding property in LOV*
Document	Contribution	http://lod.semanticsoftware.info/pubo/pubo#hasAnnotation
Author	Affiliation	http://purl.org/vocab/relationship/employedBy

3   Implementation

We implemented our text mining pipeline described in Sect. 2 based on the *General Architecture for Text Engineering* (GATE) framework [4]. The pipeline accepts scientific literature in PDF, HTML or plain text format from local or remote URLs as input and stores the extracted entities in form of an RDF document in a knowledge base as output.

3.1   Text Pre-processing

When the input document is in PDF format, we first use Xpdf[12] to extract its textual content into a plain text file. We have observed that the extraction process often introduces erroneous characters to the output text, especially for accented letters. Therefore, in order to prevent cascading such defects to the downstream processing resources, we first normalize the text by replacing faulty character encodings with their correct Unicode. Next, we use GATE's ANNIE plugin [5] to pre-process the document's text into smaller meaningful units, such as word tokens and sentences. The Gazetteer processing resource then generates so-called *Lookup* annotations from word tokens that match entries in its

---

[11] Originally called the *"RDF Mapper"*, it is now an independent open source project available at http://www.semanticsoftware.info/lodexporter.

[12] Xpdf, http://www.foolabs.com/xpdf/.

dictionary. We also use GATE's Morphological Analyzer resource to detect the root form of all word tokens, such as plurals and various verb tenses, so they can be directly matched against the gazetteers terms. Finally, the annotated text is passed onto the Rule Transducer component to classify the document's sentences.

3.2 Rule-Based Extraction of Contextual Entities

The rules of our pipeline's transducers are implemented using GATE's JAPE language that provides for defining regular expressions over a document's annotations (by internally transforming them into finite-state transducers). The transducing process is conducted in an incremental manner: First, various segments of the document (e.g., Abstract, Main Body, References) are detected so that further analysis can be properly focused, for example, Authors and Affiliations are only detected in the Metadata_body segment of the document. Then, several other JAPE rules are executed sequentially to find Authors, Affiliations, References, Ontology and Funding Agency mentions in text,[13] as described in Sect. 2.2.

For rhetorical entities, multiple JAPE rules are executed sequentially to detect deictic phrases and metadiscourse elements. Finally, depending on the type of the sentence's main verb phrase, the transducer annotates the boundary of the sentence under study with RhetoricalEntity as its type and a reference to the LOV, such as the Contribution class in the SALT Rhetorical Ontology, as its semantic class. Figure 2 shows a sequence of JAPE rules to detect the authors and title of a Reference entity (left) and its corresponding annotation in GATE Developer environment (right).

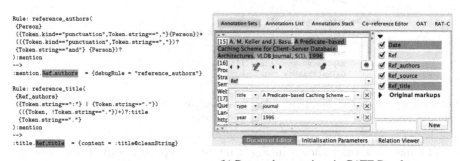

(a) Example JAPE rules   (b) Detected annotations in GATE Developer

Fig. 2. Rule-based extraction of References with JAPE

3.3 Knowledge Base Population

The LODeXporter component is implemented as a GATE processing resource that uses the Apache Jena[14] library to export the document annotations to

---

[13] Several of our named entity extraction rules are extensions of GATE's ANNIE plugin [5].

[14] Apache Jena, http://jena.apache.org.

RDF triples, according to custom mapping rules, described in Sect. 2.3. The mapping rules themselves are stored in the knowledge base, expressed using RDF triples that explicitly define what annotation types need to be exported and what vocabularies and relations must be used to create a new triple in the knowledge base. Figure 3 shows an excerpt of the mapping rules to export Author and Affiliation annotations and their relations into semantic triples.

```
@prefix map: <http://semanticsoftware.info/mapping#> .
@prefix rdf: <http://www.w3.org/1999/02/22-rdf-syntax-ns#> .
@prefix cnt: <http://www.w3.org/2011/content#> .
@prefix rel: <http://purl.org/vocab/relationship/> .
@prefix foaf: <http://xmlns.com/foaf/0.1/> .
@prefix gn: <http://www.geonames.org/ontology#> .

### Annotation Mapping ###
map:GATEAuthor a map:Mapping ;
        map:type    foaf:Person ;
        map:GATEtype  "Author" ;
        map:hasMapping map:GATEContentMapping .

map:GATEAffiliation a map:Mapping ;
        map:type    foaf:Organization ;
        map:GATEtype  "Affiliation" ;
        map:hasMapping map:GATEContentMapping ;
        map:hasMapping map:GATELocatedInFeatureMapping .

### Feature Mapping ###
map:GATEContentMapping a map:Mapping ;
        map:type    cnt:chars ;
        GATEattribute "content" .

map:GATELocatedInFeatureMapping a map:Mapping ;
        map:type    gn:LocatedIn ;
        GATEfeature "locatedIn" .

### Relation Mapping ###
map:AuthorAffiliationRelationMapping a map:Mapping ;
        map:type rel:employedBy ;
        map:domain map:GATEAuthor ;
        map:range map:GATEAffiliation ;
        GATEattribute "employedBy" .
```

Fig. 3. Excerpt of the mapping rules for exporting Authors, Affiliations and their relations

The mapping rules shown in Fig. 3 describe exporting GATE annotations into several inter-connected triples: Each Author annotation in the document should be exported with <foaf:Person> as its type, and its verbatim content in text using the <cnt:chars> predicate. Similarly, Affiliation annotations are exported with their *"locatedIn"* feature describing their geographical position from the GeoNames ontology (<gn:locatedIn>). Subsequently, the value of the *"employedBy"* feature of each Author annotation is used to construct a <rel:employedBy> relation between an author instance and its corresponding affiliation instance in the knowledge base. We used vocabularies from our PUBO ontology wherever no equivalent entity was available in the LOV. For example, we use the <pubo:containsNE> property to build a relation between rhetorical entities and the topics that appear within their boundaries (detected by an NER tool).

Ultimately, the LODeXporter processing resource generates all of the desired RDF triples from the document's annotations, and stores them in a scalable, TDB-based[15] triplestore. In addition to the challenge queries, in [1], we demonstrated a number of complex queries that such a semantically-rich knowledge base can answer.

4   Results and Discussion

We analyzed the complete dataset set, consisting of 183 documents (101 in the training set and 82 additional papers for evaluation), with our text mining pipeline and populated the knowledge base in a TDB-based triplestore. The total number of RDF triples generated from processing the complete training set is 506,694, describing the challenge entities, their relations, rhetorical elements, named entities, as well as the triples from the mapping rules. On average, the processing time of extracting and triplification of the knowledge in the proceedings was between 7 and 52 (Mean: 17.30) seconds per volume (running on a 2.3 GHz Intel Core i7 MacBook Pro with 16 GB memory).

Evaluation on Training Set (Pre-Challenge). Prior to release of the testing dataset, we evaluated the performance of our text mining pipeline against a gold standard corpus that we manually curated. We annotated 20 random papers from the training dataset for all of the entity types described in Sect. 2.2 and compared the *Precision*[16] and *Recall*[17] of our pipeline against human judgment. Figure 4 shows the results of our evaluation and the average F1-measure,[18] using GATE's Corpus Quality Assurance tool. In particular, we observed that the precision and recall of the pipeline suffers whenever *(i)* the organization names are

		Corpus statistics	Document statistics				
Annotation	Match	Only A	Only B	Overlap	Prec.B/A	Rec.B/A	F1.0-a.
Abstract_body	13	2	1	4	0.8333	0.7895	0.8108
Affiliation	23	8	3	9	0.7857	0.6875	0.7333
Author	66	0	3	2	0.9437	0.9853	0.9640
Metadata_body	18	1	1	1	0.9250	0.9250	0.9250
Ref_authors	200	2	29	23	0.8393	0.9400	0.8868
Ref_source	175	12	14	25	0.8762	0.8844	0.8803
Ref_title	192	19	12	14	0.9128	0.8844	0.8984
References_body	10	0	1	9	0.7250	0.7632	0.7436
Title	20	0	0	0	1.0000	1.0000	1.0000
Macro summary					0.8712	0.8733	0.8714
Micro summary	717	44	64	87	0.8762	0.8968	0.8864

Fig. 4. Qualitative analysis of the pipeline performance vs. our gold standard

---

[15] Apache TDB, http://jena.apache.org/documentation/tdb/.
[16] Precision is the fraction of extracted annotations that are relevant.
[17] Recall is the fraction of relevant annotations that are extracted.
[18] F-measure is the harmonic mean between Precision and Recall.

in a different language than English, *(ii)* authors used unconventional section headers that negatively impacts text segmentation, and *(iii)* anomalies in bibliographical entries were found in text, e.g., arbitrary abbreviation of journal or venue names and author names.

Evaluation on the Complete Set (Post-Challenge). Once the testing set was released for the challenge, we populated our knowledge base with processing the complete dataset of 183 documents (see Sect. 4). We then evaluated the precision (correctness) and recall (completeness) of our populated KB, by comparing the results of our formulated SPARQL queries, shown in Table 3, against the gold standard provided by the challenge coordinators. Posing 50 queries (5 different queries for each of the challenge's 10 queries) against the populated knowledge base yielded an average F-measure of 0.24 (Precision: 0.3, Recall: 0.25). A closer inspection revealed that while our KB performed relatively well in answering **Q2.1–Q2.4**, **Q2.9** and **Q2.10** (average F-measure of 0.43), the overall F-measure suffered from zero recall in **Q2.5**,[19] **Q2.6** and **Q2.7** (and obviously, in **Q2.8** since we did not extract any of its required entities).

Table 3. Challenge queries and their equivalent interpretation in our KB (excluding Q2.8)

Challenge query	Equivalent interpretation in our knowledge base
Q2.1: (Authors &) Affiliations in a paper	For the given paper, return all annotations of type `<foaf:Organization>` (affiliations), if it appears as object of the predicate `<rel:employedBy>` and the subject is of type `<foaf:Person>` (author)
Q2.2: Papers from a country	Return all papers that have an annotation of type `<foaf:Organization>` (affiliation), which has a predicate `<gn:locatedIn>` and the object's string value is the given country
Q2.3: Cited works	For the given paper, return all annotations of type `<swrc:Publication>` (reference)
Q2.4: Recent cited works	For the given paper, return all annotations of type `<swrc:Publication>`, which have a predicate `<fabio:hasPublicationYear>` and the object's numerical value is greater than the given year
Q2.5: Cited Journal Papers	For the given paper, return all annotations of type `<swrc:Publication>`, which have a predicate `<ov:category>` and the object's string value is *"journal"*
Q2.6: Research grants	For the given paper, return all annotations of type `<frapo:Grant>`
Q2.7: Funding agencies	For the given paper, return all annotations of type `<frapo:FundingAgency>`
Q2.8: EU projects	*Not addressed in our system*
Q2.9: Related ontologies	For the given paper, return all annotations of type `<owl:Ontology>`
Q2.10: New ontologies	For the given paper, return all annotations of type `<owl:Ontology>`, which have a predicate `<opmw:hasStatus>` and the object's string value is *"new"*

Prefixes used: foaf: <http://xmlns.com/foaf/0.1/>, rel: <http://purl.org/vocab/relationship>, gn: <http://www.geonames. org/ontology#>, swrc: <http://www.geonames.org/ontology#>, fabio: <http://purl.org/spar/fabio/>, ov: <http:// open.vocab.org/terms/>, frapo: <http://purl.org/cerif/frapo/>, owl: <http://www.w3.org/2002/07/owl#>, opmw: <http://www.opmw.org/ontology/>

---

[19] The zero recall for our Q2.5 was due to an error in the mapping rules, where an entity was mapped to two different classes. Apart from that, the annotations were correctly extracted.

5   Conclusions

With the ever-growing amount of information available, students, scientist, and employees spend an ever-increasing proportion of their time searching for the right information. Semantic enrichment of scholarly literature facilitates the automated discovery of knowledge and the integration of data between otherwise disparate documents. The second edition of the Semantic Publishing Challenge aimed at fostering the development of tools for the automatic generation of such metadata. In this context, we described the details of our rule-based text mining system that can extract various semantic information from computer science workshop proceedings. We also introduced a novel, flexible system to transform the detected entities into semantic triples and populate a knowledge base, interlinked with other resources on the Linked Open Data (LOD) cloud. The resulting semantic knowledge base, thus, holds machine-interpretable scientific knowledge that can be exploited through various services, ranging from queries [1] to semantic wikis [6], custom-tailored to a user's task and information needs. In the future, we aim to iteratively improve our text mining pipeline. Working together with challenge organizers and participants, we also hope to address the aggregation of each group's results: Since no data model was enforced in the challenge rules, the individual, submitted results were based on a diverse set of models and vocabularies. A collaboratively generated knowledge base could serve as a unified, clean open dataset for future research and development in semantic publishing initiatives.

References

1. Sateli, B., Witte, R.: What's in this paper? Combining rhetorical entities with linked open data for semantic literature querying. In: Semantics, Analytics, Visualisation: Enhancing Scholarly Data (SAVE-SD 2015), Florence, Italy, ACM (2015)
2. Constantin, A., Peroni, S., Pettifer, S., David, S., Vitali, F.: The Document Components Ontology (DoCO). The Semantic Web Journal (2015) (in press). http://www.semantic-web-journal.net/system/files/swj1016_0.pdf
3. Groza, T., Handschuh, S., Möller, K., Decker, S.: SALT - semantically annotated LaTeX for scientific publications. In: Franconi, E., Kifer, M., May, W. (eds.) ESWC 2007. LNCS, vol. 4519, pp. 518–532. Springer, Heidelberg (2007)
4. Cunningham, H., Maynard, D., Bontcheva, K., Tablan, V., Aswani, N., Roberts, I., Gorrell, G., Funk, A., Roberts, A., Damljanovic, D., Heitz, T., Greenwood, M.A., Saggion, H., Petrak, J., Li, Y., Peters, W.: Text Processing with GATE (Version 6). University of Sheffield, Department of Computer Science (2011)
5. Cunningham, H., Maynard, D., Bontcheva, K., Tablan, V.: GATE: a framework and graphical development environment for robust NLP tools and applications. In: Proceedings of the 40th Anniversary Meeting of the Association for Computational Linguistics (ACL 2002) (2002)
6. Sateli, B., Witte, R.: Supporting researchers with a semantic literature management Wiki. In: The 4th Workshop on Semantic Publishing (SePublica 2014). CEUR Workshop Proceedings, vol. 1155, Anissaras, Crete, Greece. CEUR-WS.org (2014)

CEUR-WS-LOD:
Conversion of CEUR-WS Workshops to Linked Data

Maxim Kolchin[1], Eugene Cherny[1,2], Fedor Kozlov[1], Alexander Shipilo[3],
and Liubov Kovriguina[1(✉)]

[1] ITMO University, Saint-petersburg, Russia
{kolchinmax,eugene.cherny}@niuitmo.ru,
{kozlovfedor,alexandershipilo,lkovriguina}@gmail.com
[2] Åbo Akademi University, Turku, Finland
[3] Saint-Petersburg State University, Saint-petersburg, Russia

Abstract. CEUR-WS.org is a well-known place for publishing proceedings of workshops and very popular among Computer Science community. Because of that it's an interesting source for different kinds of analytics, e.g. measurement of workshop series popularity or person's contribution to the field by organizing workshops and etc. For realizing an insightful and effective analytics one needs to combine information from different places that can supplement each other. And this brings a lot of challenges which can be mitigated by using Semantic Web technologies.

Keywords: Information extraction · RDF · Semantic publishing · Linked open data · CEUR-WS

1 Introduction

"Semantic publishing refers to publishing information on the Web as documents accompanied by semantic markup"[1] using RDFa or Microformats, or by publishing information as data objects using Semantic Web technologies such as RDF and OWL. One of the areas where semantic publishing is actively used is scholarly publishing, where it helps bring improvements to scientific communication "by enabling linking to semantically related articles, provides access to data within the article in actionable form, or facilitates integration of data between papers" [9].

We don't aim to survey the state-of-art of semantic publishing of scientific research in this paper, but we suggest to look at the existing works [1,5,6,9] and papers presented at the series of Workshops on Semantic Publishing[2] for more in-depth overview.

This paper presents a contribution to semantic publishing of scientific research by conversion of a well-known web-site for publishing proceedings

---

[1] Cf. http://en.wikipedia.org/wiki/Semantic_publishing.
[2] Cf. http://ceur-ws.org/Vol-1155/.

© Springer International Publishing Switzerland 2015
F. Gandon et al. (Eds.): SemWebEval 2015, CCIS 548, pp. 142–152, 2015.
DOI: 10.1007/978-3-319-25518-7_12

of workshops to Linked Data dataset. The work is carried out in framework of Semantic Publishing Challenge 2015[3], is based on the previous effort [3] extended by improving precision/recall of the information extraction and the ontology model.

Source Data. The source of data is CEUR-WS.org that publishes proceedings of workshops starting from 1995th year and is very popular among Computer Science community. At the time of writing, it contains information about 1346 proceedings and around 130 ones are added each year, over 19 000 papers and more than 33 000 people.

Challenges. As was described in the previous work [3], extraction of the needed information from the CEUR-WS's web pages faces several challenges, some of them:

- the web pages don't have uniform structured markup, therefore it's not feasible to relay on a single template for mapping data to RDF,
- 41.5 % of proceedings' web pages don't contain any markup, such as RDFa or Microformats. But even pages having the markup don't always follow its structure and semantics,
- a big part of the proceedings are jointly published by several workshops, e.g. http://ceur-ws.org/Vol-1244/ includes papers of ED2014 and GViP2014 workshops.

Table 1. Namespaces and prefixes used in the paper

Prefix	URL
swc	http://data.semanticweb.org/ns/swc/ontology#
bibo	http://purl.org/ontology/bibo/
swrc	http://swrc.ontoware.org/ontology#
owl	http://www.w3.org/2002/07/owl#
foaf	http://xmlns.com/foaf/0.1/
dcterms	http://purl.org/dc/terms/
dc	http://purl.org/dc/elements/1.1/
rdfs	http://www.w3.org/2000/01/rdf-schema#

Structure of the Paper. The structure of the paper is as follows. Section 2 presents our approach. Section 3 explains the ontology model and mappings to some well-known ontologies. Section 4 gives an overall view of the dataset and lists SPARQL query examples. Also Sect. 4 describes how the dataset is published and how users can access the data. The last section concludes the work and results. The prefixes used throughout the paper are defined in Table 1.

---

[3] Cf. http://github.com/ceurws/lod/wiki/SemPub2015.

2   System Description

In this work we apply *knowledge engineering approach* to the design of Information Extraction systems which requires expression of *rules* for the system are constructed by hand using knowledge of the application domain [2].

Although this approach is laborious, the results of the previous challenge shown that it's performance much higher than the others [4]. The system submitted last year reached overall average precision/recall equal to 0.707/0.636 correspondingly while the next best result was 0.478/0.447.

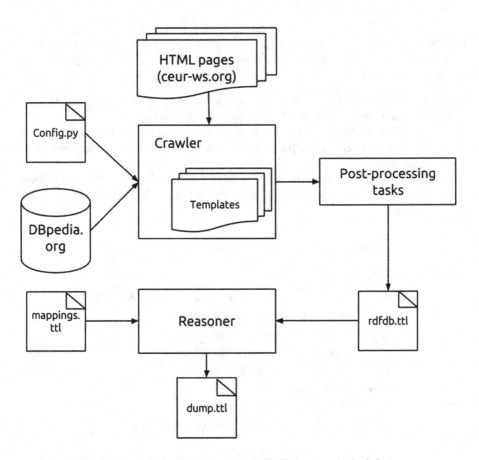

Fig. 1. Workflow of conversion CEUR-WS.org to linked data

The system developed to convert CEUR-WS.org to Linked Data dataset implements the workflow outlined in Fig. 1. The workflow consist of three major steps:

- crawling the web pages and serializing the extracted information to RDF,
- processing the resulted RDF dump to merge resources of persons with similar names, e.g. Dusan Kolář and Dusan Kolar is actually the same person, therefore he should be represented by a single resource,
- applying the mapping ontology to link the data to well-known ontologies.

The source code is open sourced and available at https://github.com/ailabitmo/ceur-ws-lod under the MIT License.

Crawling. In the system the *rules* are expressed using XPath expressions which constitute a *template* of an HTML block. The system has a separate template for each different HTML block presented on the web site's pages. These templates are run by the crawler implemented using Grab framework[4] that provides Python API for creating crawlers.

There are two *abstract templates* which aren't used by the crawler directly, but are used by the other templates as basis: *Parser* and *ListParser*. The difference between them is that *ListParser* is used for repeatable structures such as Table of Content of proceedings or list of proceedings on the index page.

The crawler groups the templates by the web site pages, such as *index, proceedings, publication.* There are 11 templates. In Table 2 all these *templates* with corresponding RegExp expressions that is used to categorize the pages are presented.

Table 2. Templates grouped by the web site's pages

Web page	RegExp	Template name
index	^http://ceurs-ws\.org/*$	ProceedingsRelations
		WorkshopSummary
		WorkshopAcronym
		WorkshopRelations
		ProceedingsSummary
proceedings	^http://ceur-ws\.org/Vol-\d+/*$	WorkshopPage
		EditorAffiliation
		EditorNameExpand
		JointWorkshopsEditors
		Publication
publication	^http://ceur-ws\.org/Vol-\d+/*\.pdf$	PublicationNumOfPages

Each such *template* is a Python class which extends *Parser* or *ListParser* classes and has one or more methods having *parse_template_* string as prefix in its name. The crawler executes these methods one by one while one of them matches the HTML block. After that the method extracts the information and passes it for the serialization.

---

[4] Cf. http://grablib.org/.

Name Disambiguation. At the post-processing step the system does the disambiguation of the peoples' names by fuzzy-matching sorted of tokenized name-string. The *fuzzywuzzy*[5] library was used for this task. For each pair of names in the dataset we have performed the following operations:

1 String normalization: convert to ASCII representation, make lowercase.
2 Split name string into tokens using whitespace separator and sort tokens in string.
3 Perform fuzzy string matching between token-sorted strings.

Entities that have similar names were interlinked with *owl:sameAs* property and exported as separate file[6].

We do not have tools to estimate correctness of the persons' interlinking, thus we only performed manual validation of the output file[7]. The results in general are good, except two moments. First, the algorithm has the $O(n^2)$ complexity and it took more than 12 hours to perform comparison of all names. Second, due to the nature of fuzzy string matching, the algorithm recognized a group of 32 persons with Asian names as one. This is due to the common names and surnames, such as "Li", and short lengths of the name-surname combination—the string matching algorithm often returns high similarity measure in such occasions.

Mapping to Well-Know Ontologies. The last step is to map the ontology used by the system to several well-known ontologies. To do it a parser based on Jena Inference API[8] was implemented which supports several RDFS and OWL constructs such as *rdfs:subClassOf, rdfs:subPropertyOf, rdf:type, owl:equivalentClass, owl:sameAs* and etc.

3   Ontology Model

We considered three ontologies for use as the basis of semantic representation of the crawled data:

– Semantic Web Conference Ontology (SWC) is an ontology for describing academic conferences,
– Semantic Web for Research Communities (SWRC) is an ontology for modeling entities of research communities such as persons, organisations, publications and their relationship,

---

[5] Cf. https://github.com/seatgeek/fuzzywuzzy.
[6] Cf. https://github.com/ailabitmo/ceur-ws-lod/releases/download/ceur-ws-crawler-v1.0.0/task-1-persons-sameas.ttl.
[7] Cf. https://github.com/ailabitmo/ceur-ws-lod/blob/master/ceur-ws-crawler/post processing/merged_persons.json.
[8] Cf. https://jena.apache.org/documentation/inference/index.html.

– Bibliographic ontology (BIBO) is an ontology providing main concepts and
properties for describing citations and bibliographic references (i.e. quotes,
books, articles, etc.).

Unfortunately, each of those ontologies alone are not sufficient to fully represent the structure of crawled information. For example, *BIBO* doesn't have an
"event is part of bigger event" semantics and with *SWRC* we can't explicitly
describe how many pages are in a publication, as *swrc:pages* could be used for
describing page region, e.g. *255–259; SWC* reuses *SWRC*, thus they share the
same limitations, and *SWC* does not introduce entities relevant for our work.
Of course, this is not full list of all incompletenesses of those ontologies, but we
think that detailed ontology comparison is out of scope of this paper, therefore
we refer the reader to existing works [7,8]. Thus, based on subjective evaluation we decided to use *SWRC* as much as possible and add terms from other
ontologies only if *SWRC* does not contain needed semantics. The structure of
resulting ontology is represented on the Fig. 2.

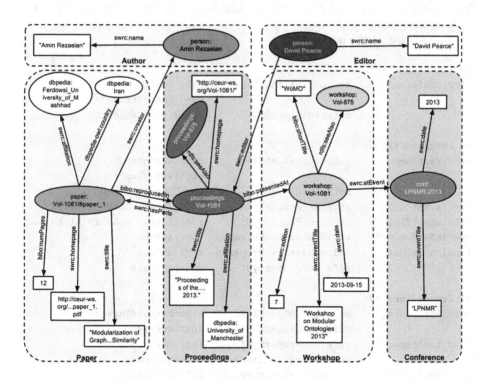

Fig. 2. Semantic representation of the crawled data

We used *SWC* ontology only once to mark a paper as invited one, making
it an individual of class *swc:InvitedPaper*, because *SWC* is the poorest of those
three ontologies in terms of semantic richness: the number of properties is much

lesser than in others, some classes have names like "Event-1" and "Role-1", a lot of them are deprecated, and, last but not least, official site of ontology is not accessible, so we were forced to download the ontology from the third-party site[9], which doesn't contain imports *SWC* depends on. All those factors suggest that development of this ontology was halted before reaching consistent usable state—this is why we tried to avoid using it in our work.

A concept "series of events" is not described in any of these ontologies, thus we choose to link workshops of the same series with the *rdfs:seeAlso* property. To keep things consistent we decided to use this approach to link "series of proceedings" and not to make additional *bibo:Series* class.

3.1   Mapping to Well-Know Ontologies

To compensate semantic inconsistencies in the resulting data set introduced by usage of properties and classes from different ontologies, we created the mappings between ontologies with *owl:eqivalentProperty* and *owl:eqivalentClass* properties. We interlinked only *BIBO* and *SWRC* ontologies, as *SWC* already has some dependencies on *SWRC*.

The full list of the mappings:

```
## Conference ##
swrc:Conference      owl:equivalentClass    bibo:Conference,
                                            swpo:Conference ;
                     rdfs:subClassOf        swc:OrganizedEvent .


## Workshop ##
swrc:Workshop        owl:equivalentClass    bibo:Workshop,
                                            swpo:Workshop ;
                     rdfs:subClassOf        swc:OrganizedEvent .
swrc:eventTitle      rdfs:subPropertyOf     rdfs:label, dcterms:title .
bibo:shortTitle      rdfs:subPropertyOf     rdfs:label, dcterms:title .
swc:isSubEventOf     owl:equivalentProperty swrc:atEvent .
timeline:atDate      owl:equivalentProperty swrc:date ;
                     rdfs:subPropertyOf     dcterms:date .


## Proceedings ##
swrc:Proceedings     owl:equivalentClass    bibo:Proceedings ;
                     rdfs:subClassOf        foaf:Document .
foaf:homepage        rdfs:subPropertyOf     foaf:page ;
                     owl:equivalentClass    swrc:homepage .
dcterms:issued       owl:equivalentProperty bibo:created,
                                            swrc:creationDate ;
                     rdfs:subPropertyOf     dcterms:date .
swrc:editor          owl:equivalentProperty bibo:editor ;
                     rdfs:subClassOf        foaf:maker,
```

---

[9] Cf. http://lov.okfn.org/dataset/lov/vocabs/swc.

```
                                                dcterms:creator .
swrc:title            owl:equivalentProperty    foaf:title ;
                      rdfs:subPropertyOf        rdfs:label, dcterms:title,
                                                dc:title .


## Paper ##
swrc:InProceedings    owl:equivalentClass       bibo:Article ;
                      rdfs:subClassOf           foaf:Document .
swrc:creator          owl:equivalentProperty    foaf:maker,
                                                dcterms:creator .


## Person ##
swrc:Person           owl:equivalentClass       bibo:Person, foaf:Person .
foaf:Person           rdfs:subClassOf           foaf:Agent .
foaf:Agent            owl:equivalentClass       dcterms:Agent .
swrc:name             owl:equivalentProperty    foaf:name ;
                      rdfs:subPropertyOf        rdfs:label .
```

4   Overview of Dataset

Publishing. The data is published using a Linked Data Fragments [10] server and available at http://data.isst.ifmo.ru. The users can use a Linked Data Fragments client for querying the data using SPARQL language. Or the data is also available as an HDT[10] dump in the GitHub repository[11].

Statistics. The dataset includes 402 648 triples and 55 893 subjects. The distribution of resource types are depicted on Fig. 3.

In absolute numbers the dataset includes information about 1 344 proceedings, 1 360 workshops, 18 875 regular and 203 invited papers, 252 conferences, 33 859 persons with 2 657 editors.

4.1   Example Queries

In this section several SPARQL queries are presented which provide some interesting insights.

Query 1. Top-10 persons how was an editor of the highest number of workshop series:

```
SELECT ?editor (COUNT(DISTINCT ?workshop) AS ?count) {
  {
    SELECT DISTINCT ?workshop {
```

---

[10] Cf. http://www.rdfhdt.org/.
[11] Cf. http://github.com/ailabitmo/ceur-ws-lod.

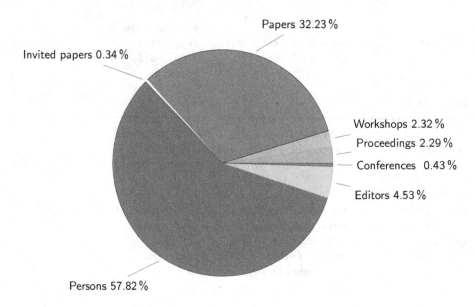

Fig. 3. Distribution of resource types in the dataset (# of triples – 402 648)

```
    ?workshop a bibo:Workshop ;
       rdfs:seeAlso ?inseries .
    FILTER NOT EXISTS { [] rdfs:seeAlso ?workshop }
  }
}
{
  ?proceedings a swrc:Proceedings ;
     swrc:editor ?editor .
  { ?proceedings bibo:presentedAt ?workshop }
  UNION
  { ?proceedings bibo:presentedAt ?inseries .
    ?workshop rdfs:seeAlso ?inseries .
  }
}
}
GROUP BY ?editor
ORDER BY DESC(?count)
LIMIT 10
```

Query 2. Top-10 workshops with the highest number of authors:

```
SELECT ?workshop (COUNT(DISTINCT ?author) as ?num_authors) {
  ?paper a swrc:InProceedings ;
     swrc:creator ?author ;
```

```
    dcterms:partOf ?proceedings .
  ?proceedings bibo:presentedAt ?workshop .
}
GROUP BY ?workshop
ORDER BY DESC(?num_authors)
LIMIT 10
```

Query 3. Latest workshops of top-10 workshop series with the longest history.

```
SELECT ?workshop (COUNT (?related) + 1 AS ?count) WHERE {
  ?workshop a bibo:Workshop ;
    rdfs:seeAlso ?related .
  FILTER NOT EXISTS { [] rdfs:seeAlso ?workshop .}
}
GROUP BY ?workshop
ORDER BY DESC(?count)
```

5 Conclusion

In this paper we described a system that converts a well-known web-site for publishing proceedings of academic events, called CEUR-WS.org, to Linked Data dataset. Also we described semantic representations (ontologies) that are used to create the dataset. The system is based on *knowledge engineering approach* to design Information Extraction systems.

To overview the resulted dataset we introduced some statistical information, such as amount of papers and proceedings. Also we presented example SPARQL queries which provide some interesting insights from the extracted information.

The presented system is developed in the framework of Semantic Publishing Challenge 2015[5] and based on the previous work [3] which was extended with richer semantic representations and was improved in terms of precision and recall.

Acknowledgments. This work has been partially financially supported by the Government of Russian Federation, Grant #074-U01.

References

1. Auer, S., Lange, C., Ermilov, T.: Towards facilitating scientific publishing and knowledge exchange through linked data. In: Bolikowski, L., Casarosa, V., Goodale, P., Houssos, N., Manghi, P., Schirrwagen, J. (eds.) TPDL 2013. CCIS, vol. 416, pp. 10–15. Springer, Heidelberg (2014). http://dx.doi.org/10.1007/978-3-319-08425-1_2
2. Eikvil, L.: Information extraction from world wide web - a survey. Technical report, July 1999. http://user.phil-fak.uni-duesseldorf.de/rumpf/SS2003/Informationsextraktion/Pub/Eik99.pdf

3. Kolchin, M., Kozlov, F.: A template-based information extraction from web sites with unstable markup. In: Presutti, V., et al. (eds.) SemWebEval 2014. CCIS, vol. 475, pp. 89–94. Springer, Heidelberg (2014). http://dx.doi.org/10.1007/978-3-319-12024-9_11

4. Lange, C., Di Iorio, A.: Semantic publishing challenge – assessing the quality of scientific output. In: Presutti, V., et al. (eds.) SemWebEval 2014. CCIS, vol. 475, pp. 61–76. Springer, Heidelberg (2014). http://dx.doi.org/10.1007/978-3-319-12024-9_8

5. Nevzorova, O., Zhiltsov, N., Zaikin, D., Zhibrik, O., Kirillovich, A., Nevzorov, V., Birialtsev, E.: Bringing math to LOD: a semantic publishing platform prototype for scientific collections in mathematics. In: Alani, H., et al. (eds.) ISWC 2013, Part I. LNCS, vol. 8218, pp. 379–394. Springer, Heidelberg (2013). http://dx.doi.org/10.1007/978-3-642-41335-3_24

6. Peroni, S.: Semantic Publishing: issues, solutions and new trends in scholarly publishing within the Semantic Web era. Ph.D. thesis, Universit di Bologna (2012). http://dx.doi.org/10.6092/unibo/amsdottorato/4766

7. Peroni, S., Shotton, D.: FaBiO and CiTO: ontologies for describing bibliographic resources and citations. Web Semant. Sci. Serv. Agents World Wide Web **17**, 33–43 (2012). http://www.sciencedirect.com/science/article/pii/S1570826812000790

8. Ruiz Iniesta, A., Corcho, O.: A review of ontologies for describing scholarly and scientific documents. http://ceur-ws.org/Vol-1155#paper-07

9. Shotton, D.: Semantic publishing: the coming revolution in scientific journal publishing. Learn. Publ. **22**(2), 85–94 (2009). http://www.ingentaconnect.com/content/alpsp/lp/2009/00000022/00000002/art00002

10. Verborgh, R., et al.: Querying datasets on the web with high availability. In: Mika, P., et al. (eds.) ISWC 2014, Part I. LNCS, vol. 8796, pp. 180–196. Springer, Heidelberg (2014). http://dx.doi.org/10.1007/978-3-319-11964-9_12

Metadata Extraction from Conference Proceedings Using Template-Based Approach

Liubov Kovriguina[1]([✉]), Alexander Shipilo[3], Fedor Kozlov[1], Maxim Kolchin[1], and Eugene Cherny[1,2]

[1] ITMO University, Saint-petersburg, Russia
{lkovriguina,alexandershipilo,kozlovfedor}@gmail.com,
{kolchinmax,eugene.cherny}@niuitmo.ru
[2] Åbo Akademi University, Turku, Finland
[3] Saint-Petersburg-State University, Saint-Petersburg, Russia

Abstract. The paper describes a number of metadata extraction procedures based on rule-based approach and pattern matching from CEUR Workshop proceedings Cf. http://ceur-ws.org and its converting to a Linked Open Data (LOD) dataset in the framework of ESWC 2015 Semantic Publishing Challenge Cf. http://github.com/ceurws/lod/wiki/SemPub2015.

Keywords: Metadata extraction · Semantic publishing · Linked open data · Semantic web · PDF parsing · Natural language processing

1 Introduction

The work that is presented in this paper aims to provide a solution for Task 2 of ESWC 2015 Semantic Publishing Challenge (see footnote 1). The task is to crawl and parse PDF papers from CEUR Workhop proceedings web site[3] and create a LOD dataset containing detailed information about the papers, citations, authors and their organizations and etc.

The source code and instructions to run the crawler are available at our GitHub repository[1].

The main goal of the paper is to provide an approach for information extraction from the textual content of the papers in PDF format and translating it to LOD format. This information should provide a deeper understanding of the context in which the paper was written. In particular, extracted information is expected to answer queries about authors' affiliations and research institutions, research grants, funding bodies, and related works. Previous work includes results presented in the paper [2].

Tasks of the paper include

- analysis of workshop paper elements and ontology development using published and frequently used vocabularies;

---

[1] Cf. http://github.com/ailabitmo/ceur-ws-lod.

© Springer International Publishing Switzerland 2015
F. Gandon et al. (Eds.): SemWebEval 2015, CCIS 548, pp. 153–164, 2015.
DOI: 10.1007/978-3-319-25518-7_13

- development of paper metadata extraction procedures from PDF files;
- development of the tool crawling PDF papers, applying metadata extraction procedures and publishing results as Linked Open Data;
- testing the developed tool using testing module and the set of SPARQL queries.

The output dataset should allow to perform the following queries.

- Q2.1 (Affiliations in a paper): Identify the affiliations of the authors of the paper X.
- Q2.2 (Papers from a country): Identify the papers presented at the workshop X and written by researchers affiliated to an organization located in the country Y.
- Q2.3 (Cited works): Identify all works cited by the paper X
- Q2.4 (Recent cited works): Identify all works cited by the paper X and published after the year Y.
- Q2.5 (Cited journal papers): Identify all journal papers cited by the paper X
- Q2.6 (Research grants): Identify the grant(s) that supported the research presented in the paper X (or part of it).
- Q2.7 (Funding agencies): Identify the funding agencies that funded the research presented in the paper X (or part of it).
- Q2.8 (EU projects): Identify the EU project(s) that supported the research presented in the paper X (or part of it).
- Q2.9 (Related ontologies): Identify the ontologies mentioned in the abstract of the paper X.
- Q2.10 (New ontologies): Identify the ontologies introduced in the paper X (according to the abstract).

2   Data Model

The output of PDF parser is written to the dataset. SPARQL queries are sent to the data of this dataset. These queries aim to provide information about paper structure, references, paper heading metadata (authors, affiliation), related projects and mentioned ontological resources. To be able to perform SPARQL queries an ontology of paper content and metadata has to be developed (see overall architecture at Fig. 2).

To develop the ontology analysis of paper content and metadata relations has to be done. CEUR website stores workshops' papers. This implies we need to introduce "Workshop" and "Paper" classes to the ontology and link them. Queries Q2.1 and Q2.2 require information about authors, their affiliations and countries so we included classes "Author", "Organization", "Country" and their relations. Queries Q2.3, Q2.4, Q2.5 concern the type of the document where the paper was published which results in adding "Document" and "Journal" classes and properties describing citation, date of publication and DOI. Queries Q2.6, Q2.7, Q2.8 concern grants, funding agencies and EU projects so corresponding classes were added to the ontology and properties describing paper funding by the funding agency and grant attributes. Class "Ontology" and corresponding properties were added for the last two queries. As a result, the developed ontology includes the following classes: "Workshop", "Paper", "Author", "Organization", "Country", "Document", "Journal", "Grant", "Funding Agency", "EU Project" and "Ontology".

Based on the elaborated ontology we chose actual vocabularies to create the ontology model. Vocabularies were selected by their relevance and popularity. Their classes and properties have to describe relations between the objects. In contradictory situations the most frequently used vocabulary was selected.

The developed ontology for workshop papers is shown in Fig. 1. It is based on the BIBO[2] (The Bibliographic Ontology Specification). The Bibliographic Ontology Specification provides main concepts and properties for describing citations and bibliographic references (i.e. quotes, books, articles, etc.) on the Semantic Web. Classes from this ontology are used to describe papers, cited documents, authors and their organizations. The properties from this ontology are used to describe citing, reviewing in the text, publications in journals, document titles, dates and DOI. To describe relations between authors and papers the FOAF[3] (Friend of a Friend) and the DC[4] (The Dublin Core) ontologies are used. To describe author's affiliation with certain organization the SWRC[5] ontology is used [4]. The DBpedia Ontology[6] is used to describe the class of organization's country. The DBpedia Ontology is a shallow, cross-domain ontology, which has been manually created based on the most commonly used infoboxes within Wikipedia. The ARPFO[7] (Academic Research Project Funding Ontology) ontology is used to describe classes of grants, funding agencies and EU projects. ARPFO provides classes and properties to describe the project funding structure of academic research, and also provides classes and properties to encode the relations.

3   Our Approach

Metadata extraction procedures are based on regular expressions, natural language processing methods, heuristics concerning html document style (font family, size, etc.), style of the elements of standard bibliographic description [1,3]. We combined all these methods while developing the current approach. Proposed rules were elaborated on the training dataset including LNCS and ACM templates but are not limited to them. Rules are applied to the HTML representation of the text.

In the next subsections we describe specific solutions which we applied for a particular query.

---

[2] Cf. http://purl.org/ontology/bibo/.
[3] Cf. http://xmlns.com/foaf/0.1/.
[4] Cf. http://purl.org/dc/elements/1.1/.
[5] Cf. http://swrc.ontoware.org/ontology.
[6] Cf. http://dbpedia.org/resource/.
[7] Cf. http://vocab.ox.ac.uk/projectfunding.

bibo: <http://purl.org/ontology/bibo/>
foaf: <http://xmlns.com/foaf/0.1/>
dcterms: <http://purl.org/dc/terms/>
swrc <http://swrc.ontoware.org/ontology#>
dbpedia: <http://dbpedia.org/ontology/>
arpfo: <http://vocab.ox.ac.uk/projectfunding#>

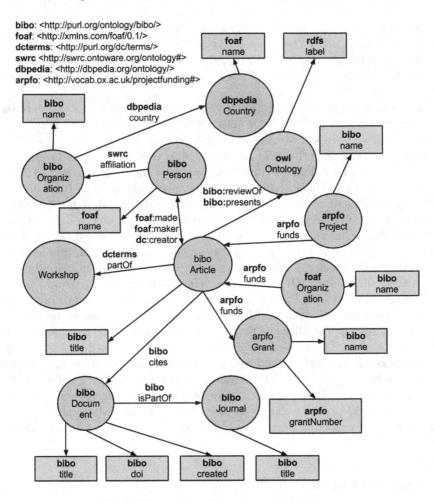

Fig. 1. The ontology for papers of workshops

Query 2.1. Queries 2.1-2.2 require heading parsing. Parsing procedure starts with splitting HTML file into pages. The heading is assumed to be the block beginning from the < div > containing string 'Page 1' to the < div > which has more than 30 words in it (excluding tags), because some papers do not have the 'Abstract' section. To extract the title of the paper we used font characteristics and text position on the page. HTML elements inside the headings are sorted according to the value of the 'top' property. Then the text, encapsulated in the blocks, having the same value of the 'font-family' property, is extracted as title. An example is provided below, title of the paper is 'Keynote: Listening to the pulse of our cities during City Scale Events'.

1. Example of the improper PDF -> HTML title parsing.

```
<div style=''position:absolute; border: textbox 1px solid;
writing-mode:lr-tb; left:142px; top:182px; width:330px;
height:14px;''>
 <span style=''font-family: YTEDIA+CMBX12; font-size:14px''>
Listening to the pulse of our cities during City
 <br>
 </span>
</div>
<div style=''position:absolute; border: textbox 1px solid;
writing-mode:lr-tb; left:275px; top:164px; width:63px;
height:14px;''>
 <span style=''font-family: YTEDIA+CMBX12; font-size:14px''>
 Keynote:
 <br>
 </span>
</div>
<div style=''position:absolute; border: textbox 1px solid;
writing-mode:lr-tb; left:263px; top:200px; width:88px;
height:14px;''>
 <span style=''font-family: YTEDIA+CMBX12; font-size:14px''>
 Scale Events
 <br>
 </span>
</div>
```

2. The same HTML block sorted by the 'top' property values.

```
<div style=''position:absolute; border: textbox 1px solid;
writing-mode:lr-tb; left:275px; top:164px; width:63px;
height:14px;''>
 <span style=''font-family: YTEDIA+CMBX12; font-size:14px''>
 Keynote:
 <br>
 </span>
</div>
<div style=''position\:absolute; border\: textbox 1px solid;
writing-mode\:lr-tb; left\:142px; top\:182px; width\:330px;
height\:14px;''>
 <span style=''font-family\: YTEDIA+CMBX12; font-size\:14px''>
 Listening to the pulse of our cities during City
 <br>
 </span>
</div>
<div style=''position\:absolute; border\: textbox 1px solid;
writing-mode\:lr-tb; left\:263px; top\:200px; width\:88px;
height\:14px;''>
```

```
<span style=''font-family\: YTEDIA+CMBX12; font-size\:14px''>
 Scale Events
 <br>
 </span>
</div>
```

Here parts of the title are mixed up: 'Keynote:' is inserted between 'City' and 'Scale'. Proper order of title parts can be restored using 'top' values: in the discussed heading 'Keynote:' has top value 164px; 'Listening to the pulse of our cities during City' has top value 182px; 'Scale Events' has top value 200px, all title parts have font-family 'YTEDIA+CMBX12'. Therefore, ascending sorting by the 'top' value settles the right sequence of title elements. After title extraction authors names and surnames are identified. We used the assumption that personal information provided in the heading is redundant. Major part of the authors choose various combinations of their name and surname as an e-mail nickname. Local part of the e-mail address frequently matches the following patterns:

- 'name.surname' ('john.smith'),
- 'first_symbol_of_the_name.surname' ('j.smith'),
- 'surname' ('smith')

Therefore, information in the local part of the e-mail address can be used to find the string containing author name.

The block after the title is split into tokens by spaces, dots, commas and colons. Then all emails are extracted and split into local and domain parts. Local parts are split by dot into tokens, the latest are searched above the e-mail in the heading. If a token matches a substring, this substring is considered as a candidate for the person's name or surname. So a block of text between the authors name and surname is extracted. This block contains affiliation. This approach is useful for the case when there are no digits pointing to the affiliation (like in LNCS template). The procedure covers 2 types of e-mail parsing: (1) authors with the same affiliation have separate e-mails (like in ACM template), (2) authors with the same affiliation have local names listed in figure brackets and common domain name. For the second case affiliation is duplicated for each author. Multiple affiliation is parsed using digits in the heading.

Query 2.2. To identify the papers presented at the workshop X and written by researchers affiliated to an organization located in the country Y, affiliation is parsed from the last symbol, comma is used as a delimiter between the tokens (thus a token may consist of more than one space-separated item, e.g. Czech Republic, United Arab Emirates). Candidate token is checked via the countries list whether it is a country. For some cases like "NY USA" only a substring of the token refers to the country name and if validating procedure returned no country, the token is split by spaces and validation is iterated for the last item.

Block of queries 2.3-2.5 requires reference parsing. The file is scanned for the first occurrence of 'references' or 'bibliography' keyword (case is ignored).

References' block is extracted starting from the found keyword to the end of HTML file. Every bibliographic reference is split into its elements: authors, title, title of periodical or conference, imprint details (publisher, publishing place, year). Beginning from the word "References" to the end of file document space is split into separate references by the paper's number.

Query 2.3. Firstly, it is necessary to set the boundaries of each bibliography item. It may start with a digit (or single token - a surname - followed by a digit) enclosed in square brackets or, if a digit is not enclosed with squares, a dot follows it (it also obligatory appears at the beginning of a line). The end of each bibliographical item is the beginning of the next one. From each reference the following data are extracted: year, title, and the name of journal it is published in (0 - if it is not a journal paper). Year matches a plain regular expression: any four digits match the year.

The title begins from the first capital letter after the end of the authors block. There were found several templates for cited paper authors extractions. They are:

1. J. Conesa "[A-Z]\. [A-Z][a-z]+". The first capital letter after the last matched regular expression is the beginning of a title
2. J. Conesa "[A-Z][a-z]+ [A-Z]\". The first capital letter after the last matched regular expression is the beginning of a title.

If the beginning of the bibliographical item doesn't match these regular expressions, we found the first dot in the string. The title ends with dot or double quote.

To identify the name of the journal we use the regular expression ", \d+(\d+)". The part of the bib item between the beginning of this regular expression and end of the title identified at the previous step.

Query 2.4. To identify all works cited by the paper X and published after the year Y, a procedure addresses the dictionary where reference attributes are stored and checks the year of the paper.

Query 2.5. To identify all journal papers cited by the paper X, principles of bibliographic reference composing are used. When a journal paper is cited, volume number and issue number are given. The last is given in round brackets, so to identify that a paper is published in the journal, part of the reference should match the regular expression "[0-9]+([0-9]+)". The journal title is a sequence between paper title and the sequence that has matched this regular expression. This rule allows to extract journals when no lexemes point to it, e.g. 'Cognitive Linguistics 4(2)'. If this regular expression returned no matches, the string is scanned for keywords 'J. —Journal—Annals—Letters'. If the latest are found, journal title is extracted as the sequence including the keyword, from the end of the title to the first space+digit combination or space + uppercase 'V' after the keyword (e.g. '*J. Data Semantics* V: 64-90', '*Annals of Pure and Applied Logics* 123', '*Information Processing Letters*, 74').

Group of queries 2.6-2.8 is performed over the 'Acknowledgements' section. The section is split into sentences. Firstly, grant numbers are identified and removed from the sentence, then a group of context-free patterns to extract funding agencies is applied, EU-funded projects are extracted after it and, finally, the rest of the funding agencies is extracted.

Query 2.6. Grant number may combine several identification elements, such as type code, activity code, institute code, serial number, support year, etc. We relied that serial number contains at least 3 digits. Therefore, grant number may contain only digits, digits and literals, hyphens and slashes. The regular expression extracting grant number, matches a token containing at least 3 digits and obligatory having a digit as its last symbol.

Query 2.7. To identify the funding agencies that funded the research presented in the paper X we started with testing Stanford Named Entity Tagger[8] but found out it does not extract all funding agencies we need. In the following examples from the training dataset paper[9] "Christian Doppler Forschungsgesellschaft" was recognized as person, "Österreichischer Austauschdienst" was not recognized at all, and "Federal Ministry of Economy, Family and Youth" was partially extracted. There are some other examples where this tool is not precise.

Example. This work was supported by the Christian Doppler Forschungsgesellschaft, the Federal Ministry of Economy, Family and Youth, Österreichischer Austauschdienst (ÖAD) and the National Foundation for Research, Technology and Development - Austria.

Considering that acknowledgements section is written in a highly standardized manner, each sentence in the 'Acknowledgements' section was scanned for the stems "support|fund|sponsor". If the sentence contained this stems two group of patterns were applied to extract funding agencies. The group of context-free patterns are applied first. These patterns are:

1. 'by ORGANIZATION under',
2. 'funding from ORGANIZATION under',
3. 'by ORGANIZATION in',
4. 'by ORGANIZATION within',
5. 'by ORGANIZATION-funded| funded'.

If nothing was extracted with these patterns, the procedure switches to project extraction, then returns to scan the sentence for the remained funding agencies. On this stage the sentence is scanned for the keywords 'by|funding| funding from', their indices are returned. Starting from the found keyword to the end of the sentence word sequences having at least one symbol in uppercase (excluding prepositions *of, and, for* are extracted. Candidates for funding agencies are split by comma. For long organization titles special regular expressions are reserved:

---

[8] Cf. http://nlp.stanford.edu/software/CRF-NER.shtml.
[9] Cf. http://ceur-ws.org/Vol-1155/paper-06.pdf.

– $[A - Z][a - z] + [A - Z][a - z]+$ of $[A - Z][a - z]+, [A - Z][a - z]+$ and
  $[A - Z][a - z]+$ ('Federal Ministry of Economy, Family and Youth'),
– $[A - Z][a - z] + [A - Z][a - z]+$ for $[A - Z][a - z]+, [A - Z][a - z]+$ and $[A - Z]$
  $[a - z]+$ ('National Foundation for Research, Technology and Development').

However, an alternative rule can be formulated to extract long titles. An extra condition has to be specified, that a funding agency whole title should have no less than 2 symbols in uppercase. In case it has 2 or less symbols they should not contain "and". Otherwise, this candidate is merged to the previous one.

Query 2.8. To select EU-funded projects keywords and keyphrases pointing to the European Union and its programmes are searched in each sentence of the 'Acknowledgement' block. The following elements were used to write the regular expressions :

– 'EU-funded',
– 'EU FP\d'
– 'FP\d European'
– 'European Union'
– 'FP\d'
– 'EU \dth Framework Program'
– 'European Union \dth Framework Program'

When any of these elements is found, its index is used. On the distance of -4; +4 tokens from this element the sentence part is scanned for a sequence(s) of tokens (or a single token) having at least one symbol in uppercase (e.g., 'NewsReader', 'LOD2', 'DM2E', 'Dr Inventor'). Token is defined as a sequence between the spaces.

Query 2.9 and Q2.10. For procedures in queries 2.9-2.10 we used a stop-list of acronyms and abbreviations related to semantic web (including ontology languages, Semantic Web standards, etc.) to avoid their extraction as candidates for ontology name and Stanford Parser[10] to do syntactic analysis of the sentence in order to remove false candidates in Q2.10. A list of existing ontologies was also used. These two queries are performed on the 'Abstract' section. Firstly, ontologies in the predefined list are searched in each sentence of the abstract and written as the output for query 2.9. Then, if a sentence includes stem 'ontolog', this sentence is sent to the Stanford Parser for syntactic analysis. The Parser returns a list of dependencies between the words in the sentence. Then it is checked, whether there is a dependency between 'introduce|present|propose|describe' and the word having 'ontolog' as a substring. If such dependency exists, part of the sentence at -5;+5 distance from the stem 'ontolog' is scanned for a word sequence where each word has at least one symbol in uppercase. It is extracted and written as a new ontology, mentioned in the abstract. If Stanford Parser gives no dependency between the words, mentioned above, part of the sentence at -5;+5

---

[10] Cf. http://nlp.stanford.edu/software/lex-parser.shtml.

distance from the stem 'ontolog' is scanned for a word sequence where each word has at least one symbol in uppercase. Such sequence(s) is written as the output of query 2.9.

To find new ontologies, hyperlinks in the 'Abstract' were also parsed. We supposed, that a link given in the abstract may identify a new project. So hyperlink's body was scanned for having 'onto' as a substring and (if true) was split by dot (similarly to the splitting of e-mails in Q2.1). Sentences in the abstract were lowercased and parts of hyperlink body were searched there. If any part was found, we returned the corresponding token from the original sentence. An example is given below. Original sentence is 'BioPortal, a web-based library of biomedical ontologies.available online at http://bioportal.bioontology.org.' includes a hyperlink. This is the list with the elements to be searched as ontology name: ['bioportal', 'bioontology']. Having obtained the index, mentioned ontology name is returned: 'BioPortal'.

4   Implementation

4.1   Overall Architecture

The tool is implemented in Python 2.7. Developed tool uses Grab Spider framework[11]. This framework allows to build asynchronous site crawlers. Crawler downloads all workshop's papers and then runs the parsing tasks. The Paper Parser uses the Metadata Extraction Library to gather information about the paper. The tool uses the Ontology Mapper module to build properties and entity relations. The Ontology Mapper module uses RDFLib[12] library to create and store triples. The overall architecture of the developed tool is shown in Fig. 2.

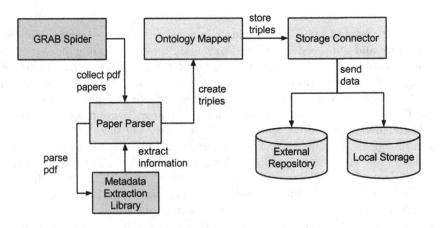

Fig. 2. The overall architecture of the developed tool

---

[11] Cf. http://grablib.org/.
[12] Cf. https://github.com/RDFLib.

4.2   Library for Context Information Extraction from the PDF Full Text of the Papers

The metadata extraction has several steps. At the first step the input PDF is converted into TXT and HTML format. This conversion is made with pdf2txt utility (a part of Python PDFminer library[13]). Then the metadata extraction library deals with obtained HTML and TXT only. We use BeautifulSoup[14] as a HTML parser library. The module is implemented using Python 2.7.

5   Results and Discussions

The developed tool produces a LOD dataset in the output, which stores information about cited papers, affiliations, agencies, mentioned ontologies, some other objects and relations for each paper. The tool was tested on the training dataset of 12 workshop proceedings having total 101 papers. Testing was accomplished by running original automated tests. Automated tests use SPARQL queries to collect information from dataset and check for equality with manually predefined results stored in CVS format. For example to identify all journal papers cited by the paper http://ceur-ws.org/Vol-1302/paper7.pdf (Q2.5) the following query should be send.

```
SELECT ?resource_iri ?doi ?paper_title ?journal_title {
 VALUES ?paper_iri {
    <http://ceur-ws.org/Vol-1302#paper7>
 }
 ?paper_iri bibo:cites ?resource_iri .
 ?resource_iri  bibo:isPartOf ?journal_iri .
 ?resource_iri  bibo:title ?paper_title .
 ?journal_iri  bibo:title ?journal_title
 OPTIONAL {?resource_iri  bibo:doi ?doi}
}
```

6   Conclusion

Analysis of workshop paper elements resulted in accomplishing the following tasks:

- development of ontology describing paper metadata and mentioned resources and named entities;
- development of metadata extraction procedures;
- development of the tool crawling PDF papers, applying metadata extraction procedures and publishing results as Linked Open Data.

---

[13] Cf. https://pypi.python.org/pypi/pdfminer/.

[14] Cf. https://pypi.python.org/pypi/BeautifulSoup/3.2.1.

Task 2 of Semantic Publishing Challenge 2015 is solved with the developed tool based on Grab Spider framework, RDFLib library and the developed library for metadata and context information extraction from the PDF full text of the papers. This tool uses BIBO, FOAF, SWRC, ARPFO and DBpedia ontologies. Metadata Extraction Library uses regular expressions based on html page style attributes, natural language processing methods, heuristics about acronym resolving and named entities extraction. Further work implies improvement of named entities extraction procedures, performing deeper syntactic analysis, adding external data sources, using validation via external sources, e.g. heading elements except e-mail can be validated via DBLP[15], candidates for mentioned ontologies can be also checked via external source[16].

Acknowledgments. This work has been partially financially supported by the Government of Russian Federation, Grant #074-U01.

References

1. Guo, Z., Jin, H.: Reference Metadata Extraction from Scientific Papers. In: 2011 12th International Conference on Applications and Technologies Parallel and Distributed Computing (PDCAT), pp. 45–49, October 2011
2. Kolchin, M., Kozlov, F.: A template-based information extraction from web sites with unstable markup. In: Presutti, V., Stankovic, M., Cambria, E., Cantador, I., Di Iorio, A., Di Noia, T., Lange, C., Reforgiato Recupero, D., Tordai, A. (eds.) SemWebEval 2014. CCIS, vol. 475, pp. 89–94. Springer, Heidelberg (2014). http://dx.doi.org/10.1007/978-3-319-12024-9_11
3. Marinai, S.: Metadata extraction from pdf papers for digital library ingest. In: 2009 10th International Conference on Document Analysis and Recognition, ICDAR 2009, pp. 251–255, July 2009
4. Sure, Y., Bloehdorn, S., Haase, P., Hartmann, J., Oberle, D.: The SWRC ontology semantic web for research communities. In: Bento, C., Cardoso, A., Dias, G. (eds.) EPIA 2005. LNCS (LNAI), vol. 3808, pp. 218–231. Springer, Heidelberg (2005). http://dx.doi.org/10.1007/11595014_22

---

[15] Cf. http://dblp.uni-trier.de.
[16] Cf. http://prefix.cc.

Semantically Annotating CEUR-WS Workshop Proceedings with RML

Pieter Heyvaert[(✉)], Anastasia Dimou, Ruben Verborgh, Erik Mannens,
and Rik Van de Walle

Multimedia Lab, Ghent University - iMinds, Ghent, Belgium
{pheyvaer.heyvaert,anastasia.dimou,ruben.verborgh,erik.mannens,
rik.walle}@ugent.be

Abstract. In this paper, we present our solution for the first task of
the second Semantic Publishing Challenge. The task requires extracting
and semantically annotating information regarding CEUR-WS workshops,
their chairs and conference affiliations, as well as their papers and their
authors, from a set of HTML-encoded workshop proceedings volumes. Our
solution builds on last year's submission, while we address a number of
shortcomings, assess the generated dataset for its quality and publish the
queries as SPARQL query templates. This is accomplished using the RDF
Mapping Language (RML) to define the mappings, the RMLProcessor to
execute them, the RDFUnit to both validate the mapping documents and
assess the generated dataset's quality, and The DataTank to publish the
SPARQL query templates. This results in an overall improved quality of
the generated dataset that is reflected in the query results.

1 Introduction

A lot of information is available on the Web through websites. However, this
information is not always processable by Semantic Web enabled systems, because
most HTML pages lack the required metadata. An example of such a website is
CEUR-WS Workshop Proceedings (CEUR-WS)[1]. CEUR-WS is a publication service
for proceedings of scientific workshops. It provides (i) a list of all the volumes
indexed in a single Web page; and (ii) a detailed Web page for each volume.
In need of assessing the scientific output quality, the Semantic Publishing Challenge (SPC14) was organized in 2014[2], followed by this year's edition[3] (SPC15).

In this paper, we propose a solution to solve the challenge's first task[4], which
includes extracting information regarding workshops, their chairs and conference
affiliations, as well as their papers and their authors, from a set of HTML-encoded
tables of workshop proceedings volumes. In order to achieve this, we build on last
year's submission [1]. The solution uses the RDF Mapping language (RML)[5] [2,3],

---

[1] http://ceur-ws.org/.
[2] http://challenges.2014.eswc-conferences.org/index.php/SemPub/.
[3] https://github.com/ceurws/lod/wiki/SemPub2015.
[4] https://github.com/ceurws/lod/wiki/Task1.
[5] http://rml.io.

© Springer International Publishing Switzerland 2015
F. Gandon et al. (Eds.): SemWebEval 2015, CCIS 548, pp. 165–176, 2015.
DOI: 10.1007/978-3-319-25518-7_14

which is a generic mapping language based on an extension over R2RML, the W3C standard for mapping relational databases into RDF. RML offers a uniform way of defining the mapping rules for data in heterogeneous formats.

We follow the same approach as last year. However, we (i) address a number of shortcomings, (ii) assess the generated dataset for its quality and (iii) publish the queries as SPARQL query templates. This is accomplished using RML (see Sect. 4) to define the mappings, the RMLProcessor to execute them, the RDFUnit to both validate the mapping documents and assess the generated dataset's quality (see Sect. 8.2), and The DataTank to publish the SPARQL query templates (see Sect. 8.3).

This paper that supports our submission to the SPC15 is structured as follows: we state the problem in Sect. 2, and give an overview of our approach in Sect. 3. In Sect. 4 we elaborate on the basis of the solution, namely RML. After defining how the data is modeled in Sect. 5, we elaborate on how the mapping is done in Sect. 6. We discuss how the queries of the task are evaluated in Sect. 7. In Sect. 8 we explain the used tools: RMLProcessor (Sect. 8.1), the RDFUnit (Sect. 8.2) and The DataTank (Sect. 8.3). Finally, in Sect. 9, we discuss our solution and its results, after which we form our conclusions.

2   Problem Statement

The conclusions of the Semantic Publishing Challenge 2014 [4] show that the submitted solutions provided satisfying results. However, they also highlight that there is still room for improvement. With the Semantic Publishing Challenge 2015, the organizers continue pursuing the objective of assessing the quality of scientific output and of evolving the dataset bootstrapped in 2014 to take also into account the wider ecosystem of publications. The challenge consists of the following three tasks:

Task 1 Extraction and assessment of workshop proceedings information,
Task 2 Extracting contextual information from the papers text in PDF, and
Task 3 Interlinking

In this paper we explain how we tackle the first task of the challenge. The participants are asked to extract information from a set of HTML tables published as Web pages in the CEUR-WS workshop proceedings. The information is obtained from the HTML pages' content which is semantically annotated and represented using the RDF data model. The extracted information is expected to answer queries about the quality of these workshops, for instance by measuring growth, longevity, and so on. The task is an extension of the SPC14's first task. The most challenging quality indicators from last year's challenge are reused. However, a number of them are defined more precisely, and new indicators are added. This results in the following three subtasks:

SubTask 1.1   Extract information from the HTML input pages;
SubTask 1.2   Annotate the information with appropriate ontologies and vocabularies; and
Subtask 1.3   Publish the semantically enriched representation with the RDF data model.

Table 1. Submission's output

Output	Location
RML mapping documents	http://rml.io/data/SPC2015/mappings
RDF dataset	http://rml.io/data/SPC2015/dataset.ttl
SPARQL templates	http://rml.io/data/SPC2015/sparql_templates
Query results	http://rml.io/data/SPC2015/query_results
List of queries on The DataTank	http://ewi.mmlab.be/spc

3   Overview of Our Approach

Our approach includes: (i) the generation of the RDF dataset and (ii) the evaluation of the SPARQL queries. The first is achieved with the following workflow:

1. define the mapping documents, using RML;
2. assess the mapping documents, using the RDFUnit;
3. generate the dataset, by executing the mappings, using the RMLProcessor;
4. assess the quality of the dataset, using theRDFUnit, and
5. publish the dataset, using The DataTank.

After the generation of the RDF dataset, the queries of the task are evaluated (see Sect. 7). In order to achieve this, the following are considered:

1. define the queries, using SPARQL templates, using The DataTank,
2. instantiate and execute the SPARQL queries, and
3. provide the results.

The components and output of our solution and where they can be found are summarized in Table 1.

4   RML

RDF Mapping Language (RML) [2,3] is a generic language defined to express customized mapping rules from data in heterogeneous formats to the RDF data model. RML is defined as a superset of the W3C-standardized mapping language R2RML [5], extending its applicability and broadening its scope. RML keeps the mapping definitions as in R2RML and follows the same syntax, providing a generic way of defining the mappings that is easily transferable to cover references to other data structures, combined with case-specific extensions, making RML highly extensible towards new source formats.

4.1   Structure of an RML Mapping Document

In RML, the mapping to the RDF data model is based on one or more Triples Maps that define how RDF triples should be generated. A Triples Map consists of three main parts: (i) the Logical Source (`rml:LogicalSource`), (ii) the Subject Map, and (iii) zero or more Predicate Object Maps.

The Subject Map (`rr:SubjectMap`) defines the rule that generates unique identifiers (URIs) for the resources which are mapped and is used as the subject of all RDF triples generated from this Triples Map. A Predicate Object Map consists of Predicate Maps, which define the rule that generates the triple's predicate and Object Maps or Referencing Object Maps, which define the rule that generates the triple's object. The Subject Map, the Predicate Map and the Object Map are Term Maps, namely rules that generate an RDF term (an IRI, a blank node or a literal).

4.2 Leveraging HTML with RML

A Logical Source (`rml:LogicalSource`) is used to determine the input source with the data to be mapped. RML deals with different data serializations which use different ways to refer to their content. Thus, RML considers that any reference to the Logical Source should be defined in a form relevant to the input data, e.g., XPATH for XML files or JSONPATH for JSON files. The Reference Formulation (`rml:referenceFormulation`) indicates the formulation (for instance, a standard or a query language) to refer to its data. Any reference to the data of the input source must be valid expressions according to the Reference Formulation stated at the Logical Source. This makes RML highly extensible towards new source formats.

At the current version of RML, the `ql:CSV`, `ql:XPath`, `ql:JSONPath` and `ql:CSS3` Reference Formulations are predefined (where *ql* is the prefix for http:// semweb.mmlab.be/ns/ql). For the task we use the `ql:CSS3` Reference Formulation to access the elements within the document. CSS3[6] selectors are standardized by W3C, they are easily used and broadly-known as they are used for selecting the HTML elements both for cascading styles and for jQuery[7]. CSS3 selectors can be used to refer to data in HTML documents. However, they can also be used for XML documents.

5   Data Modeling

In order to model the workshop proceedings information, we use the following ontologies:

- The Bibliographic Ontology[8] (with prefix *bibo*),
- DCMI Metadata Terms[9] (with prefix *dcterms*),
- Friend of a Friend[10] (with prefix *foaf*),

---

[6] http://www.w3.org/TR/selectors/.

[7] http://jquery.com.

[8] http://purl.org/ontology/bibo/.

[9] http://purl.org/dc/terms/.

[10] http://xmlns.com/foaf/0.1/.

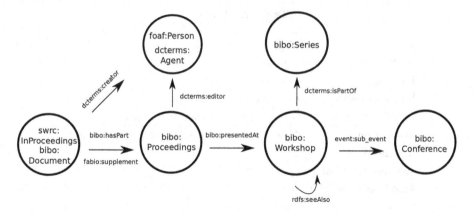

Fig. 1. An overview of the interaction between the classes and properties used to model the workshops proceedings information.

- RDF Schema[11] (with prefix *rdfs*),
- FRBR-aligned Bibliographic Ontology[12] (with prefix *fabio*)
- The Event Ontology[13] (with prefix *event*)
- Semantic Web for Research Communities[14] (with prefix *swrc*)

The classes used to determine the type of the entities are denoted in Table 2.

The properties used to annotate the entities and determine the relationships among them are denoted in Table 3. The properties listed here are not exhaustive, and for a complete overview of the used properties we refer to the mapping documents[15]. An overview of the entities and the relationships between the entities and the properties that determine them is shown in Fig. 1. Overall, the modelling of the data is driven by the queries that need to be answered as part of the challenge.

We extracted information related to workshop (`bibo:Workshop`) entities from the index page. Furthermore, we extracted information that models the relationship among different workshops (`rdfs:seeAlso`) of the same series, that denotes which proceedings are presented at a workshop (`bibo:presentedAt`) and states the conference that the workshop was co-located with (`dcterms:isPartOf`). To determine the workshops we iterated over the volumes, because, except for the joint volumes, all of them represent a separate workshop. Finally, the workshops related to the current one are added by following the 'see also' links in its description.

Each volume page represents a proceedings entity (`bibo:Proceedings`). This HTML page contains information about the papers (`swrc:InProceedings`, `bibo:Document`), which are connected to the proceedings (`bibo:hasPart`).

---

[11] http://www.w3.org/2000/01/rdf-schema.

[12] http://purl.org/spar/fabio/.

[13] http://purl.org/NET/c4dm/event.owl.

[14] http://swrc.ontoware.org/ontology.

[15] http://rml.io/data/spc2015/mappings.

Table 2. Classes

Class	Entity
bibo:Workshop	workshop
bibo:Series	workshop series
bibo:Proceedings	proceedings of a workshop
bibo:Conference	event where a workshop took place
foaf:Person dcterms:Agent	editor of a proceedings and author of a paper
swrc:InProceedings bibo:Document	paper

Table 3. Properties

Property	Relationship
dcterms:creator	person who is author of a paper
dcterms:hasPart	proceedings that a paper belong to
fabio:supplement	proceedings that a supplemental document (e.g., invited paper) belong to
dcterms:editor	person who is editor of proceedings
bibo:presentedAt	workshops that the papers, hence, the proceedings, are presented
dcterms:isPartOf	workshop series that a workshop is part of
rdfs:seeAlso	workshop that is related to this workshop
event:sub_event	event that the workshop is a subevent of

We make a distinction between non-invited and invited papers (using `fabio:supplement` instead of `bibo:hasPart`). The authors (`foaf:Person`, `dcterms:Agent`) are defined (using `dcterms:creator`) of each paper, as well as the editors (`foaf:Person`, `dcterms:Agent`) of the proceedings (`dcterms:editor`). Finally, from the workshop's name its series (`bibo:Series`) is determined and the workshop's co-located event (`bibo:Conference`) is determined (using `event:sub_event`). The extraction of additional information (location, date, edition), annotated with datatype properties, is defined in the mapping documents. Due to the repetitive nature of the corresponding definitions, we refer to the mapping documents for more details.

6   Mapping CEUR-WS from HTML to RDF

The task refers to two types of HTML pages that serve as input. On the one hand it is the index page listing all the volumes, namely http://ceur-ws.org. On the other hand, for each volume there is an HTML page that contains more detailed information, e.g., http://ceur-ws.org/Vol-1165/.

6.1 Defining the Mappings

Excerpts of a mapping document for one of the volumes are indicatively presented. First, the input source (Listing 1.1, line 5) that is used by this Triples Map (Listing 1.1, line 4) is stated, together with the Reference Formulation, in this case the CSS3 selectors (Listing 1.1, line 7), that states how we refer to the input and the iterator (Listing 1.1, line 6) over which the iteration occurs, as in Listing 1.1:

```
1  @prefix rml: <http://semweb.mmlab.be/ns/rml#>.
2
3  <#VolumeMapping>
4    rml:logicalSource [
5      rml:source <http://ceur-ws.org/Vol-1128> ;
6      rml:iterator "body";
7      rml:referenceFormulation ql:CSS3 ].
```

Listing 1.1. Defining the source of a mapping for a volume page

To define how the subject of all RDF triples will be generated using this Triples Map (Listing 1.2, line 4), we define a Subject Map (Listing 1.2, line 5). A unique URI will be generated for each volume with the volume number that is present on each page. This number is addressable by the CSS3 expression `span.CEURVOLNR` (Listing 1.2, line 6). The class of the workshop is set to `swrc:Proceedings` (Listing 1.2, line 7). The definition of a complete Subject Map can be found in Listing 1.2:

```
1  @prefix rr: <http://www.w3.org/ns/r2rml#>.
2  @prefix swrc: <http://swrc.ontoware.org/ontology#> .
3
4  <#VolumeMapping>
5    rr:subjectMap [
6      rr:template "http://ceur-ws.org/{span.CEURVOLNR}/";
7      rr:class swrc:Proceedings ].
```

Listing 1.2. Defining the subject of mapping for a volume page

For each RDF triple of the volume we need to define a Predicate Object Map (Listing 1.3, line 7). In our example (see Listing 1.3), we add the predicate for the label (`rdfs:label`) to the volume (Listing 1.3, line 6). The value of the object is specified as the content of the link (`<a>`) inside the `<span>` with the class CEURVOLTITLE, which results in the CSS3 selector `span.CEURVOLTITLE a` (Listing 1.3, line 8). The definition of a complete Subject Map is indicatively presented at Listing 1.3:

```
1  @prefix rdfs: <http://www.w3.org/2000/01/rdf-schema#>.
2  @prefix rr: <http://www.w3.org/ns/r2rml#>.
3
4  <#VolumeMapping>
5    rr:predicateObjectMap [
6      rr:predicate rdfs:label;
7      rr:objectMap [
8        rml:reference "span.CEURVOLTITLE a" ] ].
```

Listing 1.3. Defining the Objects (as literals) for the subject for a volume page

For the object's generation, RML is not limited to literals, as in the previous example. A reference to another Triples Map (Listing 1.4, line 8), instead of an rml:reference, is used to generate resources instead of literal values. In Listing 1.4, we state that all subjects of <#EditorMapping> are editors (bibo:editor) of the volume:

```
1    @prefix bibo: <http://purl.org/ontology/bibo/>.
2    @prefix rr: <http://www.w3.org/ns/r2rml#>.
3
4    <#VolumeMapping>
5      rr:predicateObjectMap [
6        rr:predicate bibo:editor;
7        rr:objectMap [
8          rr:parentTriplesMap <#EditorMapping> ] ].
```

Listing 1.4. Defining the objects (as resources) for the editors of a volume

6.2   Executing the Mappings

Executing an RML mapping requires a mapping document that summarizes all Triples Maps and points to an input data source. The mapping document is executed by an RML processor and the corresponding RDF output is generated. Each Triples Map is processed and the defined Subject Map and Predicate Object Maps are applied to the input data. For each reference to the input HTML, the CSS3 extractor returns an extract of the data and the corresponding triples are generated. The resulting RDF can be exporting in a user-specified serialization format. This solves subtask 1.3.

Data cleansing is out of RML's scope. However, the values extracted from the input is not always exactly as desired to be represented in RDF and the situation aggravates when mapping e.g. live HTML documents on-the-fly, where neither pre-processing is possible nor being as selective as desired purely based on CSS3 expressions to retrieve extracts from HTML pages. To this end, we defined and used rml:process, rml:replace and rml:split to further process the values returned from the input source as defined within a mapping rule. To be more precise, rml:process and rml:replace were used to define regular expressions whenever it is required to be more selective over the returned value and replaced by a part of the value or another value. For instance, a reference to h3 span.CEURLOCTIME returns Montpellier, France, May 26, 2013 and since there is no further HTML annotation, we cannot be more selective over the returned value. In these cases rml:process is used to define a regular expression, e.g. ([a-zA-Z]*), [a-zA-Z]*, [a-zA-Z]* [0-9]*, [0-9]*, and rml:replace is used to define the part of the value that is used for a certain mapping rule, e.g., $1, for the aforementioned case to map the city Montpellier. Furthermore, rml:split allows to split the value based on a delimiter and to map each part separately. The possibility to chain them enables even more fine-grained selections. These adjustments contribute in solving subtask 1.2.

Challenge-Specific Adjustments. In order to cope with a number of non-trivial structures of the challenge-specific HTML input sources, the default CSS3 selectors are not expressive enough. To this extent, we added the CSS3 function :until(x) to CSSelly[16], a Java implementation of the W3C CSS3 specification, used by the RMLProcessor. This function matches the first x found element in the HTML document.

The structure of the index page does not allow to use the default CSS3 selectors to extract the required information. However, implementing a custom function is not possible in this case, due to the extensibility limitations of CSSelly. To this extent, we reformatted[17] the index page to make it processable using the available selectors.

Last, a number of HTML pages contain invalid HTML syntax. To cope with this, we used JTidy[18] to produce valid versions of the HTML pages[19]. These adjustments allow to solve subtask 1.1.

7   Query Evaluation

The queries for Task 1 of the challenge can be found at https://github.com/ceurws/lod/wiki/QueriesTask1. Based on the description of each query, we created the corresponding SPARQL queries based on our data model (Sect. 5). Because of the queries templated nature, we defined our queries as SPARQL templates[20] and published them using The DataTank (sect. 8.3), allowing easy access to the queries for different values. For example, the SPARQL template for the query 1.1 can be found in Listing 1.5. It is the same as the original query with exception of line 9, where $workshop is added. If we want to execute the query with the value Vol-1085 for the variable workshop, we consider the following URI http://rml.io/data/spc2015/tdt/queries/q01.json?workshop=Vol-1085. This returns the results of the query in JSON format.

```
1   PREFIX bibo: <http://purl.org/ontology/bibo/>
2   PREFIX swrc: <http://swrc.ontoware.org/ontology#>
3   PREFIX rdfs: <http://www.w3.org/2000/01/rdf-schema#>
4
5   SELECT DISTINCT ?W ?name
6   WHERE {
7       ?W a swrc:Proceedings ; bibo:editor ?editor .
8       ?editor rdfs:label ?name.
9       FILTER (?W = <http://ceur-ws.org/${workshop}/> ) }
```

Listing 1.5. Sparql Template of Query 1.1

8   Tools

The execution of our publishing workflow is accomplished based on two tools: the RMLProcessor that is used to execute the mapping definitions and generate the RDF dataset and RDFUnit that is used to validate and improve the quality of both the defined schema and the generated dataset. Besides the publishing workflow, we used another tool, The DataTank to publish the SPARQL queries.

---

[16] http://jodd.org/doc/csselly/.

[17] This tool is available at http://rml.io/data/spc2015/reformat_tool.

[18] http://jtidy.sourceforge.net/.

[19] The valid HTML pages are available at http://rml.io/data/spc2015/valid_html.

[20] http://rml.io/data/spc2015/sparql_templates.

8.1 RML Processor

Our RMLProcessor[21], implemented in Java on top of db2triples[22], was used to perform the mappings. The RMLProcessor follows the mapping-driven processing approach, namely it reads the mapping definitions as defined with RML, and executes the mapping rules to generate the corresponding RDF dataset. The RMLProcessor has a modular architecture where the extraction and mapping modules are executed independently of each other. When the RML mappings are processed, the mapping module deals with the mappings' execution as defined in the mapping document in RML syntax, while the extraction module deals with the target languages expressions, in our case CSS3 expressions. To be more precise, the RMLProcessor uses CSSelly, a Java implementation of the W3C CSS3 specification.

8.2 RDFUnit

RDFUnit [6] is an RDF validation framework inspired by test-driven software development. In RDFUnit, every vocabulary, ontology, dataset or application can be accompanied by a set of data quality Test Cases (TCs) that ensure a basic level of quality. Assigning TCs in ontologies results in tests that can be reused by datasets sharing the same schema. All TCs are executed as SPARQL queries using a pattern-based transformation approach. In our workflow, we use RDFUnit to assure that (i) the mapping documents validate against the RML ontology, (ii) the schema, as a combination of several ontologies and vocabularies, is valid and (iii) the generated dataset does not contain violations in respect to the schema used.

8.3 The DataTank

The DataTank[23] is a RESTful data management system written in PHP and maintained by OKFN Belgium[24]. It enables publishing several data formats into Web readable formats. The source data can be stored in text based files, such as CSV, XML and JSON, or in binary structures, such as SHP files and relational databases. The DataTank reads the data out of these files and/or structures and publishes them on the Web using a URI as an identifier. It can provide the data in any format depending on the users needs, independently of the original format. Next to publishing data, The DataTank allows to publish (templated) SPARQL queries. SPARQL templates make it possible to define a variable's value at runtime (by the user). As a result, those queries have improved reusability and their scope fits well in the challenge's needs.

---

[21] https://github.com/mmlab/RMLProcessor.
[22] https://github.com/antidot/db2triples/.
[23] http://thedatatank.com/.
[24] http://www.openknowledge.be/.

9 Discussion and Conclusion

It is beneficial that CSS3 selectors become part of a formalization that performs mappings of data in HTML. Considering that the RML processor takes care of executing the mappings while the CSS3 extractor parses the document, the data publishers' contribution is limited in providing only the mapping document. As RML enables reusing same mappings over different files, the effort they put is even less. For the challenge, same mapping documents and/or definitions were re-used for different HTML input sources.

It is reasonable to consider CSS3 selectors to extract content from HTML pages because nowadays most websites use templates, formed with CSS3 selectors. Thus the content of their Web pages is structured in a similar way, which is the same point of reference as the one used by RML. This allows us to use RML mapping documents as a 'translation layer' over the published content of HTML pages.

Furthermore, as the mappings are partitioned in independent Triples Maps, data publishers can select the Triples Maps they want to execute at any time. For instance, in the case of the challenge, if violations were identified using the RDFUnit because of incorrect mappings, we can isolate the Triples Map that generated those triples, correct the relevant mapping definitions and re-execute them, without affecting the rest mapping definitions or the overall dataset. This becomes even easier considering that the mappings in RML are defined as triples themselves and, thus, the triples' provenance can be tracked and used to identify the mappings and data that cause the erroneous RDF result.

Beyond re-using the same mapping documents, RML allows to combine data from different input sources either they are in the same format or not. This leads to enhanced results as integration of data from different sources occurs during the mapping and relations between data appearing in different resources can be defined instead of interlinking them afterwards. For instance, the proceedings appearing in HTML can be mapped in an integrated fashion with the results of the extraction of the information from the PDF's of the papers published at the workshops, aligning with the results of Task 2. This results in enriching dataset when the two original datasets are combined.

Compared to last year's submission, we made the following improvements: (i) more information was extracted from the index page, while we keep the volume mapping documents simpler; (ii) the information extraction was focused on answering the challenge's queries; and (iii) series and workshops were modeled as separate entities, adding more semantic meaning to the resulting dataset; (iv) we use single mapping documents for multiple Web pages of the CEUR-WS HTML input sources. These improvements occur thanks to the updated syntax and the more stable release of RMLProcessor, leading to a higher number of supported queries.

Acknowledgements. The described research activities were funded by Ghent University, iMinds, the Institute for the Promotion of Innovation by Science and Technology in Flanders (IWT), the Fund for Scientific Research Flanders (FWO Flanders), and the European Union.

References

1. Dimou, A., Vander Sande, M., Colpaert, P., De Vocht, L., Verborgh, R., Mannens, E., Van de Walle, R.: Extraction and semantic annotation of workshop proceedings in HTML using RML. In: Presutti, V., et al. (eds.) SemWebEval 2014. CCIS, vol. 475, pp. 114–119. Springer, Heidelberg (2014)
2. Dimou, A., Vander Sande, M., Colpaert, P., Verborgh, R., Mannens, E., Van de Walle, R.: RML: a generic language for integrated RDF mappings of heterogeneous data. In: Workshop on Linked Data on the Web (2014)
3. Dimou, A., Vander Sande, M., Slepicka, J., Szekely, P., Mannens, E., Knoblock, C., Van de Walle, R.: Mapping hierarchical sources into RDF using the RML mapping language. In: Proceedings of the 8th IEEE International Conference on Semantic Computing (2014)
4. Lange, C., Di Iorio, A.: Semantic publishing challenge – assessing the quality of scientific output. In: Presutti, V., et al. (eds.) SemWebEval 2014. CCIS, vol. 475, pp. 61–76. Springer, Heidelberg (2014)
5. Das, S., Sundara, S., Cyganiak, R.: R2RML: RDB to RDF mapping language. In: Working group recommendation, W3C, September 2012. http://www.w3.org/TR/r2rml/
6. Kontokostas, D., Westphal, P., Auer, S., Hellmann, S., Lehmann, J., Cornelissen, R., Zaveri, A.: Test-driven evaluation of linked data quality. In: Proceedings of the World Wide Web Conference, pp. 747–758 (2014)

On the Automated Generation of Scholarly Publishing Linked Datasets: The Case of CEUR-WS Proceedings

Francesco Ronzano[(✉)], Beatriz Fisas, Gerard Casamayor del Bosque, and Horacio Saggion

TALN Research Group, Universitat Pompeu Fabra,
C/Tanger 122, 08018 Barcelona, Spain
{francesco.ronzano,beatriz.fisas,gerard.casamayor,
horacio.saggion}@upf.edu

Abstract. The availability of highly-informative semantic descriptions of scholarly publishing contents enables an easier sharing and reuse of research findings as well as a better assessment of the quality of scientific productions. In the context of the ESWC2015 Semantic Publishing Challenge, we present a system that automatically generates rich RDF datasets from CEUR-WS workshop proceedings and exposes them as Linked Data. Web pages of proceedings and textual contents of papers are analyzed through proper text processing pipelines. Semantic annotations are added by a set of SVM classifiers and refined by heuristics, gazetteers and rule-based grammars. Web services are exploited to link annotations to external datasets like DBpedia, CrossRef, FundRef and Bibsonomy. Finally, the data is modelled and published as an RDF graph.

Keywords: Semantic Web · Information extraction · Scholarly publishing · Open Linked Data

1 Extract and Semantically Model Scholarly Publishing Contents

During the last few years several approaches have been proposed to turn on-line information into Linked Datasets, dealing with contents coming from a huge variety of domains and ranging from structured to semi-structured and unstructured sources. Proper languages [3] and tools [4,5] to *map a relational database schema to ontologies and automate the generation of RDF triples from it* have been developed [2]. *Semantic annotation and generation of RDF graphs from textual contents* have also been deeply investigated. In this context, information extraction techniques and tools are widely exploited to mine concepts and relations from texts, ranging from the identification of shallow linguistic patterns

The work described in this paper has been funded by the European Project Dr. Inventor (FP7-ICT-2013.8.1 - Grant no: 611383).

© Springer International Publishing Switzerland 2015
F. Gandon et al. (Eds.): SemWebEval 2015, CCIS 548, pp. 177–188, 2015.
DOI: 10.1007/978-3-319-25518-7_15

typical of open-domain approaches [18] to methodologies that strongly rely on semantic knowledge models like ontologies [19,20]. On-line tools and Web services to extract Named Entities from documents and disambiguate them by associating proper URIs are currently extensively available. Systems like NERD [6] and the RDFa Content Editor [7] compare many of these tools and mix their output. Current approaches to create RDF graphs by processing unstructured texts often rely on deep parsing and semantic annotation of textual contents to support the generation of RDF triples. Examples of this kind of systems are LODifier [8] and the text analysis pipeline presented by [9].

In such a context of extensive creation and exploitation of semantic data, scholarly publishing represents a knowledge domain that would strongly benefit from an enhanced structuring, interlinking and semantic modeling of its contents [10]. This goal represents the core objective of **semantic publishing** [1,11]. Semantic Web technologies are an enabling factor towards this vision [12]. They provide the means to structure and semantically enrich scientific publications so as to support the generation of Linked Data from them [13,14], thus fostering the reproducibility and reusability of their outcomes [21]. Recently, a few scientific publication repositories including DBLP[1], ACM[2] and IEEE[3] have been also published as Open Linked Data. In general, however, they expose only basic bibliographic information that is too generic to properly support the diffusion and the assessment of the quality of scientific publications.

With the purpose of experimenting with new approaches to generate rich and highly descriptive scholarly publishing Open Linked Datasets, in the context of the ESWC2015 Semantic Publishing Challenge (2015 SemPub Challenge), in this paper we present a system that automatically analyses the contents of the workshop proceedings of CEUR-WS Web portal, both Web pages and PDF papers, and exports them as an RDF graph. Our system extends our approach to the 2014 SemPub Challenge [22] by dealing with the new information extraction and data modeling needs identified by the 2015 SemPub Challenge. In particular, the 2015 SemPub Challenge proposes two different tasks focused on the extraction of information respectively from CEUR-WS Web pages (SemPub Task 1) and from the content of PDF papers published by CEUR-WS (SemPub Task 2). In Sect. 2 we introduce our system motivating our information extraction approach to both Tasks. Section 3 provides a detailed description of all the data processing phases that characterize our system. In Sect. 4 we explain how we semantically model the information extracted from workshop proceedings as an RDF graph by reusing and extending existing ontologies. Section 5 discusses the evaluation of the RDF datasets generated. In Sect. 6 we analyze the lessons we learned when building our system and outline future work.

---

[1] http://dblp.l3s.de/d2r/.
[2] http://acm.rkbexplorer.com/.
[3] http://ieee.rkbexplorer.com/.

2 Turning On-line Workshop Proceedings into RDF Graphs: Overall Approach

The ultimate goal of the data processing pipelines we developed is to generate rich semantic descriptions of scientific workshops and conferences. In particular, we mined CEUR-WS on-line workshop proceedings to semantically model *detailed descriptive information of each workshop* from Web pages and *data concerning authors, affiliations, cited papers and mentions of funding bodies and ontologies* from PDF papers[4]. In this way we can easily relate and aggregate information across multiple workshops in order to track their evolution and experiment with new metrics to evaluate them.

CEUR-WS on-line workshop proceedings are organized into volumes; at time of writing there are 1343 published volumes. Each volume contains the proceedings of one or more workshops that are usually co-located at the same conference. Each volume is described by an HTML page including links to the PDF documents of the papers presented at the workshop. Microformats[5] and RDFa[6] annotations are available for some of these HTML documents, and missing in others.

In the context of the 2015 SemPub Challenge, we rely on the following considerations to properly process workshop proceedings:

– Since 2010, 20 microformat classes (CEURVOLEDITOR, CEURTITLE, CEURAUTHORS, etc.) have been adopted to annotate HTML pages detailing the contents of each proceeding volume. The occurrences of each class provide a set of examples of relevant kinds of information required to be extracted by SemPub Task 1. **This data can be exploited to train an automatic text annotation system** in order to add these annotations to proceedings where they are not present.
– Several scholarly publishing resources accessible on-line refer and partially replicate CEUR-WS contents in a structured or semi-structured format. Among them there are Bibsonomy[7], DBLP[8] , Wiki CFP[9], the CrossRef Database[10], and FundRef[11]. These resources can be exploited **to support the information extraction process and to make the RDF contents generated by our system strongly linked with related datasets**. In this context, links to DBpedia[12] can also be established by means of SPARQL

---

[4] For a detailed description of how workshop related data are modeled as an RDF graph, refer to Sect. 4.

[5] A semantic markup approach that conveys metadata and other attributes in Web pages by existing HTML/XHTML tags.

[6] A semantic markup useful to embed RDF triples within XHTML documents.

[7] http://www.bibsonomy.org/.

[8] http://dblp.uni-trier.de/.

[9] http://www.wikicfp.com/cfp/.

[10] http://crossref.org/.

[11] http://www.crossref.org/fundref/.

[12] http://dbpedia.org/.

queries or by relying on more complex Semantic Web Named Entities disambiguation tools like DBpedia Spotlight[13] [17].

On the basis of the previous considerations, we have designed and implemented two data processing pipelines that respectively convert CEUR-WS proceeding volumes and PDF papers into rich RDF datasets.

3   Data Analysis Pipelines

In this Section we describe in detail the data processing pipelines that mine respectively the Web pages of CEUR-WS proceedings (SemPub Task 1, Subsect. 3.1) and the contents of PDF papers (SemPub Task 2, Subsect. 3.2).

3.1   Task 1: Processing CEUR-WS HTML Contents

We mine the information contained in each on-line proceeding by relying on an extended version of the processing pipeline we introduced in the 2014 SemPub Challenge [22]. In particular, we increase the number of external datasets and Web services exploited to support information extraction. We also refine the heuristics useful to validate, sanitize and normalize the data extracted. We keep out from this pipeline the parts that are devoted to process the contents of PDF papers from CEUR-WS proceedings. These components, properly extended, have been integrated in the PDF processing pipeline exploited in the context of Sem-Pub Task 2 (see Subsect. 3.2). Figure 1 outlines the high level architecture of our system. This pipeline is implemented by relying on the GATE Text Engineering Framework[14] [15], and complemented by external tools and interactions with on-line Web services and knowledge repositories. We functionally describe each pipeline component hereafter.

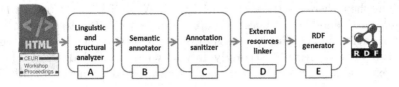

Fig. 1. Task 1: CEUR-WS Proceeding data processing pipeline

(T1.A) Linguistic and Structural Analyzer. Given a set of CEUR-WS proceeding Web pages, their contents are retrieved and characterized by means of linguistic and structural features, useful to support the execution of the following processing steps. In particular, the textual contents of each proceeding are properly split into lines containing homogeneous information by relying on

---

[13] http://spotlight.dbpedia.org/.
[14] https://gate.ac.uk/.

both HTML markup and custom heuristics. Linguistic analysis is performed in order to tokenize and POS-tag these texts exploiting the information exaction framework ANNIE[15]. Occurrences of paper titles and authors names, acronyms of conferences and workshops, names of institutions, cities and states are pointed out by means of a set of gazetteers; they rely on lists of expressions compiled by crawling WikiCFP, processing the XML dump of DBLP and parsing European Projects information retrieved from the European Union Open Data Portal[16]. Text tokens that denote common names related to research institution (like 'department', 'institute', etc.) or refer to ordinal numbers are also properly spotted.

(T1.B) Semantic Annotator. This component automatically adds semantic annotations to the textual contents of proceedings without semantic markups (volumes up to 558). To this purpose we exploited a set of chunk-based and sentence-based Support Vector Machine (SVM) classifiers [16]. We trained these classifiers over the CEUR-WS microformat annotations existing in proceedings volumes from 559 to 1343. We considered the 14 most frequent microformat classes adopted by CEUR-WS (CEURTITLE, CEURAUTHORS, ect.), thus compiling 14 training corpora. Each corpus includes all the CEUR-WS volumes available on-line that are annotated with the corresponding microformat class. Since we want to model the affiliation of workshop editors and there is no CEUR-WS microformat class for it, we introduced an additional dedicated annotation type, CEURAFFILIATION. We created a training corpus by randomly choosing 75 proceedings that were manually annotated with editor affiliations, thus generating 256 training examples. The first three columns of Table 1 show, for each type of annotation, the number of proceeding volumes where such annotation is present and the total number of annotation examples that are available.

The features added to the textual contents of each proceeding by the *Linguistic and structural analyzer* are exploited to characterize textual chunks and sentences so as to enable their automatic classification. For each annotation type we trained a chunk-based and a sentence-based SVM classifier to automatically perform the annotation task. We chose to automatically annotate proceedings that do not have or include incomplete microformat annotations by exploiting the classifier that better performs for each annotation type (best F1 score, see Table 1).

In general, token-based classifiers perform better with annotation types covering a small number of consecutive tokens that are characterized by a highly distinctive set of features and can be easily discriminated from preceding and following sets of tokens. On the contrary, sentence-based classifiers obtain better results with classes that can be better characterized by sentence level features rather than token level ones.

(T1.C) Annotation Sanitizer. A set of heuristics are applied to fix cases when the annotation borders are incorrectly identified or to delete annotations

---

[15] http://gate.ac.uk/sale/tao/splitch6.html.
[16] https://open-data.europa.eu/en/data.

Table 1. For each annotation type, number of proceeding volumes including such annotations, number of training examples, precision, recall and F1 score (10-fold cross validation) of token-based and sentence-based SVM classifiers; in bold the classifier chosen to be applied in our system - (*) = manual annotation

Annotation type	Num. Proc.	Num. Examp.	Prec/Rec/F1 (Token)	Prec/Rec/F1 (Sent.)
CEURVOLACRONYM	429	429	0.995/0.980/**0.987**	0.953/0.975/0.963
CEURURN	785	785	1.000/1.000/**1.000**	0.988/1.000/0.994
CEURLOCTIME	785	785	0.973/0.920/0.945	0.966/0.986/**0.975**
CEURVOLTITLE	782	782	0.981/0.909/**0.942**	0.759/0.732/0.745
CEURPUBDATE	581	581	1.000/0.926/0.961	0.997/1.000/**0.999**
CEURVOLEDITOR	785	2901	0.832/0.570/0.676	0.951/0.957/**0.954**
CEURVOLNR	786	786	1.000/0.998/**0.999**	0.998/1.000/0.999
CEURTITLE	784	12807	0.641/0.328/0.434	0.951/0.994/**0.972**
CEURAUTHORS	777	777	0.673/0.376/0.482	0.936/0.982/**0.958**
CEURFULLTITLE	778	778	0.854/0.710/0.775	0.992/0.918/**0.953**
CEURPUBYEAR	777	777	0.998/0.998/0.998	0.998/1.000/**0.999**
CEURPAGES	522	7387	0.983/0.985/**0.984**	0.964/0.987/0.975
CEURSESSION	463	1740	0.930/0.871/0.899	0.876/0.940/**0.906**
CEURCOLOCATED	242	242	0.927/0.928/0.924	0.945/0.975/**0.958**
CEURAFFILIATION (*)	75	256	0.841/0.601/0.699	0.938/0.972/**0.953**

that are not compliant with the normal sequence of annotations of a proceeding (e.g. editor affiliations annotated after the list of paper titles and authors). In addition, links between pairs of related annotations are created (e.g. authors and papers by considering the sequence of annotations or editors and affiliations by means of their markups).

(T1.D) External Resources Linker. This component extends annotations with information retrieved from external resources. Bibsonomy REST API are exploited to link CEURTITLEs to Bibsonomy entries and import the related BibTeX meta-data, if any. DBpedia Spotlight Web Service is exploited to identify DBpedia URIs of occurrences of States, Cities and Organizations in CEUR-LOCTIMEs and CEURAFFILIATIONs.

(T1.E) RDF Generator. All the information gathered by the previous processing steps is aggregated and normalized so as to generate a highly-informative Open Linked Dataset. The contents of each proceeding are modelled by reusing and extending widespread semantic publishing ontologies. Section 4 provides further details about RDF data modelling.

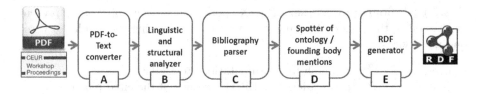

Fig. 2. Task 2: PDF papers data processing pipeline

3.2   Task 2: Mining PDF Papers

In order to extract information from PDF papers as required by SemPub Task 2, we set up a dedicated text analysis pipeline that takes as input one or more PDF papers published by CEUR-WS proceedings and generates an RDF graph. As in SemPub Task 1, the pipeline is based on the GATE Text Engineering Framework. This pipeline takes advantage of part of the external tools and online Web services and knowledge repositories exploited in Task 1. The high level architecture of the pipeline is outlined in Fig. 2. We functionally describe its components.

(T2.A) PDF to Text Converter. We rely on two different PDF-to-text conversion tools: the Web service **PDFX**[17] and the command line utility **Poppler**[18]. Even if the following text analysis phases are mainly based on the textual conversion generated by PDFX, we exploit the output of Poppler to complement it since Poppler preserves information concerning the layout of the original PDF paper. We use this information to support the identification of authors names and to match authors and affiliations in paper headers. PDFX is a PDF-to-text conversion Web service that implements a rule-based iterative PDF analyzer. The style and layout of PDF documents are exploited by PDFX to extract basic meta-data and structural / rhetorical segmentation.

(T2.B) Linguistic and Structural Analyzer. In a similar way to Task 1, the textual contents of each paper are split into lines, tokenized and POS-tagged thanks to the information exaction framework ANNIE[19]. The same gazetteer lists referenced in Task 1 are exploited to point out occurrences of authors names as well as names of institutions, cities and states. Information retrieved from the European Union Open Data Portal and the FundRef founding agencies database is exploited to spot full names, identification numbers and acronyms of European Projects as well as full and abbreviated names of funding agencies. Text tokens that denote common names related to research institution (like 'department', 'institute', etc.) are also identified.

---

[17] http://pdfx.cs.man.ac.uk/.

[18] http://poppler.freedesktop.org/.

[19] http://gate.ac.uk/sale/tao/splitch6.html.

(T2.C) Bibliography Parser. PDFX spots each bibliographic entry present at the end of the paper. We parse this text by aggregating the results of three on-line services:

– *CrossRef API*[20]: to match free-form citations to DOIs;
– *Bibsonomy API*[21]: to retrieve the BibTeX record of the cited paper;
– *Freecite on-line citation parser*[22]: to identify the constituent elements of a bibliographic entry (author, title, year, journal name, etc.) by applying a sequence tagging algorithm over its tokens.

We enrich each bibliographic entry by merging the processing output of these three services. This information is properly exploited in order to generate the RDF triples modelling the bibliography of the paper.

(T2.D) Spotter of Ontology and Founding Body mentions. This component implements a set of JAPE grammars[23] useful to spot mentions of *ontologies* and *founding bodies* (EU projects, grants, founding agencies). Mention spotting relies on a set of textual patterns that match the annotations produced by the Linguistic and structural analyzer. JAPE grammars have been created by manually analysing the context of occurrences of mentions of *ontologies* and *founding bodies* in the papers of the training set of SemPub Task 2. When mentions of *founding bodies* are matched to entries of the lists of FundRef founding agencies or European Projects, we can enrich such mentions with meta-data like the FundRef URI of the founding agency. These meta-data will contribute to generate a richer RDF graph.

(T2.E) RDF Generator. All the paper-related information gathered by the previous processing steps is aggregated and normalized so as to generate a highly-informative Open Linked Dataset. We exploit widespread semantic publishing ontologies to model the contents of each paper. Section 4 provides further details about RDF data modeling.

4 Modeling Workshop Data as an RDF Graph

In order to properly model the information concerning workshop proceedings and papers we exploited and extended widespread semantic publishing ontologies. In particular, we relied on:

– the *Semantic Web for Research Communities Ontology* (prefix swrc) that is useful to shape many relevant domain concept and relationships;

---

[20] http://search.crossref.org/help/api.
[21] http://www.bibsonomy.org/help/doc/api.html.
[22] http://freecite.library.brown.edu/.
[23] https://gate.ac.uk/sale/tao/splitch8.html.

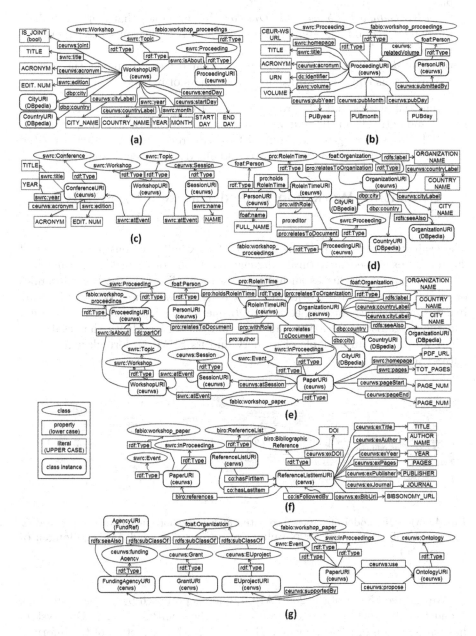

Fig. 3. RDF data models of workshops (a), proceedings (b), conferences (c), editors (d), papers and authors (e)

– the *Bibliographic Reference Ontology* (prefix biro) that is useful to model the bibliographic information of a paper;
– the *FRBR-aligned Bibliographic Ontology* (prefix fabio) that is useful to better characterize bibliographic records of scholarly endeavours like papers and proceedings;
– the *Publishing Role Ontology* (prefix pro) that is useful to model the roles of researchers as editors of workshops and authors of papers.

From the classes and the properties modeled by these ontologies, we have reused and derived - in the ceur-ws namespace - sub-classes and sub-properties: the RDF Datasets we generate from CEUR-WS Proceedings include the related T-BOX axioms. Figure 3 visually represents our data modeling approach.

5   Evaluating Workshop Linked Datasets by SPARQL Queries

The evaluation procedure of the 2015 SemPub Challenge consisted of a set of 20 queries expressed in natural language, each one of them aggregating data of a workshop or serving as an indicator of its quality (e.g. list the full names of all authors who have (co-)authored a paper in workshop W). Participants had to rewrite these queries as SPARQL queries so that the organizers could run them against the participants RDF dataset and evaluate the results. In Fig. 4 we provide an example of a query and its SPARQL formulation for our dataset model.

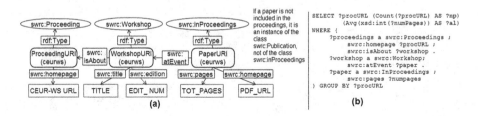

Fig. 4. (a) RDF model of papers presented at a workshop, included in a proceeding volume; (b) SPARQL query for **Numbers of papers** (?np) and **Average length of papers** (?al)

We covered 15 out of the 20 SPARQL queries proposed by the SemPub Task 1 and the 10 SPARQL queries proposed by the SemPub Task 2. Our system has large margin of improvement with respect to the extraction of the information required in the context of the challenge from the Web pages of CEUR-WS Proceedings (SemPub Task 1). The performance of our pipeline improves when it deals with the extraction of authors' names, country and affiliation and the analysis of bibliographic entries from PDF papers (SemPub Task 2).

6 Conclusions and Future Work

We described a system that extracts structured information from CEUR-WS on-line proceedings by parsing both Web pages and PDF papers and modeling their contents as Linked Datasets.

Our system design has been motivated by the need of flexibility and robustness in the face of different ways in which information is written, structured or annotated in the input dataset. Despite that, we found that **customized and often laborious information extraction and post processing steps are essential to correctly deal with borderline information structures that are difficult to generalize**, like unusual markups, infrequent ways to link authors and affiliations, etc.

In general, we hope that the increasing availability of structured and rich scientific publishing Linked Datasets will enable larger communities to easily discover and reuse research outcomes as well as to propose and test new metrics to better understand and evaluate research outputs. In this context we believe that, in parallel to the investigation of approaches to automate the creation of semantic datasets by mining partially structured inputs, it is also essential to push scientific communities towards standardized, shared and opened procedures to expose their outcomes in a structured way.

References

1. Shotton, D.: Semantic publishing: the coming revolution in scientific journal publishing. Learned Publishing **22**(2), 85–94 (2009)
2. Spanos, D.E., Stavrou, P., Mitrou, N.: Bringing relational databases into the semantic web: a survey. Semant. Web **3**(2), 169–209 (2012). IOS Press
3. World Wide Web Consortium: R2RML: RDB to RDF mapping language. W3C Recommendation (2012)
4. Bizer, C., Cyganiak, R.: D2r server-publishing relational databases on the semantic web. In: Poster at the 5th International Semantic Web Conference (2006)
5. Knoblock, C.A., Szekely, P., Ambite, J.L., Goel, A., Gupta, S., Lerman, K., Muslea, M., Taheriyan, M., Mallick, P.: Semi-automatically mapping structured sources into the semantic web. In: Simperl, E., Cimiano, P., Polleres, A., Corcho, O., Presutti, V. (eds.) ESWC 2012. LNCS, vol. 7295, pp. 375–390. Springer, Heidelberg (2012)
6. Rizzo, G., Troncy, R., Hellmann, S., Bruemmer, M.: NERD meets NIF: lifting NLP extraction results to the linked data cloud. In: Proceedings of the Linked Data on the Web Workshop (2012)
7. Khalili, A., Auer, S., Hladky, D.: The RDFa content editor - from WYSIWYG to WYSIWYM. In: Proceedings of the IEEE Computer Software and Applications Conference, COMPSAC (2012)
8. Augenstein, I., Padó, S., Rudolph, S.: LODifier: generating linked data from unstructured text. In: Simperl, E., Cimiano, P., Polleres, A., Corcho, O., Presutti, V. (eds.) ESWC 2012. LNCS, vol. 7295, pp. 210–224. Springer, Heidelberg (2012)
9. Exner, P., Nugues, P.: Entity extraction: from unstructured text to DBpedia RDF triples. In: Proceedings of the Web of Linked Entities Workshop, WoLE (2012)

10. Stegmaier, F., et al.: Unleashing semantics of research data. In: Rabl, T., Poess, M., Baru, C., Jacobsen, H.-A. (eds.) WBDB 2012. LNCS, vol. 8163, pp. 103–112. Springer, Heidelberg (2014)

11. Eefke, S., Van Der Graaf, M.: Journal article mining: the scholarly publishers' perspective. Learned Publishing 25(1), 35–46 (2012)

12. Bizer, C.: Linking data and publications expert report, global research data infrastructure of European Union (2012)

13. Ciancarini, P., Di Iorio, A., Nuzzolese, A.G., Peroni, S., Vitali, F.: Semantic annotation of scholarly documents and citations. In: Baldoni, M., Baroglio, C., Boella, G., Micalizio, R. (eds.) AI*IA 2013. LNCS, vol. 8249, pp. 336–347. Springer, Heidelberg (2013)

14. Attwood, T.K., Kell, D.B., McDermott, P., Marsh, J., Pettifer, S.R., Thorne, D.: Utopia documents: linking scholarly literature with research data. Bioinformatics 26(18), 568–574 (2010)

15. Cunningham, H., Maynard, D., Bontcheva, K., Tablan, V.: GATE: a framework and graphical development environment for robust NLP tools and applications. In: Proceedings of the 40th Anniversary Meeting of the Association for Computational Linguistics, ACL (2002)

16. Li, Y., Bontcheva, K., Cunningham, H.: Adapting SVM for Data sparseness and imbalance: a case study on information extraction. Nat. Lang. Eng. 15, 241–271 (2009). Cambridge University Press

17. Mendes, P.N., Jakob, M., Garca-Silva, A., Bizer, C.: DBpedia spotlight: shedding light on the web of documents. In: Proceedings of the 7th International Conference on Semantic Systems, pp. 1–8. ACM (2011)

18. Etzioni, O., Banko, M., Soderland, S., Weld, D.S.: Open Information Extraction from the Web. Communications of the ACM - Surviving the data deluge 51(12), 68–74 (2008)

19. Wimalasuriya, D.C., Dou, D.: Ontology-based Information Extraction: An Introduction and a Survey of Current Approaches. Journal of Information Science 36(3), 306–323 (2010)

20. Saggion, H., Funk, A., Maynard, D., Bontcheva, K.: Ontology-based information extraction for business intelligence. In: Aberer, K., et al. (eds.) ASWC 2007 and ISWC 2007. LNCS, vol. 4825, pp. 843–856. Springer, Heidelberg (2007)

21. Bechhofer, S., et al.: Why linked data is not enough for scientists. Future Gener. Comput. Syst. Spec. Sect. Recent Adv. e-Sci. 29(2), 599–611 (2013). Elsevier

22. Ronzano, F., del Bosque, G.C., Saggion, H.: Semantify CEUR-WS proceedings: towards the automatic generation of highly descriptive scholarly publishing linked datasets. In: Presutti, V., et al. (eds.) SemWebEval 2014. CCIS, vol. 475, pp. 83–88. Springer, Heidelberg (2014)

Schema-Agnostic Queries over Large-Schema Databases Challenge (SAQ-2015)

The Schema-Agnostic Queries (SAQ-2015) Semantic Web Challenge: Task Description

André Freitas[1]([✉]) and Christina Unger[2]

[1] Department of Computer Science and Mathematics,
University of Passau, Passau, Germany
andre.freitas@uni-passau.de
[2] Semantic Computing Group, Cognitive Interaction Technology,
Center of Excellence (CITEC), Bielefeld University, Bielefeld, Germany

Abstract. As datasets grow in schema-size and heterogeneity, the development of infrastructures which can support users querying and exploring the data, without the need to fully understand the conceptual model behind it, becomes a fundamental functionality for contemporary data management. The first edition of the Schema-agnostic Queries Semantic Web Challenge (SAQ-2015) aims at creating a test collection to evaluate *schema-agnostic/schema-free* query mechanisms, i.e. mechanisms which are able to semantically match user queries expressed in their own vocabulary to dataset elements, allowing users to be partially or fully abstracted from the representation of the data.

1 Introduction

The evolution of data environments towards the consumption of data from multiple data sources and the growth in the schema size, complexity, dynamicity and decentralisation (SCoDD) of data [4,7] increases the complexity of contemporary data management. The SCoDD trend emerges as a central data management concern in Big Data scenarios, where users and applications have a demand for more complete data, produced by independent data sources, under different semantic assumptions and contexts of use, which is the typical scenario for Semantic Web/Linked Data applications.

The evolution of databases in the direction of heterogeneous data environments strongly impacts the usability, semiotic and semantic assumptions behind existing data accessibility methods such as structured queries, keyword-based search and visual query systems. With schema-less databases containing potentially millions of dynamically changing attributes, it becomes unfeasible for some users to become aware of the 'schema' or vocabulary in order to query the database. At this scale, the effort in understanding the schema in order to build a structured query can become prohibitive.

This Semantic Web Challenge focuses on catalyzing the development and evaluation of methods and tools which can help data consumers to query structured data without the understanding of the representation behind the data.

© Springer International Publishing Switzerland 2015
F. Gandon et al. (Eds.): SemWebEval 2015, CCIS 548, pp. 191–198, 2015.
DOI: 10.1007/978-3-319-25518-7_16

At the center of this discussion is the semantic gap between users and databases, which becomes more central as the scale and complexity of the data grows. Addressing this gap is a fundamental part of the Semantic Web vision.

Schema-agnostic query mechanisms aim at allowing users to be abstracted from the representation of the data, supporting the automatic matching between queries and databases [1,2,5]. This challenge aims at emphasizing the role of schema-agnosticism as a key requirement for contemporary database management, by providing a test collection for evaluating flexible query and search systems over structured data in terms of their level of *schema-agnosticism* (i.e. their ability to map a query issued with the users' terminology and structure, mapping it to the dataset vocabulary). The challenge is instantiated in the context of Semantic Web datasets.

2   Schema-Agnostic Queries

Schema-agnostic queries can be defined as query approaches over structured databases which allow users satisfying complex information needs without the understanding of the representation (schema) of the database. Similarly, [5] defines it as "search approaches, which do not require users to know the schema underlying the data". Approaches such as keyword-based search over databases allow users to query databases without employing structured queries. However, as discussed by [5]: "From these points, users however have to do further navigation and exploration to address complex information needs. Unlike keyword search used on the Web, which focuses on simple needs, the keyword search elaborated here is used to obtain more complex results. Instead of a single set of resources, the goal is to compute complex sets of resources and their relations".

The development of approaches to support natural language interfaces (NLI) over databases have aimed towards the goal of schema-agnostic queries. Complementarily, some approaches based on keyword search have targeted keyword-based queries which express more complex information needs. Other approaches have explored the construction of structured queries over databases where schema constraints can be relaxed. All these approaches (natural language, keyword-based search and structured queries) have targeted different degrees of sophistication in addressing the problem of supporting a flexible semantic matching between queries and data, which vary from the completely absence of the semantic concern to more principled semantic models.

While the demand for schema-agnosticism has been an implicit requirement across semantic search and natural language query systems over structured data, it is not sufficiently individuated as a concept and as a necessary requirement for contemporary database management systems. Recent works have started to define and model the semantic aspects involved on schema-agnostic queries [1,2,5].

3   Challenge Description

The challenge aims at providing an evaluation test collection for schema-agnostic query mechanisms, focusing on Semantic Web scenarios. The large-schema and semantically heterogeneous nature of Semantic Web datasets brings schema-agnosticism as a fundamental data management concern for this community.

The test collection supports the quantitative and qualitative evaluation of degree of schema-agnosticism of different approaches. Since addressing schema-agnostic queries is dependent on semantic approaches which need to cope with different types of semantic matching between query and dataset, the test collection explores different categories of semantic phenomena involved in the challenge of matching schema-agnostic queries. Each query is categorized according to the semantic mapping types. This categorization supports a fine-grained qualitative and quantitative interpretation of the evaluation results.

4   Evaluation Description

The challenge provides a gold standard with the correct answers for each *schema-agnostic query*. Queries are issued over DBpedia 3.10. A training dataset consisting of 30 queries is be made available for the participants. In order to participate in the challenge, each system submitted the results in the format proposed by the challenge. The organizers then automatically calculated *precision, recall, mean reciprocal rank* for each query and the associated averages. Participants are recommended to submit their *query execution time, dataset semantic enrichment time*, and *user-interaction and disambiguation effort*.

The challenge consists of addressing a set of 103 schema-agnostic queries over DBpedia 2014[1] and associated YAGO classes[2]. The training and test sets are available at[3].

The schema-agnostic queries were derived from the natural languages present at the Question Answering over Linked Data (QALD-4) test collection [6]. These natural language questions were manually converted to schema-agnostic queries, preserving its vocabulary and using a consistent set of conversion guidelines.

Two categories of schema-agnostic queries (tasks) are available: *schema-agnostic SPARQL query* and *schema-agnostic keyword query*. Evaluation systems can compete in one or in both categories.

4.1   Schema-Agnostic SPARQL Query

Consists of schema-agnostic queries following the syntax of the SPARQL standard without namespace prefixes. The syntax and semantics of operators are maintained, while different terminologies are used.

Example I:

```
SELECT ?y {
  BillClinton hasDaughter ?x .
  ?x marriedTo ?y .
}
```

---

[1] http://wiki.dbpedia.org/Downloads2014.

[2] http://data.dws.informatik.uni-mannheim.de/dbpedia/2014/links/yago_types.nt.bz
  2.

[3] https://sites.google.com/site/eswcsaq2015/resources.

which maps to the following SPARQL query in the dataset vocabulary:

```
PREFIX : <http://dbpedia.org/resource/>
PREFIX dbpedia2: <http://dbpedia.org/property/>
PREFIX dbpedia: <http://dbpedia.org/ontology/>
PREFIX skos: <http://www.w3.org/2004/02/skos/core#>
PREFIX dbo: <http://dbpedia.org/ontology/>

SELECT   ?y {
 :Bill_Clinton dbpedia:child ?x .
 ?x dbpedia2:spouse ?y .
 }
```

Example II:

```
SELECT   ?x {
         ?x isA book .
         ?x by William_Goldman .
         ?x has_pages ?p .
         FILTER (?p > 300) .
 }
```

which maps to the following SPARQL query in the dataset vocabulary:

```
PREFIX rdf: <http://www.w3.org/1999/02/22-rdf-syntax-ns#>
PREFIX : <http://dbpedia.org/resource/>
PREFIX dbpedia2: <http://dbpedia.org/property/>
PREFIX dbpedia: <http://dbpedia.org/ontology/>
SELECT ?x {
         ?x rdf:type dbpedia:Book .
         ?x dbpedia2:author :William_Goldman .
         ?x dbpedia:numberOfPages ?p .
                 FILTER(?p > 300) .
}
```

4.2   Schema-Agnostic Keyword Query

Consists of schema-agnostic queries using keyword queries. In this case the syntax and semantics of operators are different from the SPARQL syntax.

Example I: "Bill Clinton daughter married to"

Example II: "Books by William Goldman with more than 300 pages"

4.3   Returned Result

In order to participate in the challenge, systems submitted the results in the format proposed by the challenge. For queries which return a list of URIs (uri1, uri2) or values:

```
<dataset id="saq-2015_test">
<query id="1">
<answers>
<answer> uri1 </answer>
<answer> uri2 </answer>
</answers>
</query>

<query id="2">
<answers>
<answer> value </answer>
</answers>
</query>

</dataset>
```

For queries of the type YES/NO:

```
<dataset id="saq-2015_test">
<query id="1">
<answers>
<answer> true </answer>
</answers>
</query>
</dataset>
```

Teams had 24 h after receiving the test query set to return their results.

5   Schema-Agnostic Mappings

In the test set, each schema-agnostic query contains a classification of the query-data alignments. For example:

```
<query id="14">
<keyword_query lang="en">
<![CDATA[ships called after Benjamin Franklin]]>
</keyword_query>
<schema_agnostic_query>
<![CDATA[
SELECT DISTINCT ?uri
WHERE {
        ?uri type Ship .
        ?uri calledAfter Benjamin_Franklin .
}
]]>
```

```
</schema_agnostic_query>
<resolved_query><![CDATA[
PREFIX res: <http://dbpedia.org/resource/>
PREFIX dbp: <http://dbpedia.org/property/>
SELECT DISTINCT ?uri
WHERE {
        ?uri dbp:shipNamesake res:Benjamin_Franklin.
}
]]>
</resolved_query>
<alignments>
<alignment> Ship (c o) -> shipNamesake (p) | substring </alignment>
<alignment> Benjamin_Franklin (i o) -> Benjamin_Franklin (i o) | substring </alignment>
<alignment> calledAfter (p) -> shipNamesake (p) | related </alignment>
<op> select -> select </op>
</alignments>
<answers>
<answer>http://dbpedia.org/resource/HMS_Canopus_(1798)</answer>
<answer>http://dbpedia.org/resource/USS_Franklin_(1815)</answer>
<answer>http://dbpedia.org/resource/USS_Franklin_(1795)</answer>
<answer>http://dbpedia.org/resource/Ben_Franklin_(PX-15)</answer>
</answers>
</query>
```

In the alignment below, the schema-agnostic query term 'calledAfter' is associated with a predicate '(p)' data type, mapping to the predicate 'shipNamesake' in the dataset, and that the type of relationship between two terms are described as *semantically related*.

```
<alignment> calledAfter (p) -> shipNamesake (p) | related </alignment>
```

Alignments are categorized according to 6 categories:

- **semantically related:** If a query term and its associated database entity are *semantically related*. Example: *languageOf* in the query maps to *spokenIn* in the dataset.
- **semantically similar:** If a query term and its associated database entity are *semantically similar*, i.e. it follows a taxonomic relation. Example: *wifeOf* in the query maps to *spouseOf* in the dataset.
- **synonym:** If a query term and its associated database entity are *synonyms*. Example: *startDate* in the query maps to *beginDate* in the dataset.
- **string similar:** If a query term has a *string similarity* relationship to its associated database entity. Example: *startDate* in the query maps to *beginDate* in the dataset.
- **substring:** If a query term is a *substring* of its associated database entity or vice-versa. Example: *wifeOf* in the query maps to *wife* in the dataset.
- **functional content:** Consists on the mapping of *function words* (e.g. prepositions) in the query to *other function words* or *content words* in the dataset entity. Example: *in* in the query maps to *location* in the dataset.
- **abbreviation:** If a query term is an *abbreviation* of its associated database entity or vice-versa. Example: *extinct* in the query maps to *'EX'* in the dataset.

Other examples of alignments (including compositions of different categories) include:

```
<alignment> languageOf (p) -> spokenIn (p) | related </alignment>
<alignment> writtenBy (p) -> author (p) | substring, related </alignment>
<alignment> in (p) -> location (p) | functional_content </alignment>
<alignment> in (p) -> isPartOf (p) | functional_content </alignment>
<alignment> FemaleFirstName (c o) -> gender (p) | substring, related </alignment>
<alignment> state (p) -> locatedInArea (p) | related </alignment>
<alignment> extinct (p) -> conservationStatus (p) | related </alignment>
<alignment> extinct (p) -> 'EX' (v o) | substring, abbreviation </alignment>
<alignment> startAt (p) -> sourceCountry (p) | substring, synonym </alignment>
<alignment> U.S._State (c o) -> StatesOfTheUnitedStates (c o) | string_similar </alignment>
<alignment> calledAfter (p) -> shipNamesake (p) | related </alignment>
<alignment> wifeOf (p) -> spouse (p) | substring, similar </alignment>
<alignment> constructionDate (p) -> beginningDate (p) | substring, related </alignment>
```

Alignment terms are classified according to their data model types, with regard to the position within the triple (*subject* (s), *predicate* (p), *object* (o)) and entity type (*instance* (i), *class* (c), *property* (p), *value* (v)).

The alignment classifications are a simplification of the schema-agnostic alignments described in [1].

6   Results

Just one system competed officially in the SAQ-2015 Semantic Web Challenge: the UMBC_Ebiquity-SFQ system from the University of Maryland Baltimore County (Syed et al. [3]).

The results are described in Table 1:

Table 1. Evaluation of the participating system for the SAQ-2015 challenge.

System	Avg. precision	Avg. recall	Avg. f1-measure	% of answered queries
UMBC_Equity-SFQ	0.33	0.36	0.31	0.44

7   Summary

The ability to abstract users from the specifics of the representation of the data, including its vocabulary and structural relations is a fundamental functionality for large-scale and heterogeneous data. The Schema-agnostic Queries Semantic Web Challenge (SAQ-2015) aims at providing a test collection for supporting the development of schema-agnostic query mechanisms, i.e. query approaches which supports automatically crossing the semantic gap between users and the data. The test collection provides a categorized set of schema-agnostic queries, covering a range of different alignments from string variations to different types of semantic relations. The performance of the participating system indicates that state-of-the-art systems are able to provide an initial solution for the problem. However, the initial results show that schema-agnostic queries are still a challenging problem and that there is space for major improvements.

References

1. Freitas, A., Da Silva, J.C.P., Curry, E.: On the semantic mapping of schema-agnostic queries: a preliminary study. In: 13th International Semantic Web Conference (ISWC) Workshop of the Natural Language Interfaces for the Web of Data (NLIWoD), Rival del Garda (2014)
2. Bischof, S., Krötzsch, M., Polleres, A., Rudolph, S.: Schema-agnostic query rewriting in SPARQL 1.1. In: Mika, P., et al. (eds.) ISWC 2014, Part I. LNCS, vol. 8796, pp. 584–600. Springer, Heidelberg (2014)
3. Syed, Z.: UMBC_Ebiquty-SFQ: schema free querying system. In: 12th Extended Semantic Web Conference on SAQ-2015 Semantic Web Challenge (ESWC) (2015)
4. Helland, P.: If you have too much data, then 'good enough' is good enough. Commun. ACM 54(6), 40–47 (2011)
5. Tran, T., Mathäß, T., Haase, P.: Usability of keyword-driven schema-agnostic search. In: Aroyo, L., Antoniou, G., Hyvönen, E., ten Teije, A., Stuckenschmidt, H., Cabral, L., Tudorache, T. (eds.) ESWC 2010, Part II. LNCS, vol. 6089, pp. 349–364. Springer, Heidelberg (2010)
6. Unger, C., et al.: Question answering over linked data (QALD-4). In: Proceedings of CLEF (2014)
7. Brodie, M.L., Liu, J.T.: The power and limits of relational technology in the age of information ecosystems. In: Keynote, On The Move Federated Conferences, Heraklion, Greece, 25–29 October 2010

UMBC_Ebiquity-SFQ: Schema Free Querying System

Zareen Syed[1(✉)], Lushan Han[1], Muhammad Rahman[1], Tim Finin[1],
James Kukla[2], and Jeehye Yun[2]

[1] University of Maryland Baltimore County, 1000 Hilltop Circle,
Baltimore, MD 21250, USA
{zsyed,lushan1,mrahman1}@umbc.edu, finin@cs.umbc.edu
[2] RedShred, 5520 Research Park Drive Suite 100, Baltimore, MD 21228, USA
{jkukla,jyun}@redshred.net

Abstract. Users need better ways to explore large complex linked data resources. Using SPARQL requires not only mastering its syntax and semantics but also understanding the RDF data model, the ontology and URIs for entities of interest. Natural language question answering systems solve the problem, but these are still subjects of research. The Schema agnostic SPARQL queries task defined in SAQ-2015 challenge consists of schema-agnostic queries following the syntax of the SPARQL standard, where the syntax and semantics of operators are maintained, while users are free to choose words, phrases and entity names irrespective of the underlying schema or ontology. This combination of query skeleton with keywords helps to remove some of the ambiguity. We describe our framework for handling schema agnostic or schema free queries and discuss enhancements to handle the SAQ-2015 challenge queries. The key contributions are the robust methods that combine statistical association and semantic similarity to map user terms to the most appropriate classes and properties used in the underlying ontology and type inference for user input concepts based on concept linking.

Keywords: Information storage and retrieval · User interfaces · Semantic web

1 Introduction

Developing interfaces to enable casual, non-expert users to query complex structured data has been the subject of much research over the past forty years. Since such interfaces allow users to freely query data without understanding its schema, knowing how to refer to objects, or mastering the appropriate formal query language, we call them as schema-free or schema-agnostic query interfaces. Schema-agnostic query interface systems address a fundamental problem in NLP, Database and AI: bridging the gap between a user's conceptual model of the world and the machine's representation.

Schema-agnostic query interface systems are challenged by three hard problems. First, we still lack practical interfaces. Unrestricted natural language interfaces (NLIs) are easy for people to use but hard for machines to process accurately. Today's NLP

© Springer International Publishing Switzerland 2015
F. Gandon et al. (Eds): SemWebEval 2015, CCIS 548, pp. 199–208, 2015.
DOI: 10.1007/978-3-319-25518-7_17

technology is still not reliable enough to extract the relational structure from natural language questions with high accuracy. Keyword-based query interfaces, on the other hand, are easy to use but have limited expressiveness and still suffer from the ambiguity inherent in the natural language terms used as keywords.

A second problem is that people have many different ways to express the same meaning, which can result in vocabulary and structure mismatches between the user's query and the machine's representation. This is often referred to as the semantic heterogeneity problem. Today we still heavily rely on ad hoc and labor-intensive approaches to deal with the semantic heterogeneity problem.

Third, the Web has seen increasing amounts of open-domain semantic data with heterogeneous or unknown schemas. Processing such data presents challenges to traditional NLI systems, which typically require well-defined schemas.

In this paper, we present our system to address these problems. We introduce a new schema-free query interface that we call the SFQ interface, in which the user explicitly specifies the relational structure of the query as a graphical "skeleton" and annotates it with freely chosen words, phrases and entity names. By using SFQ interface, we work around the unreliable step of extracting complete relations from natural language queries.

One motivation for our work is an enhancement to a system we are developing with RedShred, LLC that will help people identify and analyze business documents that include RFPs, RFQ, calls for proposals, BAAs, solicitations and similar business documents. Our prototype uses document analysis, information retrieval, NLP information extraction and question answering techniques and is largely domain independent. It understands general RFP-related concepts (e.g., proposal deadlines, duration, deliverables, security requirements, points of contacts, etc.) and can extract and organize information to help someone quickly evaluate opportunities. However, it does not have built-in knowledge of any particular domain, such as software development or material science, and is thus unable to address potentially critical characteristics involving them. For RFPs about software development, for example, we may need to know if the work requires a particular programming language (e.g., Java), is targeted for a given system or architecture (e.g., iOS), or has special requirements (e.g., 3DES encryption).

Given the breadth and variety of domains of interest, manually developing and maintaining custom ontologies, language models and systems for each is not viable. We are currently working on a system for automatic discovery of slots and fillers from RFP documents similar to infoboxes in Wikipedia and that are linked to DBpedia ontology. We plan to build on the results of this work to be able to provide schema free query support over extracted slots and fillers from RFP documents.

Our framework makes three main contributions. It uses robust methods that combine statistical association and semantic similarity to map user terms to the most appropriate classes and properties used in the underlying ontology. Second, it uses a novel type inference approach based on concept linking for predicting classes for subjects and objects in the query. Third, it implements a general property mapping algorithm based on concept linking and semantic text similarity.

The remainder of the paper proceeds as follows. Section two describes our word similarity model. Sections three and four give an overview of our concept level association model trained on DBpedia and our query mapping approach. Sections five and six describe our enhancements to support the challenge queries and generating final SPARQL queries and in section seven we present the conclusions.

2 Semantic Similarity Component

We need to compute semantic similarity between concepts in the form of noun phrases, such as City and Soccer Club, and between relations in the form of short phrases, such as crosses and birth date. A common approach is using distributional similarity [5], which is a statistical approach that uses a term's collective context information drawn from a large text corpus to represent the meaning of the term. Distributional similarity is usually applied to words but it can be generalized to phrases [7]. However, the large number of potential input phrases precludes pre-computing and storing distributional similarity data and computing it dynamically as needed would take too long. Thus, we assume that the semantic of a phrase is compositional on its component words and we apply an algorithm to compute semantic similarity between two phrases using word similarity.

We pair words from two phrases in a way such that it maximizes the sum of word similarities of the resulting word-pairs, similar to [9]. The maximized sum of word similarities is further normalized by the number of word-pairs. Computing semantic similarity between noun phrases requires additional work. Before running algorithm on two noun phrases, we compute the semantic similarity of their head nouns. If it exceeds an experimentally determined threshold we run the algorithm and if not, the phrases have similarity of zero. Thus we know that dog house is not similar to house dog.

Our word similarity measure is based on distributional similarity and latent semantic analysis, which is further enhanced using human crafted information from WordNet. Our distributional similarity approach, based on [11], yields a correctness of 92 % on TOEFL synonym test, which is the best performance to date. By using a simple context of bag of words, the similarity between words even with different parts of speech can also be computed.

Although distributional similarity has an advantage that it can compute similarity between words that are not strictly synonyms, the human judgments of synonymy found in WordNet are more reliable. Therefore, we give higher similarity to word pairs which are in the same WordNet synset or one of which is a near hypernym of the other by adding 0.5 and 0.2 to their distributional similarities, respectively. We also boost similarity between a word and its derivationally related forms by increasing their distributional similarity by 0.3. We do so because a word can often represent the same relation as its derivationally related forms in our context. As examples, "writer" work as the almost same relation to "write" and so does "produce" to "product" because "writer" means the subject that writes and "product" means the thing being produced.

In our case, the lexical categories of words are not important and only their semantics matters. However, the value of distributional similarity of words is significantly lowered if they are not in the same lexical category. To counteract this drawback, we put words into the same lexical category using their derivational forms and compute distributional similarity between their aligned forms. Then we compare this value with their original similarity and use the larger one as their similarity.

The DBpedia ontology is a shallow ontology and many subclasses of Person class are not included. Consequently, it is possible that some person subtypes appearing in the user query have no similarity to any existing person class in the DBpedia ontology. To address this problem, we enforce a lower bound similarity, 0.25, between person and any person subtype so that these subtypes can at least be mapped to the DBpedia Person class.

We use WordNet to find whether a concept in the semantic graph is a person subtype or not. An ideal semantic similarity measure in our scenario should give high similarity to the terms that can work as synonymous substitution and low similarity to those not. The order of terms with high similarity score is not critical because statistical association can discriminate them and find the most reasonable one. Our implementation has been developed using this strategy. Semantic similarity is an active research field in natural language processing community and has been improved steadily over the years [4, 8]. This component can be enhanced further to benefit from recent progress in this field.

3 Concept Level Association Knowledge Model (CAK Model)

We use fully automatic approaches to obtain necessary domain knowledge for interpreting SFQs. Instead of a manually maintained lexicon, we employ a computational semantic similarity measure for the purpose of locating candidate ontology terms for user input terms. Semantic similarity measures enable our system to have a broader linguistic coverage than that offered by synonym expansion by recognizing non-synonymous terms that have very similar meaning. For example, the properties author of and college are good candidates for the user terms "wrote" and "graduated from", respectively. Semantic similarity measures can be learned from a domain-dependent large corpus.

We know birds can fly but trees cannot and that a database table is not kitchen table. Such knowledge is essential for human language understanding. We refer to this as Concept level Association Knowledge (CAK). Domain and range definitions for properties in ontologies, argument constraint definitions of predicates in logic systems and schemata in databases all belong to this knowledge. However, manually defining this knowledge for broad or open domains is a tedious task at best. We therefore, learn Concept-level Association Knowledge statistically from instance data (the "ABOX" of RDF triples) and compute degree of associations between concepts based on co-occurrences. We count co-occurrences between schema terms indirectly from co-occurrences between entities because entities are associated with types. We then apply a statistical measure, Pointwise Mutual Information (PMI) [1, 2], to compute degree of associations between classes and properties and between two classes. The detailed approach is available in [3].

We used the learned CAK and semantic similarity measures for mapping a user query to a corresponding SPARQL query which we discuss in the next section.

4 Query Interpretation

In this section, we present the main steps in mapping terms in a SFQ to DBpedia ontology terms. The approach focuses on vocabulary or schema mapping, which is done without involving entities.

For each SFQ concept or relation, we generate a list of the k most semantically similar candidate ontology classes or properties. In the example in Fig. 1, candidate lists are generated for the five user terms in the SFQ, which asks Which author wrote the book Tom Sawyer and where was he born?. Candidate terms are ranked by their similarity scores, which are displayed to the right of the terms.

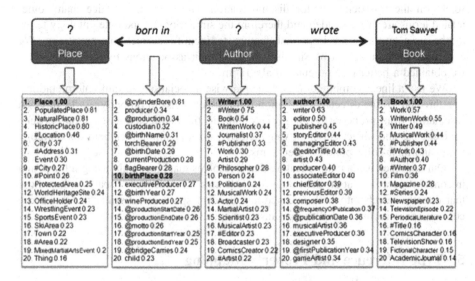

Fig. 1. A ranked list of candidate ontology terms

Each combination of ontology terms, with one term coming from each candidate list, is a potential query interpretation, but some are reasonable and others not. Disambiguation here means choosing the most reasonable interpretations from a set of candidates. An intuitive measure of reasonableness for an interpretation is the degree to which its ontology terms associate in the way that their corresponding user terms connect in the SFQ.

For example, since "Place" is connected by "born in" in Fig. 1, their corresponding ontology terms can be expected to have good association. Therefore, the combination of Place and birthPlace makes much more sense than that of Place and @cylinderBore because CAK tells us that a strong association holds between Place and birthPlace but not @cylinderBore.

As you can see, we use the degree of association from CAK to measure reasonableness. As another example, CAK data shows that both the combinations of Writer + writer and Writer + author are reasonable interpretations of the SFQ connection

"Author → wrote". However, since only author not writer has a strong association with the class Book, the combination of Writer, author and Book produces a much better interpretation than that of Writer, writer and Book for the joint SFQ connection "Author → wrote → Book".

We select two types of connections in a SFQ for computing the overall association of an interpretation. They are the connections between concepts and their relations (e.g., "Author" and "wrote") and the connections between direct connected concepts (e.g., "Author" and "Book"). We exclude indirect connections (e.g., between "Book" and "born in" or between "Book" and "Place") because they do not necessarily entail good associations.

If candidate ontology terms contained all the substitutable terms, we could rely solely on their associations for disambiguation. However, in practice many other related terms are also included and therefore the similarity of candidate ontology terms to the user terms is an important feature to identify correct interpretations. We experimentally found that by simply weighting their associations by their similarities we obtained a better disambiguation algorithm.

We use a linear combination of three pairwise associations to rank interpretations. The three are (i) the directed association from subject class to property (ii) the directed association from property to object class and (iii) the undirected association between subject class and object class, all weighted by semantic similarities between ontology terms and their corresponding user terms.

Our approach has a unique feature that it resolves mappings only using information in concept space, i.e., at the schema level. This makes it much more scalable than those that directly search into both instance and concept space for possible matches since concept space is much smaller than instance space.

5   Type Inference and Property Mapping

The SFQ system requires users to provide types or classes for subjects and objects in the query triples, however, this information is not available in many challenge queries. To bridge the gap we added a module for type inference for the challenge queries. The type inference is based on linking subject and object in the triple to Wikipedia concepts and retrieving the associated DBpedia ontology classes.

We use entity linking approach based on Wikitology [12] to link any named entities to concepts in Wikitology. We further enhanced Wikitology's entity linking system with gazetteers of named entities. For linking other topical concepts and keywords we used Wikipedia Miner service [10]. Wikipedia Miner also links named entities, however when we tested with few examples we found Wikitology's named entity linking relatively more accurate and therefore we used Wikitology for named entity linking and Wikipedia Miner for linking other types of concepts. For Wikipedia Miner we used a probability threshold of 0.4. We tested with a lower threshold to improve recall but observed decrease in accuracy. For example, for the question "Which river does the Brooklyn Bridge cross?", the service predicted a link for "cross" to "http://en.wikipedia.org/wiki/Cross" which was not relevant. A threshold of 0.4 worked much better.

After linking the subject and object to concepts in Wikipedia we retrieve the associated DBpedia ontology classes. For named entities we detect the main type of named entity i.e. Person, Place or Organization based on associated DBpedia classes or mapped Schema.org classes. For example, for "Prince William, Duke of Cambridge" the associated type in DBpedia ontology is "BritishRoyalty" which is a subclass of "Royalty" which in turn is a subclass of "Person". We restricted to detecting main named entity types instead of fine-grained entity types as many entities in Wikipedia do not have a fine grained entity type associated with them. For other topical concepts we selected the most generalized class below the "Thing" class. For cases where the property values are literals, we fetch the matching property from DBpedia ontology and fetch the xsd type for the range of the property and map all numeric types such as integer, float etc. to "Number" type which is accepted by the SFQ system.

Table 1. Type inference for challenge queries

Triples in Query	Triples input to SFQ system (after type inference)
?uri type Person. ?uri dbo:birthPlace res:Vienna. ?uri dbo:deathPlace res:Berlin.	?uri/**Person**, bornIn, Vienna/**Place** ?uri/**Person**, diedIn, Berlin/**Place**
?uri locatedOn Earth. ?uri type Mountain. ?uri height ?height.	?uri/**Mountain**, locatedOn, Earth/**CelestialBody** ?uri/**Mountain**, height, ?height/**Number**
Jane_Fonda marriedTo ?uri.	Jane_Fonda/**Person spouse** ?uri.

In addition to type inference we also try to map the user input property to DBpedia property based on linked concept. After linking the subject or the object to Wikipedia, we retrieve all associated DBpedia properties for that concept and compute similarity with the property input by the user based on the semantic text similarity module. For higher accuracy we only consider matching the property if the similarity score is at least 0.7. Table 1 shows examples of type inference and property mapping. The first example shows type inference for Vienna and Berlin to "Place". The second example shows numeric type inference of height to "Number". The third example shows property mapping from "marriedTo" to "spouse" using concept linking to *Jane_Fonda* and then retrieving the most similar property to the given property using semantic similarity.

6   SPARQL Query Generation and Selection

After user terms are disambiguated and mapped to appropriate ontology terms, translating a SFQ to SPARQL is straightforward. Figure 2 shows a sample SPARQL query produced by the system. Classes are used to type the instances, such as ?x a dbo:Writer, and properties used to connect instances as in ?0 dbo:author ?x. The bif:contains property is a built-in text search function which find literals containing specified text.

The named entities in the SFQ can often be disambiguated by the constraints in the SPARQL query. In this example, Tom Sawyer has two constraints: it is in the label of some book and is written by some writer. For the challenge queries there were cases of aggregates, filtering and ordering. For such queries we explicitly appended the respective clauses to the SPARQL produced by the system before querying DBpedia.

```
PREFIX dbo:<http://dbpedia.org/ontology/>
SELECT DISTINCT ?x, ?y WHERE {
    ?0 a dbo:Book .
    ?0 rdfs:label ?label0 .
    ?label0 bif:contains '"Tom Sawyer"' .
    ?x a dbo:Writer .
    ?y a dbo:Place .
    {?0 dbo:author ?x} .
    {?x dbo:birthPlace ?y} .
}
```

Fig. 2. SPARQL query generated by the system

Our Schema Free Querying system generates a ranked list of SPARQL queries. Some of the queries may not return results as the corresponding DBpedia instance may not have a property with the same name. For example, "mayor" is a valid property in DBpedia but for the case of Berlin, the property used is "leader". In such cases the top ranked query may not return any results. Therefore, we iterate over ranked queries until we find a query that returns results from DBpedia.

7 System II

Since our original SFQ system relies on DBpedia ontology classes and properties and does not take entities into account, we created an independent parallel system to support entity references in SPARQL query. The system is based on entity linking and semantic similarity. For any concepts mentioned in the query, we try to link it to DBpedia using Wikitology and update the reference to the linked concept in DBpedia. Furthermore, we retrieve all properties associated with the linked concept and select the property which has the highest semantic similarity with the user input property.

8 Evaluation and Discussion

For evaluation we combined the output of both systems i.e. SFQ System and System II. Our system was the only official system to participate in the SAQ-2015 challenge. The evaluation dataset for the task had 103 queries in total. Our combined system was able

Table 2. Evaluation results of independent and combined systems for SAQ-2015 challenge

	SFQ System	System II	SFQ System + System II
Avg. precision	0.27	0.22	0.33
Avg. recall	0.27	0.24	0.36
Avg. f1-measure	0.24	0.21	0.31
# of queries answered	34	30	45
% of queries answered	0.33	0.29	0.44

to generate results for 45 queries. Table 2 presents the evaluation results for two systems independently and in combination.

We performed a detailed analysis of the incorrect queries produced by the combined system based on the types of errors. We categorized the errors into different categories as shown in Table 3. In the case of "Exception" error, the SFQ System threw an exception due to not finding any types for the subject and object which are a necessary pre-requisite for the SFQ System. This was mainly due to the fact that our type prediction system was not able to predict any types for the given subject or object. We refer to "Additional Triples" as a case where the query generated by our system had more triples compared to the gold standard and we refer to the opposite case as "Fewer Triples". "Mismatch Entity" is the case where our system linked to a wrong entity and similarity "Mismatch Property" is the case where our property prediction is wrong. Some of the queries had multiple types of errors. To improve the performance of our system we plan to focus on correcting these types of errors. We can also introduce some post processing heuristics to selectively remove additional triples in case the query does not return any results. Our model for SFQ System was trained on an older version of DBpedia i.e. version 3.6 whereas the test queries were based on DBpedia version 3.10. We believe that training the SFQ System on the newer DBpedia version would have improved the performance of the system.

Table 3. Different types of errors in queries produced by the combined system

Error Type	# of Queries
Exception	15
Additional Triples	4
Fewer Triples	2
Mismatch Entity	5
Mismatch Property	14
Mismatch Entity, Extra Triple	6
Mismatch Property, Extra Triple	3
Mismatch Entity, Mismatch Property	3
Mismatch Entity, Mismatch Property, Extra Triple	6
Total incorrect queries	**58**

9 Conclusions

The schema-free structured query approach allows people to query the DBpedia dataset without mastering SPARQL or acquiring detailed knowledge of the classes, properties and individuals in the underlying ontologies and the URIs that denote them. Our system uses statistical data about lexical semantics and RDF datasets to generate plausible SPARQL queries that are semantically close to schema-free queries. We described our framework for handling schema agnostic or schema free queries and discussed enhancements to handle SAQ-2015 challenge queries. The key contributions of our approach are the robust methods that combine statistical association and semantic similarity to map user terms to the most appropriate classes and properties used in the underlying ontology and type inference for user input concepts based on concept linking.

References

1. Cimiano, P., Haase, P., Heizmann, J.: Porting natural language interfaces between domains: an experimental user study with the ORAKEL system. In: Proceedings of 12th International Conference on Intelligent User Interfaces, pp. 180–189. ACM (2007)
2. Dredze, M., McNamee, P., Rao, D., Gerber, A., Finin, T.: Entity disambiguation for knowledge base population. In: Proceedings of the 23rd International Conference on Computational Linguistics, August 2010
3. Han, L., Finin, T., Joshi, A.: Schema-free structured querying of DBpedia data. In: Proceedings of the 21st ACM International Conference on Information and Knowledge Management, pp. 2090–2093. ACM (2012)
4. Han, L., Finin, T., McNamee, P., Joshi, A., Yesha, Y.: Improving word similarity by augmenting pmi with estimates of word polysemy. IEEE Trans. Knowl. Data Eng. IEEE Comput. Soc. 25(6), 1307–1322 (2013)
5. Harris, Z.S.: Mathematical Structures of Language. Wiley, New York (1968)
6. Kashyap, A., Han, L., Yus, R., Sleeman, J., Satyapanich, T., Gandhi, S., Finin, T.: Meerkat mafia: multilingual and cross-level semantic textual similarity systems In: Proceedings of the 8th International Workshop on Semantic Evaluation, August 2014
7. Lin, D., Pantel, P.: Discovery of inference rules for question answering. Natural Lang. Eng. 7(4), 343–360 (2001)
8. Lin, D.: Automatic retrieval and clustering of similar words. In: Proceedings of the 17th International Conference on Computational Linguistics, pp. 768–774, Montreal (1998)
9. Mihalcea, R., Corley, C., Strapparava, C.: Corpus-based and knowledge-based measures of text semantic similarity. In: Proceedings of the 21st National Conference on Artificial Intelligence, pp. 775–780 (2006)
10. Milne, D., Witten, I. H.: Learning to link with wikipedia. In: Proceedings of the 17th ACM Conference on Information and Knowledge Management, pp. 509–518. ACM (2008)
11. Rapp, R.: Word sense discovery based on sense descriptor dissimilarity. In: Proceedings of the 9th Machine Translation Summit, pp. 315–322 (2003)
12. Syed, Z., Finin, T.: Creating and exploiting a hybrid knowledge base for linked data. In: Filipe, J., Fred, A., Sharp, B. (eds.) ICAART 2010. CCIS, vol. 129, pp. 3–21. Springer, Heidelberg (2011)

Concept-Level Sentiment Analysis Challenge (CLSA2015)

ESWC 15 Challenge on Concept-Level
Sentiment Analysis

Diego Reforgiato Recupero[(✉)], Mauro Dragoni, and Valentina Presutti

Catania, Italy
diego.reforgiato@istc.cnr.it

Abstract. A consequence of the massive use of social networks, blogs, wikis, etc., is the change of users' behaviour on, and their interaction with, the Web: opinions, emotions and sentiments are now expressed differently from the past. Lexical understanding of text is not anymore enough to detect sentiment polarities. Semantics became key for sentiment detection. This generates potential business opportunities, especially within the marketing area, and key stakeholders need to catch up with the latest technology if they want to be compelling in the market. Therefore, understanding the opinions and its peculiarities from a written text involves a deep understanding of natural language text and the semantics behind it. Recently, it has been proved that the use of semantics improves the accuracy of existing sentiment analysis systems, which are mainly based on pure machine learning or other statistical approaches. The second Edition of the Concept Level Sentiment Analysis challenge aims to provide a further stimulus in this direction by offering to researchers an event where they can learn and experiment on how to employ Semantic Web features within their sentiment analysis systems, aiming at reaching higher performance.

1 Introduction

As the Web rapidly evolves, Web users are evolving with it. In an era of social connectedness, people are becoming increasingly enthusiastic about interacting, sharing, and collaborating through social networks, online communities, blogs, Wikis, and other online collaborative media. In recent years, this collective intelligence has spread to many different areas, with particular focus on fields related to everyday life such as commerce, tourism, education, and health, causing the size of the Social Web to expand exponentially.

The opportunity to automatically interpret the opinions of the general public about social events, political movements, company strategies, marketing campaigns, and product preferences has raised growing interest within the scientific community [2,22], leading to many exciting open challenges, as well as in the business world, due to the remarkable benefits deriving from marketing prediction. The distillation of knowledge from such a large amount of unstructured information is an extremely difficult task, as the contents of today's Web are perfectly suitable for human consumption, but remain hardly accessible to machines.

© Springer International Publishing Switzerland 2015
F. Gandon et al. (Eds.): SemWebEval 2015, CCIS 548, pp. 211–222, 2015.
DOI: 10.1007/978-3-319-25518-7_18

Mining opinions and sentiments from natural language, involves a deep understanding of most of the explicit and implicit, regular and irregular, syntactical and semantic rules proper of a language [6,20]. Existing approaches mainly rely on parts of text in which opinions and sentiments are explicitly expressed such as polarity terms, affect words and their co-occurrence frequencies. However, opinions and sentiments are often conveyed implicitly through latent semantics, which make purely syntactical approaches ineffective. This issue offers a research opportunity and an exciting challenge to the Semantic Web community. In fact, concept-level sentiment analysis aims to go beyond a mere word-level analysis of text and provides novel approaches to opinion mining and sentiment analysis supporting a more efficient passage from (unstructured) textual information to (structured) machine-processable data, in potentially any domain.

Concept-level sentiment analysis focuses on a semantic analysis of text through the use of web ontologies, semantic resources, or semantic networks, allowing the identification of opinion data which would be very difficult with the use of pure natural language processing techniques. By relying on large semantic knowledge bases, concept-level sentiment analysis steps away from blind use of keywords and word co-occurrence count, but rather relies on the implicit features associated with natural language concepts. Unlike purely syntactical techniques, concept-based approaches are able to detect also sentiments that are expressed in a subtle manner [9], e.g., through the analysis of concepts that do not explicitly convey any emotion, but which are implicitly linked to other concepts that do so.

The Second Edition of the Concept-level sentiment analysis challenge[1] leveraged the success and experience of the first one and provided further stimulus and motivations for research in this direction. A visible effect of the 2014 edition of the challenge was the inclusion, for the first time in the SEMEVAL 2015 workshop, of the Aspect Based Sentiment Analysis as a task within the Sentiment Analysis track[2]. Thanks to the learned lessons, one important action that was taken in this edition of the challenge was the release, in the challenge web site[3], of the Python evaluation scripts. This allowed authors to download them and test their systems for checking compliance with input and output formats. The Second Edition of the challenge focused on further development of novel approaches for semantic sentiment analysis. Participants had to design a concept-level opinion-mining engine that exploited Linked Data and Semantic Web ontologies, such as DBPedia[4].

The authors of the competing systems showed how they employed semantics to obtain valuable information that would not be caught with traditional sentiment analysis methods. Accepted systems were based on natural language and statistical approaches with an embedded semantics module, in the core approach. As happened within the First Edition [19] of the challenge, a few systems merely based on syntax/word-count were excluded.

---

[1] http://2015.eswc-conferences.org/important-dates/call-CLSA.

[2] http://alt.qcri.org/semeval2015/task12/.

[3] https://github.com/diegoref/ESWC-CLSA.

[4] http://dbpedia.org.

The rest of the chapter is organised as follows. Section 2 includes related works on semantic sentiment analysis. Section 3 details the four tasks (three technical tasks plus one related to the most innovative approach) of this Second Edition of the challenge (in the previous edition tasks were five). This section also includes the description of the evaluation datasets, their annotation, and the evaluation measures computed for each task. Section 4 includes the competing systems whereas Sect. 5 shows the results of each of them for each addressed task. Finally, Sect. 6 concludes the paper with comments and experiences gained from this challenge and drafts tips, performed actions and plan for the next edition of the challenge call that we are going to propose.

2 Related Work

ESWC for the second time this year (2015) included a challenge call and a dedicated session within its program, and for the second time it hosted the Concept Level Sentiment Analysis challenge. A book [18] collects the results of all 2014 edition challenges, and as for the semantic sentiment analysis topic, the challenge was complemented by a workshop [10] held during the same conference.

Relevant events and challenges to the sentiment analysis domain are reported in [18][5], however for completeness, it is worth to list and update them here. SemEval (Semantic Evaluation) is an ongoing series of evaluations workshops of computational semantic analysis systems which evolved from the Senseval word sense evaluation series. Since 2007 the workshop covers the sentiment analysis topic. To reflect the importance of this problem in social media, the last edition, SemEval2015[6], includes four different tasks for semantic sentiment analysis: (i) implicit polarity of events, (ii) and (iii) about sentiment analysis on twitter, and (iv) the aspect-based sentiment analysis. We remark that SemEval introduced for the first time the aspect-based sentiment analysis task after it appeared in the first edition of the Concept-Level sentiment analysis challenge at ESWC2014.

An important reference site for semantic-based sentiment analysis is SenticNet[7], where a list of relevant events including workshops and challenges are reported. Among them it is worth mentioning the series of SENTIRE workshops[8] on opinion mining, and WISDOM events[9], which focus on analysing the effect of the crowds on opinionated text on the Web.

The Semantic Web challenge, a joint event of the International Semantic Web Conference, is not specific to sentiment analysis. Its call invites any type of semantic-based innovative application and evaluates them mainly on qualitative criteria. The 2014 edition of this challenge call included 30 systems to be evaluated[10]. Among them, *SHELDON: Semantic Holistic framEwork for LinkeD*

---

[5] Chapter on Concept Level Sentiment Analysis.

[6] http://alt.qcri.org/semeval2015/.

[7] http://sentic.net/.

[8] http://sentic.net/sentire/.

[9] http://sentic.net/wisdom/.

[10] http://challenge.semanticweb.org/2014/submissions/.

ONtology data, is relevant to our topic. It is a semantic framework that can be used and called over REST API for several purposes. One of the features of SHELDON allows to perform semantic sentiment analysis. In fact, it includes a Sentic Computing[11] method called Sentilo, [9], to detect holders and topic of opinion sentences. This method is built on top of FRED, a machine reader which uses a neo-Davidsonian assumption that events and situations are the primary entities for contextualising opinions. Sentilo is able to distinguish holders, main topics, and sub-topics of an opinion. A more recent extension of this work is [20], where:

– *OntoSentilo*, the defined ontology for opinion sentences was extended,
– a new lexical resource called *SentiloNet* enabling the evaluation of opinions expressed by means of events and situations was introduced,
– and a novel scoring algorithm for opinion sentences, which uses a combination of two lexical resources, SentiWordNet [1] and SenticNet [5], was developed.

Other approaches for concept-level sentiment analysis use affective knowledge bases such as ANEW [4], WordNet-Affect [21], and ISEAR [25]. ConceptNet [15] is used in [23], for the propagation of sentiment values in a two steps method that includes iterative regression and random walk with in-link normalisation to build a concept-level sentiment dictionary.

[16] presents a methodology to create a resource from automatically merging SenticNet and WordNet-Affect. Authors trained a classifier on the subset of SenticNet concepts present in WordNet-Affect and used several concept similarity measures as well as various psychological features available in ISEAR.

Authors in [12] extract from SentiWordNet the objective words and assess the sentimental relevance of such words and their associated sentiment sentences. A support vector machines classifier is adopted for the classification of sentiment data.

In [3] the authors survey existing works related to the development of an opinion mining corpus. Moreover the authors present Senti-TUT, an ongoing Italian project where a corpus for the investigation of irony within the political and social media domain is developed.

Another category of works use a mixture of knowledge-based and statistical methods. Work described in [24] consists of a hybrid approach that combines the throughput of lexical analysis with the flexibility of machine learning to cope with ambiguity and integrate the context of sentiment words.

Machine-learning is adopted in [11], where the authors developed a new approach for extracting product features and opinions from a collection of free-text customer reviews about a product or service.

Recently, solutions based on the use of information retrieval strategies for building sentiment analysis systems have been proposed [7]. The authors presented also a system using fuzzy logic for representing uncertainty associated with each word and its different polarity, related to different domains [8].

---

[11] http://sentic.net/sentics/.

3   Tasks, Datasets and Evaluation Measures

The Second Edition of the Concept-Level Sentiment Analysis challenge included four tasks: Polarity Detection, Aspect-Based Sentiment Analysis, Frames Entities Identification, The Most Innovative Approach. Participants had to submit an abstract of no up to 200 words together with a description of their system, including why the system was innovative, which features or functions the system provided, what design choices were made and what lessons were learned, how the semantics was employed. They also were required to indicate which tasks their system would address. Besides, authors had to give web access to their applications or indicate how to download their demos (in case providing account information and a set of instructions to run their program). All competing systems were evaluated for the forth task, i.e. the Most Innovative Approach, by providing a deep analysis on each of them. The evaluation criteria for this task involved innovation, computational behaviour, usability and employment of semantics.

The input of the first three tasks was a simple text. Text can be constituted by multiple sentences which were assumed to be grammatically correct in American English and had to be processed according to the input format specified at https://github.com/diegoref/ESWC-CLSA/wiki#input-and-output-format.

Following we will describe in detail each task. For the first three tasks we will also include the used evaluation datasets and the evaluation framework.

3.1   Task 1: Polarity Detection

The basic task of the challenge was binary polarity detection. The proposed semantic opinion-mining engines were assessed according to precision, recall and F-measure of the detected polarity values (positive OR negative) for each review of the evaluation dataset. As an example, for the sentence *The author hasn't even taken the trouble to put up an errata list*, the correct answer that a sentiment analysis system needed to give was *negative* and therefore it had to write 0 between the $<polarity>$, $</polarity>$ tags of the output. The problem of subjectivity detection was not addressed within this challenge, hence participants could assume that there were no neutral reviews.

10,000 sentences and their sentence-level polarities have been randomly taken from the Blitzer dataset[12]. 5000 of them had a positive polarity whereas 5000 had a negative polarity.

This task was pretty straightforward to evaluate. A precision/recall analysis was implemented to compute the accuracy of the output for this task. A true positive (tp) was defined when a sentence was correctly classified as positive. On the other hand, a false positive (fp) is a positive sentence which was classified as negative. Then, a true negative (tn) is detected when a negative sentence was correctly identified as such. Finally, a false negative (fn) happens when a negative sentence was erroneously classified as positive. With the above definitions, we defined the precision as

---

[12] http://www.cs.jhu.edu/~mdredze/datasets/sentiment/.

$$precision = \frac{tp}{tp + fp}$$

the recall as

$$recall = \frac{tp}{tp + fn}$$

the F1 measure as

$$F1 = \frac{2 \times precision \times recall}{precision + recall}$$

and the accuracy as

$$accuracy = \frac{tp + tn}{tp + fp + fn + tn}$$

3.2 Task 2: Aspect-Based Sentiment Analysis

The output of this Task was a set of aspects of the reviewed product and a binary polarity value associated to each of such aspects. As an example, for the sentence ...*but, if you 're looking for my opinion of the apex dvd player, i love it !* a correct system needed to identify 'dvd player' as the target of the positive related opinion. Engines had to be assessed according to both aspect extraction and aspect polarity detection using precision, recall and F-measure. The same approach was used for the same task in the First Edition of the Concept-Level Sentiment Analysis challenge held during ESWC2014 and re-proposed at SemEval 2015 Task 12[13]. Please refer to SemEval 2015 Task 12 for details on the precision-recall analysis. As there were no submitted systems targeting Task 2 we did not employ any tools (e.g. crowdsourcing) for the creation of an annotated test set. Therefore we refer the reader to [18] for details on the annotated test set for the same task that we developed for the First Edition of the challenge.

3.3 Task 3: Frame Entities Identification

The challenge focused on sentiment analysis at concept-level. This meant that the proposed engines needed to work beyond word/syntax level, hence addressing a concepts/semantics perspective. This task evaluated the capability of the proposed systems to identify the objects involved in a typical opinion frame according to their role: holders, topics, opinion concepts (i.e. terms referring to highly polarised concepts). For example, in a sentence such as *The mayor is loved by the people in the city, but he has been criticised by the state government* (taken from [14]), a system should be able to identify that *the people* and *state government* are opinion holders, that *is loved* and *has been criticised* are opinion concepts, and that *The mayor* is a topic (or subject) of the opinion.

---

[13] http://www.alt.qcri.org/semeval2015/task12/.

```
<sentence id='1'>
  <text>
    Robert thinks that Alex is a good and smart guy and Anna is a bad player.
  </text>
  <frame>
    <holder value="Robert"/>
    <topic value="Alex"/>
    <opinion value="good">
      <polarity>positive</polarity>
    </opinion>
  </frame>
  <frame>
    <holder value="Robert"/>
    <topic value="Alex"/>
    <opinion value="smart">
      <polarity>positive</polarity>
    </opinion>
  </frame>
  <frame>
    <holder value="Robert"/>
    <topic value="Anna"/>
    <opinion value="bad">
      <polarity>negative</polarity>
    </opinion>
  </frame>
</sentence>
```

Fig. 1. Task 3 annotated sentence example.

We randomly selected 251 texts from http://www.epinions.com and manually annotated them highlighting their opinion frame elements. Each text could have more than one associated frame, where each frame contained the quadruple $< holder, topic, opinion, polarity >$. Overall, 1481 frames were identified for 251 chosen texts. 1398 frames included information about the polarity of the opinion expressed: 871 were positive whereas 527 were negative.

Figure 1 shows an example of annotation for the sentence: *"Robert thinks that Alex is a good and smart guy and Anna is a bad player"*, including the three opinion frames that a system should be able to identify.

The systems competing for this task were evaluated by computing average precision, recall and F-measure on the detection of holders, topics, opinions, and polarities. Each element of the quadruple $< holder, topic, opinion, polarity >$ was given the same weight and, therefore, they all equally contributed to the computation of the overall precision.

3.4   Task 4: The Most Innovative Approach

This task aimed at awarding the most innovative system that in this context was identified based on a number of criteria: the use of common-sense knowledge, how the semantics was applied, the computational time, the number of features that was possible to query, the usability of the system, the appealing of the user interface, and the innovative nature of the approach, including multi-language capabilities.

4 Submitted Systems

At the time of the call for participation, we received 9 expression of interest to submission to the Second Edition of the Concept-Level Sentiment Analysis challenge. The challenge chairs created a mailing list where several authors asked questions and followed discussions before the submission deadline about the requirements that needed to be satisfied. A few systems missing a clear use of semantic features were discouraged to apply. We had a problem with timing (that was also experience during the First Edition): the call for this challenge was launched at the end of December 2014 and the first deadline was end March 2015. Therefore, time was relatively short for some authors with existing sentiment analysis systems (e.g. those applying for SemEval 2015 Task 12) to improve them towards a semantic-based approach or to adapt their input and output formats according to the challenge requirements. Finally, four participants were able to ultimate their system and submit to the challenge, and were all accepted for the competition. Participants' countries were Italy (3 systems) and Netherlands (1 system). Table 1 shows the details (title, authors, tasks participating into) of the submitted systems.

Table 1. The competing systems at the Second Edition of the Concept-Level Sentiment Analysis challenge and the tasks they addressed.

System	Task 1	Task 2	Task 3	Most Inn. Approach
Kim Schouten and Flavius Frasincar **The Benefit of Concept-based Features for Sentiment Analysis**	X			X
Giulio Petrucci and Mauro Dragoni **An Information Retrieval-based System For Multi-Domain Sentiment Analysis**	X			X
Andrea Giovanni Nuzzolese and Misael Mongiovi **Detecting sentiment polarities with Sentilo**	X			X
Francesco Corcoglioniti, Alessio Palmero Aprosio and Marco Rospocher **Opinion frame extraction from news corpus**			X	X

During the ESWC conference the participants had the opportunity to present a poster and a demo of their systems at a dedicated session, which was aimed at fostering brainstorming, research and network activities.

5   Results

A week before the ESWC conference, the two evaluation datasets (including only the sentences), one for Task 1 and the other for Task 3, were published. Participants had to run their systems and send to the challenge chairs their results by the next two days. As the precision-recall analysis script had already been released together with the test annotated datasets, the authors were able to prepare their output in compliance with the requirements. This is the reason why it was straightforward to run the precision-analysis script with the participants' output and the annotated datasets of the two tasks. In the following, we will show the results of the participants' systems.

5.1   Task 1

In Table 2 we show the precision-recall analysis of the three systems competing for Task 1. The system of *Kim Schouten and Flavius Frasincar* had the best accuracy and, therefore, was awarded with a Springer voucher of the value of 150 euros, as the winner of the task.

Table 2. Precision-recall analysis and winners for Task 1.

System	Accuracy	
Kim Schouten and Flavius Frasincar	0.4129	1
Giulio Petrucci and Mauro Dragoni	0.4078	2
Andrea Giovanni Nuzzolese and Misael Mongioví	0.3011	3

5.2   Task 3

Table 3 shows the precision-recall analysis for the system competing for Task 3. The system presented by *Francesco Corcoglioniti, Alessio Palmero Aprosio and Marco Rospocher* was the only one participating in this task, hence it was awarded with a Springer voucher of the value of 150 euros.

Table 3. Precision-recall analysis and winners for Task 3.

System	Prec	Rec	F1	Pos
Francesco Corcoglioniti, Alessio Palmero Aprosio and Marco Rospocher	0.3996	0.5336	0.4570	1

5.3   The Most Innovative Approach Task

The Innovation Prize, consisting of a Springer voucher of 150 euros, was awarded to *Andrea Giovanni Nuzzolese and Misael Mongiovi* with their presented system, Sentilo [9,20]. Sentilo builds on top of Discourse Representation Theory (DRT), relies on VerbNet for identifying and formalising events and their associated thematic roles. SENTILO uses FRED [13,17] which transforms DRT forms to RDF by following Semantic Web and Linked Data design principles, and by extending the representation model with event- and situation- semantics as formally defined by DOLCE+DnS ontology. SENTILO relies on OntoSentilo, an ontology that defines concepts and relations that characterise the entities composing the typical opinion frame (opinion trigger events, holders, topics and subtopics, opinion features). The strong semantic web-based character of SENTILO lead the evaluation committee to award it as the most innovative approach presented at this edition of the challenge.

6   Conclusions

Following the success of the First Edition, the Second Edition of the Concept-Level Sentiment Analysis challenge attracted several researchers from two sectors: (i) people within the traditional sentiment analysis research area who have investigated new opportunities provided by the Semantic Web world and have adapted their systems with Semantic Web best practices and technologies. (ii) Semantic Web experts that adapted their knowledge extraction systems in order to compute sentiment analysis tasks, such as the polarity detection.

Including the precision-recall script together with the annotated test set was a successful move. Authors of the systems were able to test their methods and, more importantly, make sure to have their output compliant with the required format. Among the learned lessons of the Second Edition of the challenge, we have clearly noticed the need of more effective dissemination and promotion actions for the event and to performed it much earlier and towards a wide set of stakeholders (industries and researchers) potentially interested. Hence, we have already acted in this direction and planned two steps to perform as soon as possible: (i) prepare the call for the next challenge proposal and (ii) identify all the potential interested stakeholders. We have identified 170 potential researchers and 32 companies (among our networks and previous participants to our challenge and to SemEval Workshop - Sentiment Analysis track) and already contacted them with an email attaching the proposed program for the Third edition of our challenge. There are a total of 25 different groups that showed interest in participating in the next edition of the challenge. This is a very promising result and gives us room for further improving the event, making it more competitive, finding sponsors, and publication venues e.g., journals, to disseminate the challenge results.

Acknowledgement. Challenge Organisers want to thank Springer for supporting the provided awards.

References

1. Baccianella, A., Esuli, S., Sebastiani, F.: SentiWordNet 3.0: an enhanced lexical resource for sentiment analysis and opinion mining. In: Calzolari, N., Choukri, K., Maegaard, B., Mariani, J., Odijk, J., Piperidis, S., Rosner, M., Tapias, D. (eds.) Proceedings of the Seventh Conference on International Language Resources and Evaluation (LREC 2010), Valletta, Malta (2010)
2. Benamara, F., Cesarano, C., Picariello, A., Reforgiato, D., Subrahmanian, V.S.: Sentiment analysis: adjectives and adverbs are better than adjectives alone. In: Proceedings of the International Conference on Weblogs and Social Media (ICWSM), Short paper (2007)
3. Bosco, C., Patti, V., Bolioli, A.: Developing corpora for sentiment analysis: the case of irony and senti-tut. IEEE Intel. Syst. **28**(2), 55–63 (2013)
4. Bradley, M., Lang, P.: Affective norms for english words (ANEW): Stimuli, instruction manual and affective ratings. Technical report, The Center for Research in Psychophysiology, University of Florida (1999)
5. Cambria, E., Olsher, D., Rajagopal, D.: Senticnet 3: A common and common-sense knowledge base for cognition-driven sentiment analysis. In: Brodley, C.E., Stone, P. (eds.) Twenty-Eight AAAI Conference on Artificial Intelligence, pp. 1515–1521. AAAI Press, Palo Alto, July 2014
6. Consoli, S., Gangemi, A., Nuzzolese, A.G., Reforgiato Recupero, D., Spampinato, D.: Extraction of topics-events semantic relationships for opinion propagation in sentiment analysis. In: Proceedings of Extended Semantic Web Conference (ESWC), Crete, GR (2014)
7. Dragoni, M.: Shellfbk: an information retrieval-based system for multi-domain sentiment analysis. In: Proceedings of the 9th International Workshop on Semantic Evaluation, SemEval 2015, pp. 502–509. Association for Computational Linguistics, Denver, June 2015. http://www.aclweb.org/anthology/S15-2084
8. Dragoni, M., Tettamanzi, A.G.B., da Costa Pereira, C.: Propagating and aggregating fuzzy polarities for concept-level sentiment analysis. Cogn. Comput. **7**(2), 186–197 (2015)
9. Gangemi, A., Presutti, V., Reforgiato Recupero, D.: Frame-based detection of opinion holders and topics: A model and a tool. IEEE Comput. Intel. Mag. **9**(1), 20–30 (2014). http://dblp.uni-trier.de/db/journals/cim/cim9.html#GangemiPR14
10. Gangemi, A., Alani, H., Nissim, M., Cambria, E., Reforgiato Recupero, D., Lanfranchi, V., Kauppinen, T. (eds.) Joint Proceedings of the 1th Workshop on Semantic Sentiment Analysis (SSA2014), and the Workshop on Social Media and Linked Data for Emergency Response (SMILE 2014) co-located with 11th European Semantic Web Conference (ESWC 2014), vol. 1329, CEUR Workshop Proceedings, Crete, Greece. CEUR-WS.org, 25 May, 2014
11. Garcia-Moya, L., Anaya-Sanchez, H., Berlanga-Llavori, R.: Retrieving product features and opinions from customer reviews. IEEE Intel. Syst. **28**(3), 19–27 (2013)
12. Hung, C., Lin, H.-K.: Using objective words in sentiwordnet to improve word-of-mouth sentiment classification. IEEE Intel. Syst. **28**(2), 47–54 (2013)
13. ISTC-CNR. FRED, December 2014. http://wit.istc.cnr.it/stlab-tools/fred
14. Liu, B.: Sentiment Analysis and Opinion Mining. Synthesis Lectures on Human Language Technologies. Morgan & Claypool Publishers (2012). http://dx.doi.org/10.2200/S00416ED1V01Y201204HLT016,   doi:10.2200/S00416ED1V01Y201204HLT016

15. Liu, H., Singh, P.: Conceptnet: A practical commonsense reasoning toolkit. BT Technol. J. **22**, 211–226 (2004)
16. Poria, S., Gelbukh, A.F., Hussain, A., Howard, N., Das, D., Bandyopadhyay, S.: Enhanced senticnet with affective labels for concept-based opinion mining. IEEE Intel. Syst. **28**(2), 31–38 (2013)
17. Presutti, V., Draicchio, F., Gangemi, A.: Knowledge extraction based on discourse representation theory and linguistic frames. In: ten Teije, A., Völker, J., Handschuh, S., Stuckenschmidt, H., d'Acquin, M., Nikolov, A., Aussenac-Gilles, N., Hernandez, N. (eds.) EKAW 2012. LNCS, vol. 7603, pp. 114–129. Springer, Heidelberg (2012)
18. Presutti, V., Stankovic, M., Erik Cambria, I., Di Cantador, A., Di Iorio, T., Noia, C.L., Recupero, D.R., Tordai, A.: Semantic Web Evaluation Challenge. SemWebEval 2014 at ESWC 2014, Anissaras, Crete, Greece, May 25-29, 2014, Revised Selected Papers. Springer, Heidelberg (2014). ISBN 3319120239, 9783319120232
19. Reforgiato Recupero, D., Cambria, E.: ESWC 14 challenge on concept-level sentiment analysis. In: Presutti, V., Stankovic, M., Cambria, E., Cantador, I., Di Iorio, A., Di Noia, T., Lange, C., Reforgiato Recupero, D., Tordai, A. (eds.) SemWebEval 2014. CCIS, vol. 475, pp. 3–20. Springer, Heidelberg (2014)
20. Recupero, D.R., Presutti, V., Consoli, S., Gangemi, A., Nuzzolese, A.: Sentilo: Frame-based sentiment analysis. Cogn. Comput. **7**(2), 211–225 (2014)
21. Strapparava, C., Valitutti, A.: WordNet-Affect: An affective extension of WordNet. In: LREC, Lisbon, pp. 1083–1086 (2004)
22. Subrahmanian, V.S., Reforgiato, D.: Ava: Adjective-verb-adverb combinations for sentiment analysis. IEEE Intel. Syst. **23**, 43–50 (2008)
23. Tsai, A.-C.-R., Wu, C.-E., Tsai, R.T.-H., Jen Hsu, J.Y.: Building a concept-level sentiment dictionary based on commonsense knowledge. IEEE Intel. Syst. **28**(2), 22–30 (2013)
24. Weichselbraun, A., Gindl, S., Scharl, A.: Extracting and grounding context-aware sentiment lexicons. IEEE Intel. Syst. **28**(2), 39–46 (2013)
25. Weigand, E. (ed.): Emotion in Dialogic Interaction. Current Issues in Linguistic Theory 248. John Benjamins, Philadelphia (2004)

The Benefit of Concept-Based Features for Sentiment Analysis

Kim Schouten[(✉)] and Flavius Frasincar

Erasmus University Rotterdam, PO Box 1738,
3000 DR Rotterdam, The Netherlands
{schouten,frasincar}@ese.eur.nl

Abstract. Sentiment analysis is an active field of research, moving from the traditional algorithms that operated on complete documents to fine-grained variants where aspects of the topic being discussed are extracted, as well as their associated sentiment. Recently, a move from traditional word-based approaches to concept-based approaches has started. In this work, it is shown by using a simple machine learning baseline, that concepts are useful as features within a machine learning framework. In all our experiments, the performance increases when including the concept-based features.

1 Introduction

Sentiment analysis is an active field of research, and much progress has been made since the early algorithms that could only predict polarity for complete documents. Nowadays, advanced methods are available that can detect the various aspects of the topic being discussed and their associated polarity. However, methods for sentiment analysis tend to lean heavily on machine learning, leaving only a small role for natural language processing. Traditionally, a bag-of-words approach is used where the features for a machine learning algorithm are simple binary features denoting the presence or absence of a word. While these methods perform well, classifying the majority of the cases correctly, their performance has reached a plateau since word-based approaches cannot correctly classify all cases (e.g., they fail to account for the grammatical structure in the text and its associated semantics). For the remaining, harder cases, more advanced methods are required. In [4], a move from traditional word-based approaches to concept-based methods is advocated, and in this paper we would like to demonstrate the usefulness of concepts for the task of sentiment analysis.

To support the previous claim, we have set up a basic linear support vector machine (SVM) for the task of sentence polarity classification, and aspect (category) detection. Since the number of features is very large and the number of data points is relatively small, a linear SVM is best suited here. By having both word-based features, grammar-based features, and concept-based features, we show that concepts are always beneficial to add to the set of features, as in our experiments the results always improve.

© Springer International Publishing Switzerland 2015
F. Gandon et al. (Eds.): SemWebEval 2015, CCIS 548, pp. 223–233, 2015.
DOI: 10.1007/978-3-319-25518-7_19

The remainder of this paper is structured as follows: first, we describe some of the existing work in this field. Then, we discuss our baseline methods for sentence polarity classification, followed by our baseline method for aspect (category) detection. Then, to complete the package, we describe a method for aspect polarity classification. Each method is evaluated in their respective section. Last, conclusions are drawn and some pointers for future work are given.

2   Related Work

For a field as new as concept-centric sentiment analysis, there are already a number of approaches proposed. First, there is the set of works presented at last year's Semantic Web Evaluation Challenge. Furthermore, there are other pioneering works that present semantic approaches towards sentiment analysis.

In [17], a concept parser is used to first extract all the concepts in each sentence. The concept parser is a set of handcrafted rules executed on the dependency parse tree output. Then the aspects are extracted in a similar fashion, using an elaborate system of handcrafted rules. In addition to the dependency parse tree and the already found concepts, these rules utilize a manually created lexicon to detect implicit aspects and an opinion lexicon (i.e., SenticNet [3]). The sentiment analysis was also performed with a rule-based method, but when no concept was found that was in SenticNet, a basic machine learning method was employed as a fall-back mechanism. A similar method is proposed in [24], where a semantic role labeling component is used after the syntactic parser. On top of that, a set of handcrafted rules is executed that describe patterns, using semantic role information and syntactic information, that denote aspects.

The work presented in [6] presents a machine learning method for polarity detection, where the traditional bag-of-words approach is complemented with semantic features. A graph-based approach [19] is used to extract the concepts from the reviews, and then SentiConceptNet [23] is used, together with a term weighting scheme, to construct the concept features, that thus consist of a weighted concept term times the concept's sentiment score.

A lexicon-based method is given in [14], where given a seed set of adjectives where the polarity is known, new adjectives are found using the conjunction rule [10] (i.e., if an unknown adjective is conjoined to a known positive adjective with 'and', then the unknown adjective is also positive). In addition, its synonyms are also added to the known list of adjectives together with its antonyms, which will get the opposite polarity score.

An ontology forms the core element of [7], modeling the space of online reviews. It is populated with instances from DBPedia [11], using lexicalizations from the DBPedia Lexicalization Dataset [13]. These lexicalizations are expanded by analyzing words appearing in a similar context (i.e., the set of words around a term). This allows new concepts, that are not already described in the ontology to be found as well. In addition, it includes prior information, like word lists of generally positive words and generally negative words. Furthermore, it employs a list of association concepts, where prior information is encoded as a <concept, opinion, sentiment> triple (e.g., <beer, cold, positive>).

An ontology-based approach is advocated in [25], as well. Here, term frequency is used to find the most descriptive words for a given product concept in product descriptions on the Web. Then, all synonyms and hyponyms are added as lexicalizations of that concept to the ontology. In this way, a concept is described by a set of weighted terms, with weights denoting the association degree between the word and the underlying concept. This association degree is based, both on presence and absence of terms in its context. Then, all adjectives, nouns, and verbs that are not identified as aspects are considered as possible sentiment words. When these sentiment candidates can be paired to an already known aspect, the aspect-opinion pair is complete. All sentiment candidates that are not paired with a known aspect are considered as yet unknown aspects.

In [15], the labels of the classes and instances in the employed ontology are used to find the aspects described in the ontology in the text, without making use of specific lexicalizations. However, it features different weights for the different aspects, according to, for example, how often this aspect is mentioned by users in their reviews. To compute the sentiment score, SentiWordNet [1] is used.

A different approach is taken in [8], where fuzzy logic is used to model the relationships between the polarity of a concepts and the domain, as well as the aboutness. To that end, a two-level graph is used, where the first level models the relations between concepts, whereas the second level models the relations between concepts and sentiment given various domains (i.e., the same word can be positive in one domain, but negative in another). A preliminary membership function is defined using the training data, having a triangle shape. These membership functions are refined in a later step, to arrive at trapezoid functions, by propagating learned information through the two-level graph. Using this method, the various membership functions will influence each other (e.g., if a semantically related concept has a strong positive polarity in a given domain, than the current concept most likely is positive in that domain as well).

Also using fuzzy logic is [21], where a fuzzy sentiment ontology is built. It uses eight different sentiment classes (i.e., expect, joy, love, surprise, anxiety, sorrow, angry, and hate [18]). Every word has different membership values for the different sentiment classes, corresponding to the semantic similarity between that word and the word denoting the sentiment class. These values differ for different meanings of a word.

Our machine learning baseline is most similar to [6], since it also uses a machine learning algorithm with concept features. However, we use a word sense dismabiguation step to link words to concepts. The rule-based approach is not concept-centric and is presented as an additional baseline.

3   Sentence Polarity Classification

The sentence polarity classification task, is an elementary task that is concerned with finding the overall polarity of a sentence. We have two methods, a rule-based method based and a machine learning method.

The rule-based method is based on OASYS [5], but with an updated formula to compute the sentiment score for words. The sentiment of each word is computed by adding $\frac{1}{sentenceLength}$ for each positive sentence this word appears in and subtracting the same value for each negative sentence this word appears in. Furthermore, negation and amplification are taken into account as well. The computation of the sentiment score of a word then becomes

$$sentiment(w) = \frac{1}{freq(w)} \sum_{s \text{ having } w} \frac{polarity(s)}{mod_s(w) \times length(s)} \qquad (1)$$

where $sentiment(w)$ is the sentiment score computed for word w, $freq(w)$ is the number of times this word appears in the training data, s having w is a sentence that contains word w, $polarity(s)$ is either $+1$ for positive sentences, and -1 for negative sentences (as taken from the annotated training data), and $length(s)$ is the number of words in sentence s. When the current word w has a 'neg' dependency, the modifier $mod_s(w)$ is -0.9 to denote negation. When w has a 'advmod' relation with a word that is in the General Inquirer [22] 'Overstatement' list, the $mod_s(w)$ is 1.4 to denote amplification, and conversely, its value is 0.6 when the word in the 'advmod' relation is in the General Inquirer 'Understatement' list.

Furthermore, an offset value is computed as the average of: the average sentiment score of positive sentence and the average sentiment score of negative sentences. This is to offset any inbalance between positive and negative sentences in the dataset.

When processing unseen sentences, the sentiment of the sentence is the sum of the word sentiment scores, computed as

$$sentiment(s) = \frac{1}{length(s)} \sum_{w \in [s]} mod_s(w) \times sentiment(w), \qquad (2)$$

where $sentiment(w)$ is the sentiment score for that word, as defined above, $lengths(s)$ is the number of words in sentence s, $[s]$ denotes the bag of words representation of sentence s, and $mod_s(w)$ represents a modifier for negation and amplification as in Eq. 1.

The machine learning method is based on a linear Support Vector Machine, using a variety of features. The first set of features is constructed by encoding the presence or absence of the lemmas of corpus words in a sentence ($\mathcal{L}$). In a similar fashion, the next set of features consists of the concepts that these words represent ($\mathcal{C}$). We use the Lesk [12] algorithm for word sense disambiguation, linking the lemmas to concepts in WordNet [9]. Then, we encode the presence or absence of each concept in a sentence. A third set of features is made by encoding grammatical lemma bigrams ($\mathcal{LG}$) of the form "lemma – grammatical relation type – lemma" (e.g., "house-amod-big", where 'amod' stands for adjectival modifier). A fourth set of feature is created by encoding grammatical polarity bigrams ($\mathcal{PG}$) of the form "word polarity – grammatical relation type – word polarity" (e.g., "neutral-amod-positive'). Last, we encode some general polarity characteristics of the sentence ($\mathcal{PC}$): whether there are more positive than negative words, whether there are positive words in the sentence, and whether there are negative words in the sentence. To get the word polarities, we use the General Inquirer lexicon [22], using the 'Positiv' and 'Negativ' word list. In the future, we would like to also incorporate polarity information from SentiWordNet, as this is concept-based instead of word-based like the General Inquirer.

3.1   Data

For the sentence polarity classification task, the data set used is the Multi-Domain Sentiment Dataset from Blitzer et al. [2]. It contains 2429 sentences, taken from Amazon reviews, from various product domains (e.g., books, movies, games, etc.). We use the binary version of the polarity annotations, where polarity is simply positive or negative. Some sentences are very short and contain only a few words, while others are extremely long, with more than 150 words. About 58 % of the sentences is labeled positive, with the remaining 42 % being labeled as negative.

3.2   Evaluation

To evaluate the proposed method, we use ten-fold cross-validation. The training data is split into ten equal parts, and the algorithm is tested on each of the ten parts, having been trained on the nine other parts. Since sentences are assigned randomly to one of the ten folds, the results can vary a little bit with each run.

From the results in Table 1 one can clearly see that the traditional bag-of-words approach is well-performing. However, a small but noticeable improvement can be seen when adding concepts from WordNet to the feature set. Whatever

Table 1. Results for task 1: sentence polarity classification.

Used feature sets					Precision
Majority Baseline					58.46
Rule-based					74.90
$\mathcal{L}$					73.69
	$\mathcal{C}$				71.76
		$\mathcal{LG}$			65.34
			$\mathcal{PG}$		62.49
				$\mathcal{PC}$	58.46
$\mathcal{L}$	$\mathcal{C}$				75.71
$\mathcal{L}$	$\mathcal{C}$	$\mathcal{LG}$			76.33
$\mathcal{L}$	$\mathcal{C}$	$\mathcal{LG}$	$\mathcal{PG}$		76.16
$\mathcal{L}$	$\mathcal{C}$	$\mathcal{LG}$	$\mathcal{PG}$	$\mathcal{PC}$	76.12
$\mathcal{L}$		$\mathcal{LG}$	$\mathcal{PG}$	$\mathcal{PC}$	75.05
$\mathcal{L}$		$\mathcal{LG}$	$\mathcal{PG}$		74.80
$\mathcal{L}$		$\mathcal{LG}$			75.21

combination of features is used, it is always better to also include the WordNet concepts, showing the added value of these kinds of features.

In Tables 2 and 3, the results of the rule-based method and the machine learning method using all feature sets are shown for the individual positive and negative labels. Interestingly, where precision for positive and negative are similar, recall is much lower for negative labels than for positive labels. A possible reason for this is that people generally use the same kind of language to denote a positive opinion, whereas there are many more ways of saying something negative about a product or service (e.g., people try to write a critical review in a polite manner, but also the wide variety of negative words). This bigger variety poses problems for recall, since the algorithm will encounter new forms of negative opinions which it has not seen before in the training data.

Table 2. Rule-based learning results for positive and negative labels when using all feature sets.

	Precision	Recall	F_1-score
Overall	74.90	74.90	74.90
Negative	71.24	66.37	68.72
Positive	77.21	80.96	79.04

Table 3. Machine learning results for positive and negative labels when using all feature sets.

	Precision	Recall	F_1-score
Overall	76.12	76.12	76.12
Negative	74.07	65.41	69.47
Positive	77.31	83.73	80.39

4   Aspect Detection

For aspect detection we use a limited set of aspects, which is known beforehand, so we can train a binary classifier for each aspect. We use a linear Support Vector Machine, with similar setup to the sentence polarity task. The feature sets used are the lemmas of the words in the sentence ($\mathcal{L}$), the concepts to which the words in a sentence refer to ($\mathcal{C}$), and the grammatical lemma bigrams ($\mathcal{LG}$). The polarity oriented feature sets used in the sentence polarity task are not used here, since classifying sentiment is not performed in this task.

4.1   Data

The dataset used for this task the is the official SemEval-2015 training data on restaurants [16]. It contains 277 reviews on restaurants, each containing one or more sentences. Each sentence is annotated with zero or more opinions, with each opinion having multiple information slots. The first slot contains the actual words in the sentence on which this opinion was voiced. For implicit opinions, that are not literally mentioned in the sentence, this slot is empty. The second slot is the category of the aspect, denoted as the combination of entity and attribute. The entity part represents high-level concepts, like 'Food', 'Location', 'Service', etc. The attribute part represents a subclass or attribute of that high-level concept. Example of attributes used in the restaurant data are 'Quality', 'Prices', 'General', etc. Combining the two yields both specific categories like 'Food#Quality', but also very general categories like 'Restaurant#General'. Note that the SVM described above learns these categories without taking the fact into account that they consist of two semantically related parts. A list of all category labels can be found in Table 4 below.

Table 4. The set of category labels for the SemEval restaurant data.

Category	Attribute	Frequency
Ambience	General	183
Drinks	Prices	15
Drinks	Quality	34
Food	General	1
Food	Prices	54
Food	Quality	581
Food	Style Options	93
Location	General	20
Restaurant	General	269
Restaurant	Miscellaneous	62
Restaurant	Prices	48
Service	General	268

4.2   Evaluation

The various combinations of the three feature sets are evaluated using ten-fold cross-validation. Since reviews, and the sentences they contain, are randomly assigned to one of the folds, the results may differ slightly with each run. The results can be seen in Table 5 below.

Similar to the sentence polarity classification task, we can see the contribution of the concept-based features. Note that concepts on their own do not work as well as lemmas, since not all words are related to a concept, and hence, information is lost by only having concepts as features. This explains why especially recall is much lower for concepts than for lemmas. Nevertheless, precision is better for concepts then for lemmas, showing the adequacy of accounting for word semantics.

Table 5. Results for task 2: aspect category classification.

Features			Precision	Recall	F_1-measure
$\mathcal{L}$			86.91	44.56	58.91
	$\mathcal{C}$		88.97	37.06	52.33
		$\mathcal{LG}$	91.36	24.30	38.40
$\mathcal{L}$	$\mathcal{C}$		85.04	51.57	64.21
$\mathcal{L}$		$\mathcal{LG}$	86.06	48.91	62.37
	$\mathcal{C}$	$\mathcal{LG}$	89.62	45.41	60.27
$\mathcal{L}$	$\mathcal{C}$	$\mathcal{LG}$	84.61	53.51	65.56

The current set of features is highly accurate, but does not have enough coverage as shown by the recall score. For that, more robust features, that generalize well to unseen data, are needed. In future work, we would like to exploit the relational structure of domain ontologies to increase the coverage of concept-based approaches.

5 Aspect Polarity Classification

For the polarity classification of the opinions on aspects, we use the same method as reported in [20]. We start by creating a sentiment lexicon from the annotated opinions. This domain-specific lexicon is then used to determine the sentiment of the opinions that have no sentiment annotation. The intuition behind this method is that the sentiment of words depends on the domain, and hence, it is convenient to automatically extract the word sentiment from the annotated corpus. Words that often appear close to positive aspects are likely to be positive, whereas words that often appear close to negative aspects are likely to be negative. Since sentiment is carried by expressions and not by single words alone, we also create lexicon entries for bigrams and trigrams. In each sentence, the distance between each n-gram and each aspect is computed and the sentiment of the aspect, discounted by the distance, is added to the overall sentiment value for that n-gram. This is shown in Eq. 3.

$$sentiment_g = \frac{1}{freq_g} \cdot \sum_{s \in S_g} p \cdot t_{order(g)} \cdot \sum_{a \in A_s} \frac{polarity_a}{(distance_{a,g})^m}, \qquad (3)$$

where g is the n-gram (i.e., word unigram, bigram, or trigram), $freq_g$ is the frequency of n-gram g in the data set, s is a sentence in S_g, which is the set of sentences that contain n-gram g, p is a parameter to correct for the overall positivity of the data set, t is a parameter that corrects for the relative influence of the type of n-gram (i.e., different values are used for unigrams, bigrams, and trigrams), a is an aspect in A_s, which is the set of aspects in sentence s, $polarity_a$ is 1 when aspect a is positive and -1 when a is negative, and m is a parameter that determines how strong the discounting by the distance should be. The distance $distance_{a,g}$ is computed as the minimum amount of words between the aspect a and the n-gram g (i.e., both an n-gram and an aspect can consist of multiple words, in which case the closest two are used to compute this distance). We set $t_{order(g)}$ to 1, 5, and 4 for unigrams, bigrams, and trigrams, respectively. Furthermore we set $p = 2$ and $m = 1$. These values were determined by manual experimentation.

The sentiment of an aspect is computed by taking the sentiment value of each n-gram from the lexicon, dividing it by the distance between that n-gram and the aspect, and summing it up, as shown in Eq. 4. For this, it is assumed that each aspect only appears once in a sentence.

$$sentiment_{a,s_a} = \sum_{g \in s_a} \frac{sentiment_g}{(\min distance_{g,a})^m},$$ (4)

where, in addition to the definitions in the previous equation, g is an n-gram in s_a, which is the sentence in which aspect a occurs. For each occurrence of an n-gram, its sentiment value is added to a total score for that aspect. When this score exceeds zero, it will be annotated as 'positive', and with a score below zero, it will be annotated as 'negative'. Since there are only a few neutral cases in our data set, and many more positive than negative aspects, we default to 'positive', when the total score is zero (e.g., this can also happen when no sentiment-bearing words are in this sentence). Neutral sentiment, although present in the training data, is ignored in this method.

For implicit opinions, where the target slot is 'null', the distance in the above formulas cannot be computed, and hence a distance of 1 is used instead.

5.1   Evaluation

This method is also evaluated on the official SemEval-2015 restaurant training data (cf. Sect. 4.1). The data set is heavily biased towards positive opinions: 1198 opinions are positive, 403 are negative, and 53 are neutral. As with the other methods, the aspect polarity classification method is evaluated using ten-fold cross-validation. Results are shown in Table 6 below.

Table 6. Results for the aspect polarity classification algorithm.

	Precision	Recall	F_1-score
Overall	76.30	76.30	76.30
Negative	54.55	52.11	53.30
Positive	83.03	87.81	85.35
Neutral	0	0	0

6   Conclusion

In this work, we have shown that including concept-based features always leads to improved performance. Since this is already the case, even in a relatively straightforward setup like this, it is clear that more advanced ways of handling semantic information will increase performance even more.

In terms of future work, we would like to incorporate sentiment lexicons, like sentic.net and SentiWordNet, as well as general knowledge bases like DBPedia, domain ontologies, and semantic lexicons like WordNet. This enables us to include more information about relations between concepts. Now, only grammatical relations were included, but conceptual relations are all the more interesting.

Acknowledgment. The authors are partially supported by the Dutch national program COMMIT.

References

1. Baccianella, S., Esuli, A., Sebastiani, F.: SentiWordNet 3.0: an enhanced lexical resource for sentiment analysis and opinion mining. In: Proceedings of the 7th Language Resources and Evaluation Conference (LREC 2010), pp. 2200–2204 (2010)
2. Blitzer, J., Dredze, M., Pereira, F.: Biographies, Bollywood, Boom-boxes and Blenders: Domain Adaptation for Sentiment Classification. In: Proceedings of the Association for Computational Linguistics, pp. 187–205. ACL (2007)
3. Cambria, E., Olsher, D., Rajagopal, D.: SenticNet 3: A common and common-sense knowledge base for cognition-driven sentiment analysis. In: Proceedings of AAAI 2014, pp. 1515–1521 (2014)
4. Cambria, E., Schuller, B., Xia, Y., Havasi, C.: New avenues in opinion mining and sentiment analysis. IEEE Intel. Syst. **28**(2), 15–21 (2013)
5. Cesarano, C., Dorr, B., Picariello, A., Reforgiato, D., Sagoff, A., Subrahmanian, V.: Oasys: An opinion analysis system. In: AAAI Spring Symposium on Computational Approaches to Analyzing Weblogs (2004)
6. Chung, J.K.-C., Wu, C.-E., Tsai, R.T.-H.: Polarity detection of online reviews using sentiment concepts: NCU IISR team at ESWC-14 challenge on concept-level sentiment analysis. In: Presutti, V., et al. (eds.) SemWebEval 2014. CCIS, vol. 475, pp. 53–58. Springer, Heidelberg (2014)
7. Coden, A., Gruhl, D., Lewis, N., Mendes, P.N., Nagarajan, M., Ramakrishnan, C., Welch, S.: Semantic lexicon expansion for concept-based aspect-aware sentiment analysis. In: Presutti, V., et al. (eds.) SemWebEval 2014. CCIS, vol. 475, pp. 34–40. Springer, Heidelberg (2014)
8. Dragoni, M., Tettamanzi, A.G.B., da Costa Pereira, C.: A fuzzy system for concept-level sentiment analysis. In: Presutti, V., et al. (eds.) SemWebEval 2014. CCIS, vol. 475, pp. 21–27. Springer, Heidelberg (2014)
9. Fellbaum, C.: WordNet: An Electronic Lexical Database. MIT Press, Cambridge (1998)
10. Hatzivassiloglou, V., McKeown, K.R.: Predicting the semantic orientation of adjectives. In: Proceedings of the 35th Annual Meeting of the Association for Computational Linguistics and Eighth Conference of the European Chapter of the Association for Computational Linguistics (ACL1998), pp. 174–181. Association for Computational Linguistics (1997). http://dx.doi.org/10.3115/976909.979640

11. Lehmann, J., Isele, R., Jakob, M., Jentzsch, A., Kontokostas, D., Mendes, P.N., Hellmann, S., Morsey, M., van Kleef, P., Auer, S., Bizer, C.: DBpedia - a large-scale, multilingual knowledge base extracted from Wikipedia. Semantic Web **6**(2), 167–195 (2015)

12. Lesk, M.: Automatic sense disambiguation using machine readable dictionaries: how to tell a pine cone from an ice cream cone. In: 5th Annual International Conference on Systems Documentation (SIGDOC 1986), pp. 24–26. ACM (1986)

13. Mendes, P.N., Jakob, M., Bizer, C.: DBpedia: A Multilingual cross-domain knowledge base. In: Proceedings of the Eight International Conference on Language Resources and Evaluation (LREC 2012), pp. 1813–1817 (2012)

14. Ofek, N., Rokach, L.: Unsupervised fine-grained sentiment analysis system using lexicons and concepts. In: Presutti, V., et al. (eds.) SemWebEval 2014. CCIS, vol. 475, pp. 28–33. Springer, Heidelberg (2014)

15. Peñalver-Martinez, I., Garcia-Sanchez, F., Valencia-Garcia, R., Rodríguez-García, Á., Moreno, V., Sánchez-Cervantes, J.L.: Feature-based opinion mining through ontologies. Expert Syst. Appl. **41**(13), 5995–6008 (2014)

16. Pontiki, M., Galanis, D., Papageogiou, H., Manandhar, S., Androutsopoulos, I.: SemEval-2015 Task 12: Aspect Based Sentiment Analysis. In: Proceedings of the 9th International Workshop on Semantic Evaluation (SemEval 2015) (2015)

17. Poria, S., Ofek, N., Gelbukh, A., Hussain, A., Rokach, L.: Dependency tree-based rules for concept-level aspect-based sentiment analysis. In: Presutti, V., et al. (eds.) SemWebEval 2014. CCIS, vol. 475, pp. 41–47. Springer, Heidelberg (2014)

18. Quan, C., Ren, F.: A blog emotion corpus for emotional expression analysis in chinese. Comput. Speech Lang. **24**(4), 726–749 (2010)

19. Rajagopal, D., Cambria, E., Olsher, D., Kwok, K.: A graph-based approach to commonsense concept extraction and semantic similarity detection. In: Proceedings of the 22nd International Conference on World Wide Web Companion, WWW 2013 Companion, pp. 565–570. International World Wide Web Conferences Steering Committee (2013)

20. Schouten, K., Frasincar, F., de Jong, F.: Commit-p1wp3: A co-occurrence based approach to aspect-level sentiment analysis. In: Proceedings of the 8th International Workshop on Semantic Evaluation (SemEval 2014), pp. 203–207. Association for Computational Linguistics and Dublin City University (2014)

21. Shi, W., Wang, H., He, S.: Sentiment analysis of chinese microblogging based on sentiment ontology: a case study of '7.23 wenzhou train collision'. Connection Sci. **25**(4), 161–178 (2013)

22. Stone, P.J., Dunphy, D.C., Smith, M.S., Ogilvie, D.M.: The General Inquirer: A Computer Approach to Content Analysis. MIT Press (1966)

23. Tsai, A.R., Wu, C.E., Tsai, R.H., Hsu, J.: Building a concept-level sentiment dictionary based on commonsense knowledge. IEEE Intel. Syst. **28**(2), 22–30 (2013)

24. Virk, S.M., Lee, Y.-H., Ku, L.-W.: Sinica Semantic Parser for ESWC'14 Concept-Level Semantic Analysis Challenge. In: Presutti, V., et al. (eds.) SemWebEval 2014. CCIS, vol. 475, pp. 48–52. Springer, Heidelberg (2014)

25. Yin, P., Wang, H., Guo, K.: Feature-opinion pair identification of product reviews in chinese: a domain ontology modeling method. New Rev. Hypermedia multimedia **19**(1), 3–24 (2013)

An Information Retrieval-Based System for Multi-domain Sentiment Analysis

Giulio Petrucci[1,2] and Mauro Dragoni[1(✉)]

[1] FBK–IRST, Trento, Italy
{petrucci,dragoni}@fbk.eu
[2] University of Trento, Trento, Italy

Abstract. This paper describes the SHELLFBK system that participated in ESWC 2015 Sentiment Analysis challenge. Our system takes a
supervised approach that builds on techniques from information retrieval.
The algorithm populates an inverted index with pseudo-documents that
encode dependency parse relationships extracted from the sentences in
the training set. Each record stored in the index is annotated with the
polarity and domain of the sentence it represents; this way, it is possible to have a more fine-grained representation of the learnt sentiment
information. When the polarity of a new sentence has to be computed,
the new sentence is converted to a query and a two-steps computation is
performed: firstly, a domain is assigned to the sentence by comparing the
sentence content with domain contextual information learnt during the
training phase, and, secondly, once the domain is assigned to the sentence, the polarity is computed and assigned to the new sentence. Preliminary results on an in-vitro test case demonstrated promising results.

1 Introduction

Sentiment analysis is a natural language processing task whose aim is to classify
documents according to the opinion (polarity) they express on a given subject [1].
Generally speaking, sentiment analysis aims at determining the attitude of a
speaker or a writer with respect to a topic or the overall tonality of a document.
This task has created a considerable interest due to its wide applications. In
recent years, the exponential increase of the Web for exchanging public opinions
about events, facts, products, etc., has led to an extensive usage of sentiment
analysis approaches, especially for marketing purposes.

By formalizing the sentiment analysis problem, a "sentiment" or "opinion"
has been defined by [2] as a quintuple:

$$\langle o_j, f_{jk}, so_{ijkl}, h_i, t_l \rangle, \tag{1}$$

where o_j is a target object, f_{jk} is a feature of the object o_j, so_{ijkl} is the sentiment value of the opinion of the opinion holder h_i on feature f_{jk} of object o_j
at time t_l. The value of so_{ijkl} can be positive (by denoting a state of happiness,
bliss, or satisfaction), negative (by denoting a state of sorrow, dejection, or dis-
appointment), or neutral (it is not possible to denote any particular sentiment),

© Springer International Publishing Switzerland 2015
F. Gandon et al. (Eds.): SemWebEval 2015, CCIS 548, pp. 234–243, 2015.
DOI: 10.1007/978-3-319-25518-7_20

or a more granular rating. The term h_i encodes the opinion holder, and t_l is the time when the opinion is expressed.

Such an analysis, may be *document-based*, where the positive, negative, or neutral sentiment is assigned to the entire document content; or it may be *sentence-based* where individual sentences are analyzed separately and classified according to the different polarity values. In the latter case, it is often desirable to find with a high precision the entity attributes towards which the detected sentiment is directed.

In the classic sentiment analysis problem, the polarity of each term within the document is computed independently of the domain which the document's domain. However, conditioning term polarity by domain has been found to improve performance [3]. We illustrate the intuition behind domain specific term polarity. Let us consider the following example concerning the adjective "small":

1. The sideboard is **small** and it is not able to contain a lot of stuff.
2. The **small** dimensions of this decoder allow to move it easily.

In the first sentence, we considered the Furnishings domain and, within it, the polarity of the adjective "small" is, for sure, "negative" because it highlights an issue of the described item. On the other hand, in the second sentence, where we considered the Electronics domain, the polarity of such an adjective may be considered "positive".

Unlike the approaches already discussed in the literature (and presented in Sect. 2), we address the multi-domain sentiment analysis problem by applying Information Retrieval (IR) techniques for representing information about the linguistic structure of sentences and by taking into account both their polarity and the domain.

The rest of the work is structured as follows. Section 2 presents a survey on works about sentiment analysis. Section 3 provides a description of the SHELLFBK system by described how information are stored during the training phase and exploited during the test one. Section 4 reports an in-vitro evaluation of the system and the results obtained in Semantic Sentiment Analysis Challenge of ESWC 2015. Finally, Sect. 5 concludes the paper.

2   Related Work

The topic of sentiment analysis has been studied extensively in the literature [2,4], where several techniques have been proposed and validated.

Machine learning techniques are the most common approaches used for addressing this problem, given that any existing supervised methods can be applied to sentiment classification. For instance, in [1,5], the authors compared the performance of Naive-Bayes, Maximum Entropy, and Support Vector Machines in sentiment analysis on different features like considering only unigrams, bigrams, combination of both, incorporating parts of speech and position information or by taking only adjectives. Moreover, beside the use of standard machine learning method, researchers have also proposed several custom techniques specifically for sentiment classification, like the use of adapted score function based on the evaluation of positive or negative words in product reviews [6], as well as by defining weighting schemata for enhancing classification accuracy [7].

An obstacle to research in this direction is the need of labeled training data, whose preparation is a time-consuming activity. Therefore, in order to reduce the labeling effort, opinion words have been used for training procedures. In [8] and [9], the authors used opinion words to label portions of informative examples for training the classifiers. Opinion words have been exploited also for improving the accuracy of sentiment classification, as presented in [10], where a framework incorporating lexical knowledge in supervised learning to enhance accuracy has been proposed. Opinion words have been used also for unsupervised learning approaches like the ones presented in [11,12].

Another research direction concerns the exploitation of discourse-analysis techniques. [13,14] discuss some discourse-based supervised and unsupervised approaches for opinion analysis; while in [15], the authors present an approach to identify discourse relations.

The approaches presented above are applied at the document-level, i.e., the polarity value is assigned to the entire document content. However, for improving the accuracy of the sentiment classification, a more fine-grained analysis of the text, i.e., the sentiment classification of the single sentences, has to be performed. In the case of sentence-level sentiment classification, two different sub-tasks have to be addressed: (i) to determine if the sentence is subjective or objective, and (ii) in the case that the sentence is subjective, to determine if the opinion expressed in the sentence is positive, negative, or neutral. The task of classifying a sentence as subjective or objective, called "subjectivity classification", has been widely discussed in the literature [16–20]. Once subjective sentences are identified, the same methods as for sentiment classification may be applied. For example, in [21] the authors consider gradable adjectives for sentiment spotting; while in [22,23] the authors built models to identify some specific types of opinions.

The growth of product reviews was the perfect floor for using sentiment analysis techniques in marketing activities. However, the issue of improving the ability of detecting the different opinions concerning the same product expressed in the same review became a challenging problem. Such a task has been faced by introducing "aspect" extraction approaches that were able to extract, from each sentence, which is the aspect the opinion refers to. In the literature, many approaches have been proposed: conditional random fields (CRF) [24,25], hidden Markov models (HMM) [26–28], sequential rule mining [29], dependency tree kernels [30], and clustering [31]. In [32,33], a method was proposed to extract both opinion words and aspects simultaneously by exploiting some syntactic relations of opinion words and aspects.

A particular attention should be given also to the application of sentiment analysis in social networks. More and more often, people use social networks for expressing their moods concerning their last purchase or, in general, about new products. Such a social network environment opened up new challenges due to the different ways people express their opinions, as described by [34,35], who mention "noisy data" as one of the biggest hurdles in analyzing social network texts.

One of the first studies on sentiment analysis on micro-blogging websites has been discussed in [36], where the authors present a distant supervision-based approach for sentiment classification.

At the same time, the social dimension of the Web opens up the opportunity to combine computer science and social sciences to better recognize, interpret, and process opinions and sentiments expressed over it. Such multi-disciplinary approach has been called *sentic computing* [37]. Application domains where sentic computing has already shown its potential are the cognitive-inspired classification of images [38], of texts in natural language, and of handwritten text [39].

Finally, an interesting recent research direction is domain adaptation, as it has been shown that sentiment classification is highly sensitive to the domain from which the training data is extracted. A classifier trained using opinionated documents from one domain often performs poorly when it is applied or tested on opinionated documents from another domain, as we demonstrated through the example presented in Sect. 1. The reason is that words and even language constructs used in different domains for expressing opinions can be quite different. To make matters worse, the same word in one domain may have positive connotations, but in another domain may have negative connotations; therefore, domain adaptation is needed. In the literature, different approaches related to the Multi-Domain sentiment analysis have been proposed. Briefly, two main categories may be identified: (i) the transfer of learned classifiers across different domains [3,40–44], and (ii) the use of propagation of labels through graph structures [45–48]. Independently of the kind of approach, works using concepts rather than terms for representing different sentiments have been proposed and only recently, solutions based on the use of information retrieval strategies for building sentiment analysis systems have been presented [49].

3   The **SHELLFBK** System

The proposed system is based on the implementation of an IR approach for inferring both the polarity of a sentence and, if requested, the domain to which the sentence belongs to. The rational behind the usage of such an approach is that by using indexes, the computation of the Retrieval Status Value (RSV) [50] of a term or expression, automatically takes into account which are the elements that are more significant in each index with respect to the ones that, instead, are not important with respect to the index content. In this section, we present the steps we carried out to implement our IR based sentiment and theme classification system.

3.1   Indexes Construction

The proposed approach, with respect to a classic IR system, does not use a single index for containing all information, but a set of indexes are created in order to facilitate the identification of the correct polarity and domain, of a sentence during the validation phase. In particular, we built the following set of indexes:

- **Domain Indexes:** a different index has been built for each domain identified in the training set. This way, it is possible to store information about which terms, or expression, are relevant for each domain.
- **Polarity Indexes:** from the training set, the positive, negative, and neutral sentences have been indexed separately for each domain.

For each document of the training set, we exploited the Stanford CoreNLP toolkit (see [51]) for extracting the dependencies between the terms. From such dependencies, we extract the information used as input in the indexing procedure. As an example, let's consider the following sentence:

"I came here to reflect my happiness by fishing."

This sentence has a positive polarity and belongs to the "outdoor_activity" domain. By applying the Stanford parser, the dependencies that are extracted are the following ones:

```
nsubj(came-2, I-1)
nsubj(reflect-5, I-1)
root(ROOT-0, came-2)
advmod(came-2, here-3)
aux(reflect-5, to-4)
xcomp(came-2, reflect-5)
poss(happiness-7, my-6)
dobj(reflect-5, happiness-7)
prep_by(reflect-5, fishing-9)
```

Each dependency is composed by three elements: the name of the "relation" (R), the "governor" (G) that is the first term of the dependency, and the "dependent" (D) that is the second one. We extract, from each dependency, the structure "field - content" shown in Table 1 by using as example the dependency "dobj(reflect-5, happiness-7)". Such a structure is then given as input to the index, taking care of storing single words for fields G and R only if they are nouns, verbs, adverbs or adjectives.

Table 1. Field structure and corresponding content stored in the index.

Field name	Content
RGD	"dobj-reflect-happiness"
RDG	"dobj-happiness-reflect"
GD	"reflect-happiness"
DG	"happiness-reflect"
G	"reflect"
D	"happiness"

The structure shown in Table 1 is created for each dependency extracted from the sentence and the aggregation of all structures are stored as final record in the index.

3.2   Domain and Polarity Computation

Once the indexes are built, both the polarity and the domain of each sentence that need to be evaluated, are computed by performing a set of queries on the indexes. In our approach, we implemented a variation of classic IR scoring formula for our purposes. In the classical TF-IDF IR model [52], the *inverse document frequency* value is used for identifying which are the most significant documents with respect to a particular query. This value is useful when we want to identify the uniqueness of a document with respect to a term contained in a query, with respect to the other documents stored into the index. In our case, the scenario is different because if a term, or expression, occurs often in the index, this aspect has to be emphasized instead of being discriminated. Therefore, in our scoring formula we consider, as final score of a term or an expression, the document frequency (DF) value (i.e., the inverse of the IDF). This way, we are able to infer if a particular term or expression is significant or not for a given polarity value or domain.

The queries are built with the same procedure used for creating the records stored in the indexes. For each sentence to evaluate, a set of queries, one for each dependency extracted from the sentence is performed on the indexes and the results are aggregated for inferring both the polarity and domain of the sentence.

As example of how the system works, let's consider the following sentence:

"I feel good and I feel healthy."

For simplicity, we only consider the following two extracted dependencies:

```
acomp(feel-2, good-3)
acomp(feel-6, healthy-7)
```

From these two dependencies, we generate the following two queries:

```
Q1:''RGD:"acomp-feel-good"
     OR RDG:"acomp-good-feel"
     OR GD:"feel-good"OR DG:"good-feel"
     OR G:"feel"OR D:"good"
Q2:"RGD:"acomp-feel-healthy"
     OR RDG:"acomp-healthy-feel"
     OR GD:"feel-healthy"OR DG:"healthy-feel"
     OR G:"feel"OR D:"healthy"
```

For each index I the value representing the RSV is the sum of the DF evaluated for each field F of the query:

$$
\begin{aligned}
RSV(I) = \ & DF(RGD_{Q1}) + DF(RDG_{Q1}) + \\
& DF(GD_{Q1}) + DF(DG_{Q1}) + DF(G_{Q1}) + \\
& DF(D_{Q1}) + DF(RGD_{Q2}) + DF(RDG_{Q2}) + \\
& DF(GD_{Q2}) + DF(DG_{Q2}) + DF(G_{Q2}) + \\
& DF(D_{Q2})
\end{aligned}
\tag{2}
$$

In this way, we can easily assign a domain to a sentence evaluating its RSV over each domain index and assign it the top scoring one:

$$
\text{Domain}(S) = \operatorname*{argmax}_{i \in 1 \ldots k} RSV(S, D_i)
\tag{3}
$$

Table 2. Precision-recall analysis and winners for Task 1.

System	Accuracy	
Kim Schouten and Flavius Frasincar	0.4129	1
Giulio Petrucci and Mauro Dragoni	0.4078	2
Andrea Giovanni Nuzzolese and Misael Mongioví	0.3011	3

If more domains end up having the same RSV the are all considered. Once the domain has been assigned, we compute the polarity performing the same queries against the three indexes containing polarized records for the domain resulting from the previous phase: positive (POS_D), negative (NEG_D), and neutral (NEU_D)

$$\text{Polarity}(S) = \underset{P \in POS_D, NEU_D, NEG_D}{\text{argmax}} RSV(S, P) \tag{4}$$

4 In-Vitro Evaluation and Challenge Results

In this Section, we present the results of a preliminary in-vitro evaluation performed on the Blitzer dataset and the results obtained by the system during the second edition of the ESWC Challenge on Semantic Sentiment Analysis.

4.1 In-Vitro Evaluation

We reported here a small evaluation conducted on the Blitzer dataset.[1] We built the indexes by using a random selection of 95 % of the reviews contained in such dataset. The remaining 5 % has been used, instead, for testing purpose, ending up in 1873 items. The system correctly classified the polarity of 1273 (i.e. 67.98 %) in the test set.

In order to replicate the experiments, the package containing the executable file, the used data, and the indexes we constructed is available online[2].

4.2 Participation at ESWC 2015 Challenge on Semantic Sentiment Analysis

Our system participated at the binary polarity detection challenge. 10, 000 sentences and their sentence-level polarities have been randomly taken from the Blitzer dataset[3]. 5000 of them had a positive polarity whereas 5000 had a negative polarity.

Systems were evaluated by computing their accuracy values.

---

[1] http://www.cs.jhu.edu/~mdredze/datasets/sentiment/.

[2] The package containing instructions for replicating the experiments can be downloaded at http://dkmtools.fbk.eu/moki/demo/SentIRe.zip.

[3] http://www.cs.jhu.edu/~mdredze/datasets/sentiment/.

In Table 2, we show the accuracy analysis of the three systems competing for Task 1.

As it is possible to see, our system obtained an accuracy very close to the one obtained by the winners. This result is encouraging for improving the system.

5   Conclusion

In this paper, we described the SHELLFBK system that partecipated in ESWC 2015 Sentiment Analysis challenge. Our system, relying on a large dataset, exploits IR techniques to classify sentences by domain and then by polarity, effectively providing domain specific sentiment analysis. Even if the metric used was as simple as possible, the system obtained reasonable prformances in an in-vitro evaluation. Future work will address the possibility to exploit more sophisticated metrics considering the belonging of a text to a certain domain not in a binary but in a *fuzzy* fashion, measuring some sort of semantic relatedness of the sentence under test with each domain and using such measures as weights for the polarity detection phase. Moreover, we intend to explore the integration of sentiment knowledge bases [53] in order to move toward a more cognitive approach.

References

1. Pang, B., Lee, L., Vaithyanathan, S.: Thumbs up? sentiment classification using machine learning techniques. In: Proceedings of the Conference on Empirical Methods in Natural Language Processing (EMNLP), pp. 79–86. Association for Computational Linguistics, Philadelphia, July 2002
2. Liu, B., Zhang, L.: A survey of opinion mining and sentiment analysis. In: Aggarwal, C.C., Zhai, C.X. (eds.) Mining Text Data, pp. 415–463. Springer, New York (2012)
3. Blitzer, J., Dredze, M., Pereira, F.: Biographies, bollywood, boom-boxes and blenders: domain adaptation for sentiment classification. In: ACL, pp. 187–205 (2007)
4. Pang, B., Lee, L.: Opinion mining and sentiment analysis. Found. Trends Inf. Retrieval 2(1–2), 1–135 (2008)
5. Pang, B., Lee, L.: A sentimental education: sentiment analysis using subjectivity summarization based on minimum cuts. In: ACL, pp. 271–278 (2004)
6. Dave, K., Lawrence, S., Pennock, D.M.: Mining the peanut gallery: opinion extraction and semantic classification of product reviews. In: WWW, pp. 519–528 (2003)
7. Paltoglou, G., Thelwall, M.: A study of information retrieval weighting schemes for sentiment analysis. In: ACL, pp. 1386–1395 (2010)
8. Tan, S., Wang, Y., Cheng, X.: Combining learn-based and lexicon-based techniques for sentiment detection without using labeled examples. In: SIGIR, pp. 743–744 (2008)
9. Qiu, L., Zhang, W., Hu, C., Zhao, K.: Selc: a self-supervised model for sentiment classification. In: CIKM, pp. 929–936 (2009)
10. Melville, P., Gryc, W., Lawrence, R.D.: Sentiment analysis of blogs by combining lexical knowledge with text classification. In: KDD, pp. 1275–1284 (2009)

11. Taboada, M., Brooke, J., Tofiloski, M., Voll, K.D., Stede, M.: Lexicon-based methods for sentiment analysis. Comput. Linguist. **37**(2), 267–307 (2011)

12. Turney, P.D.: Thumbs up or thumbs down? semantic orientation applied to unsupervised classification of reviews. In: ACL, pp. 417–424 (2002)

13. Somasundaran, S.: Discourse-level relations for Opinion Analysis. Ph.D. thesis, University of Pittsburgh (2010)

14. Asher, N., Benamara, F., Mathieu, Y.Y.: Distilling opinion in discourse: a preliminary study. In: COLING (Posters), pp. 7–10 (2008)

15. Wang, H., Zhou, G.: Topic-driven multi-document summarization. In: IALP, pp. 195–198 (2010)

16. Riloff, E., Patwardhan, S., Wiebe, J.: Feature subsumption for opinion analysis. In: EMNLP, pp. 440–448 (2006)

17. Wiebe, J., Wilson, T., Bruce, R.F., Bell, M., Martin, M.: Learning subjective language. Comput. Linguist. **30**(3), 277–308 (2004)

18. Wilson, T., Wiebe, J., Hwa, R.: Just how mad are you? finding strong and weak opinion clauses. In: AAAI, pp. 761–769 (2004)

19. Wilson, T., Wiebe, J., Hwa, R.: Recognizing strong and weak opinion clauses. Comput. Intell. **22**(2), 73–99 (2006)

20. Yu, H., Hatzivassiloglou, V.: Towards answering opinion questions: separating facts from opinions and identifying the polarity of opinion sentences. In: Proceedings of the 2003 Conference on Empirical Methods in Natural Language Processing, EMNLP 2003, pp. 129–136. Association for Computational Linguistics, Stroudsburg (2003)

21. Hatzivassiloglou, V., Wiebe, J.: Effects of adjective orientation and gradability on sentence subjectivity. In: COLING, pp. 299–305 (2000)

22. Kim, S.M., Hovy, E.H.: Crystal: analyzing predictive opinions on the web. In: EMNLP-CoNLL, pp. 1056–1064 (2007)

23. Kim, S.M., Pantel, P., Chklovski, T., Pennacchiotti, M.: Automatically assessing review helpfulness. In: EMNLP, pp. 423–430 (2006)

24. Jakob, N., Gurevych, I.: Extracting opinion targets in a single and cross-domain setting with conditional random fields. In: EMNLP, pp. 1035–1045 (2010)

25. Lafferty, J.D., McCallum, A., Pereira, F.C.N.: Conditional random fields: probabilistic models for segmenting and labeling sequence data. In: ICML, pp. 282–289 (2001)

26. Freitag, D., McCallum, A.: Information extraction with hmm structures learned by stochastic optimization. In: AAAI/IAAI, pp. 584–589 (2000)

27. Jin, W., Ho, H.H.: A novel lexicalized HMM-based learning framework for web opinion mining. In: Proceedings of the 26th Annual International Conference on Machine Learning, ICML 2009, pp. 465–472. ACM, New York (2009)

28. Jin, W., Ho, H.H., Srihari, R.K.: Opinionminer: a novel machine learning system for web opinion mining and extraction. In: KDD, pp. 1195–1204 (2009)

29. Liu, B., Hu, M., Cheng, J.: Opinion observer: analyzing and comparing opinions on the web. In: WWW, pp. 342–351 (2005)

30. Wu, Y., Zhang, Q., Huang, X., Wu, L.: Phrase dependency parsing for opinion mining. In: EMNLP, pp. 1533–1541 (2009)

31. Su, Q., Xu, X., Guo, H., Guo, Z., Wu, X., Zhang, X., Swen, B., Su, Z.: Hidden sentiment association in chinese web opinion mining. In: WWW, pp. 959–968 (2008)

32. Qiu, G., Liu, B., Bu, J., Chen, C.: Expanding domain sentiment lexicon through double propagation. In: IJCAI, pp. 1199–1204 (2009)

33. Qiu, G., Liu, B., Bu, J., Chen, C.: Opinion word expansion and target extraction through double propagation. Comput. Linguist. **37**(1), 9–27 (2011)

34. Barbosa, L., Feng, J.: Robust sentiment detection on twitter from biased and noisy data. In: COLING (Posters), pp. 36–44 (2010)
35. Bermingham, A., Smeaton, A.F.: Classifying sentiment in microblogs: is brevity an advantage? In: CIKM, pp. 1833–1836 (2010)
36. Go, A., Bhayani, R., Huang, L.: Twitter sentiment classification using distant supervision. CS224N Project Report, Stanford University (2009)
37. Cambria, E., Hussain, A.: Sentic Computing: Techniques, Tools, and Applications. SpringerBriefs in Cognitive Computation. Springer, Dordrecht (2012)
38. Cambria, E., Hussain, A.: Sentic album: content-, concept-, and context-based online personal photo management system. Cognitive Comput. **4**(4), 477–496 (2012)
39. Wang, Q.F., Cambria, E., Liu, C.L., Hussain, A.: Common sense knowledge for handwritten chinese recognition. Cognitive Comput. **5**(2), 234–242 (2013)
40. Yang, H., Callan, J., Si, L.: Knowledge transfer and opinion detection in the TREC 2006 blog track. In: TREC (2006)
41. Pan, S.J., Ni, X., Sun, J.T., Yang, Q., Chen, Z.: Cross-domain sentiment classification via spectral feature alignment. In: WWW, pp. 751–760 (2010)
42. Bollegala, D., Weir, D.J., Carroll, J.A.: Cross-domain sentiment classification using a sentiment sensitive thesaurus. IEEE Trans. Knowl. Data Eng. **25**(8), 1719–1731 (2013)
43. Xia, R., Zong, C., Hu, X., Cambria, E.: Feature ensemble plus sample selection: domain adaptation for sentiment classification. IEEE Int. Syst. **28**(3), 10–18 (2013)
44. Yoshida, Y., Hirao, T., Iwata, T., Nagata, M., Matsumoto, Y.: Transfer learning for multiple-domain sentiment analysis–identifying domain dependent/independent word polarity. In: AAAI, pp. 1286–1291 (2011)
45. Ponomareva, N., Thelwall, M.: Semi-supervised vs. cross-domain graphs for sentiment analysis. In: RANLP, pp. 571–578 (2013)
46. Tsai, A.C.R., Wu, C.E., Tsai, R.T.H., Hsu, J.Y.: Building a concept-level sentiment dictionary based on commonsense knowledge. IEEE Int. Syst. **28**(2), 22–30 (2013)
47. Tai, Y.J., Kao, H.Y.: Automatic domain-specific sentiment lexicon generation with label propagation. In: iiWAS, pp. 53:53–53:62. ACM (2013)
48. Huang, S., Niu, Z., Shi, C.: Automatic construction of domain-specific sentiment lexicon based on constrained label propagation. Knowl. Based Syst. **56**, 191–200 (2014)
49. Dragoni, M.: Shellfbk: an information retrieval-based system for multi-domain sentiment analysis. In: Proceedings of the 9th International Workshop on Semantic Evaluation, SemEval '2015, pp. 502–509. Association for Computational Linguistics, Denver, June 2015
50. da Costa Pereira, C., Dragoni, M., Pasi, G.: Multidimensional relevance: prioritized aggregation in a personalized information retrieval setting. Inf. Process. Manage. **48**(2), 340–357 (2012)
51. Manning, C.D., Surdeanu, M., Bauer, J., Finkel, J., Bethard, S.J., McClosky, D.: The Stanford CoreNLP natural language processing toolkit. In: Proceedings of 52nd Annual Meeting of the Association for Computational Linguistics: System Demonstrations, pp. 55–60. Association for Computational Linguistics, Baltimore, June 2014
52. van Rijsbergen, C.J.: Information Retrieval. Butterworth, London (1979)
53. Dragoni, M., Tettamanzi, A.G., da Costa Pereira, C.: Propagating and aggregating fuzzy polarities for concept-level sentiment analysis. Cognitive Comput. **7**(2), 186–197 (2015)

Detecting Sentiment Polarities with Sentilo

Andrea Giovanni Nuzzolese[✉] and Misael Mongiovì

Semantic Technology Lab, ISTC-CNR, Rome, Catania, Italy
{andrea.nuzzolese,misael.mongiovi}@istc.cnr.it

Abstract. We present the tool used for the Concept-Level Sentiment Analysis Challenge ESWC-CLSA 2015 Task #1, concerning binary polarity detection of the sentiment of a sentence. Our tool is a little modification of *Sentilo* [7], an unsupervised, domain-independent system, previously developed by our group, that performs sentiment analysis by hybridizing natural language processing techniques with semantic web technologies. Sentilo is able to recognize the opinion holder and measure the sentiment expressed on topics and sub-topics. The knowledge extracted from the text is represented by means of an RDF graph. Holders and topics are linked to external knowledge. Sentilo is available as a REST service as well as a user-friendly demo.

1 Introduction

Sentiment Analysis (SA) is a widely studied problem in Natural Language Processing (NLP). Recent studies have shown that including semantic features to SA algorithms improves their performance [8]. However, existing approaches are mainly supervised and hence they rely on the availability of manually annotated samples and are usually domain-dependent. The approach we used for this challenge (Sentilo) is different in that it is a domain-independent, unsupervised approach that exploits natural language processing and semantic technologies.

Another common aspect of most existing SA methods is that they neglect the identification of holders and topics of an opinion as a task *per se*. They mainly focus on interpreting the *tone* of a sentence by identifying terms that carry a particular sentiment polarity; it has been demonstrated that including topic detection in models used by algorithms for SA improves their results [2,5,9].

For example, given the following opinion: *"This phone is not a good product, but its producer made a good job with other phones."*, an ideal system would be able to identify several topics referred by such opinionated sentence: "the phone", "the producer" and "the job made by the producer with other phones". Additionally, such an ideal system would be able to analyze that the sentiment expressed on "the phone" is negative, while the sentiment expressed on the job made by the producer, and the producer itself is positive, and that the whole sentence carries both positive and negative sentiments.

In this paper we present Sentilo, the system we used for this challenge. Sentilo was designed to enable the described ideal behavior: it identifies the holder of an opinion, the topics and sub-topics of that opinion, and the sentiment expressed

© Springer International Publishing Switzerland 2015
F. Gandon et al. (Eds.): SemWebEval 2015, CCIS 548, pp. 244–250, 2015.
DOI: 10.1007/978-3-319-25518-7_21

on each of them by the holder as well as the sentiment of the overall sentence. Topics, holder, and sentiments are represented in an RDF (Resource Description Framework) graph, and topics and holders are linked to public data sources.

Sentilo[1] can be used through a graphical user interface (GUI) or through a REST API. Sentilo is also a component of SHELDON [6], a complete text processing tool. The GUI serves mainly as a demonstrator of its capability, while the REST service allows client applications to use it. Potential users may be Amazon, TripAdvisor, iTunes, Magazines and News, etc., all stakeholders that deal with opinions or reviews and have interest in performing data analytics on such opinions. Additionally, political parties as well as marketing companies would also be potential users of Sentilo. A more detailed description of Sentilo can be found here [7].

This paper is structured as follows: Sect. 2 introduces the architecture of Sentilo and explains how it performs polarity detection. Section 3 describe the task of the challenge and how we addressed it. Section 4 reports the results obtained by Sentilo at the challenge. Finally Sect. 5 concludes the paper.

2   Description of Sentilo

Sentilo implements a novel approach to the sentiment analysis based on sentic computing and it is able to compute topic-level as well as sentence-level sentiment scores. In fact, it represents opinion sentences by using an ontology that defines the main concepts and relations among holders and topics in opinion sentences and assigns separate scores to topics.

This ontology enables Sentilo to model opinion sentences according to the neo-Davidsonian events: events and situations are considered first class entities and they are used in order to gather contextual information for evaluating sentiment expressions in opinion sentences.

Figure 1 shows the architecture of Sentilo. The components are described in [7]. Please refer to this work for further details.

We describe Sentilo with an example. Consider the sentence *"We hope that the company will be condemned"*. Figure 2 shows (a fragment of) the RDF graph representing this sentence. Sentilo identifies the node "fred:person_1" (corresponding to "we") as the holder of the opinion, "fred:condemn_1" (corresponding to the condemn of the company) as the topic and "fred:company_1" (the company) as a subtopic. The reader can easily inspect the whole resulting graph by running the Sentilo demo on the sample sentence[2].

The graph in Fig. 2 is derived by Sentilo from the RDF graph produced by FRED (see Fig. 1), which represents the logical form of the original sentence according to Semantic Web and Linked Data design principles [1,3], and by extending the representation model with event- and situation-semantics as formally defined by DOLCE+DnS[3] ontology [4]. Figure 3 shows the output of FRED for this sentence.

---

[1] http://wit.istc.cnr.it/stlab-tools/sentilo.

[2] http://wit.istc.cnr.it/stlab-tools/sentilo/service.

[3] Dolce Ultra Lite Ontology. http://ontologydesignpatterns.org/ont/dul/DUL.owl.

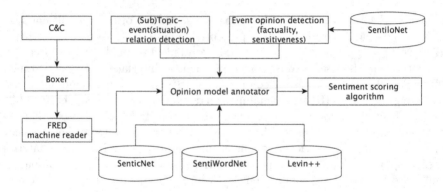

Fig. 1. Architecture of Sentilo [7].

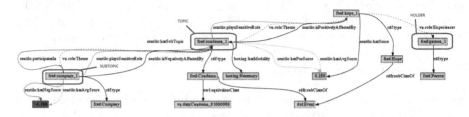

Fig. 2. RDF graph for the sentence *We hope that the company will be condemned.*

The graph returned by FRED (Fig. 3) is enriched by Sentilo (Fig. 2), using SentiloNet and OntoSentilo as background knowledge. The opinion holder expresses a positive opinion on the event "condemn", therefore this event is associated with a positive score. The "company" plays a sensitive role in the "condemn" event since it is the theme of the condemn. More precisely, the company is affected negatively by the "condemn" event. Therefore expressing a positive sentiment on the condemnation of the company cognitively implies having a negative opinion on the company. Sentilo captures very well these relations thanks to

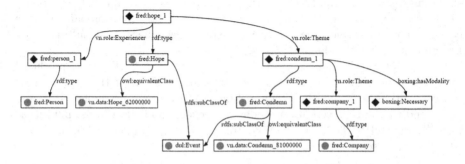

Fig. 3. FRED graph for the sentence *We hope that the company will be condemned.*

the SentiloNet resource, which provides a cognitive-oriented background knowledge that includes the concepts of *role sensitivity* and *factual impact*.

For the purpose of this challenge, after analyzing the sentence with Sentilo, we compute a polarity score for the whole sentence by averaging the polarities of its topics/subtopics.

3   Addressing the Concept-Level Sentiment Analysis Challenge

The Concept-Level Sentiment Analysis Challenge is defined in terms of different tasks, i.e., Task #1, Task #2, and Task #3.

The Task #1 is about binary (positive or negative) polarity detection of opinion sentences. The systems are assessed according to precision, recall and F-measure of detected polarity values of each review of the evaluation dataset. The problem of subjectivity detection is not addressed within this Challenge.

The Task #2 is about aspect-based sentiment analysis. The output required by this Task is a set of aspects of the reviewed product and a binary polarity value associated to each of such aspects. So, for example, while for the Elementary Task an overall polarity (positive or negative) is expected for a review about a mobile phone, this Task requires a set of aspects (such as *speaker, touchscreen, camera*, etc.) and a polarity value associated with each of such aspects.

The Task #3 is about frame entities identification. In consists of evaluating the capability of the proposed systems to identify the objects involved in a typical opinion frame according to their role: holders, topics, opinion concepts (i.e. terms referring to highly polarised concepts). For example, in a sentence such as *The mayor is loved by the people in the city, but he has been criticized by the state government*, an approach should be able to identify that *the people* and *state government* are the opinion holders, *is loved* and *has been criticized* represent the opinion concepts, and *The mayor* identifies a topic of the opinion.

We have configured a version of Sentilo that is properly designed in order to address the Task #1 of the Concept-Level Sentiment Analysis Challenge. Sentilo returns a set of polarity values associated with each topic/subtopics of an opinion sentence. These polarity values range on a scale from -1 (negative polarity) to +1 (positive polarity). In order to have a polarity value for a whole sentence we extended Sentilo in order to

- compute the average $A_{sentilo}$ of the polarities of the topics/subtopics;
- normalise the average polarity value $A_{sentilo}$ (ranging from -1 to +1) to address the dichotomous score required by Task #1, i.e., 0 meaning negative polarity and 1 meaning positive polarity.

The normalisation is performed by applying the following rationale:

- the polarity is negative (its value is 0) if $A_{sentilo} < 0$;
- the polarity is positive (its value is 1) if $A_{sentilo} >= 0$;

As an example, given the following input:

```
<sentence id='18'>
    <text>
    Koontz finds his footing in the final chapters, a Lovecraftian
    showdown between Frankenstein and his   artificial creations inside a
    series of tunnels beneath a dump.
    </text>
    <polarity>null</polarity>
</sentence>
```

Sentilo produces the following output according to the requiments of Task #1:

```
<sentence id='18'>
    <text>
    Koontz finds his footing in the final chapters, a Lovecraftian
    showdown between Frankenstein and his   artificial creations inside a
    series of tunnels beneath a dump.
    </text>
    <polarity>1</polarity>
</sentence>
```

where the polarity value has been set to 1 (i.e., meaning positive polarity). This value is not provided in input (i.e., the value was `null`).

The performance of Sentilo was then assessed by using the guidelines provided by Task #1. Namely, we used the $F1$ measure defined as follows:

$$F1 = \frac{2 * precision * recall}{precision + recall}$$

Having:

$$precision = \frac{tp}{tp + fp}$$

$$recall = \frac{tp}{tp + fn}$$

Where:

– a true positive, i.e., tp, occurs when a sentence is correctly classified as positive;
– a false positive, i.e., fp occurs when a sentence is classified as negative;
– a true negative, i.e., tn occurs when a negative sentence is correctly identified as such.

4   Results

The evaluation dataset for the Task #1 of the Concept Level Analysis Challenge counts of 10,000 sentences along with their sentence-level polarities. These sentences have been randomly taken from the Blitzer dataset[4] according to the following rationale: 5000 of them had a positive polarity whereas 5000 had a

[4] http://www.cs.jhu.edu/~mdredze/datasets/sentiment/.

negative polarity. The dataset can be downloaded from the main pages of the challenge[5].

Table 1 shows the results of the challenge in term of accuracy of the three systems competing for Task 1.

Table 1. Results of the Task #1 of the challenge.

System	Accuracy
Kim Schouten and Flavius Frasincar	0.4129
Giulio Petrucci and Mauro Dragoni	0.4078
Sentilo	0.3011

Results show that the accuracy for the polarity detection of opinion sentences in Sentilo still needs a significant improvement. Probably, computing the polarity of an opinion sentence by taking into account the average of all its topic and subtopics is fairly straightforwards. We believe that better results can be obtained by filtering and weighting the topics/subtopics holding a sentiment score in order to assign a higher confidence to those topics and subtopics that are more relevant with respect to the sentence context. Nevertheless, Sentilo was awarded with the most innovative approach prize. This demonstrates the our solution is novel and fairly promising.

5   Conclusions

In this paper we presented the algorithm used for the Concept-Level Sentiment Analysis Challenge ESWC-CLSA 2015 Task #1. The method is based on Sentilo, a tool developed by our group that computes sentiment scores for topics and subtopics of a sentence. Sentilo is available as a demo[6] and accessible through a REST API.

Acknowledgement. The research leading to these results has received funding from the European Union Horizons 2020 – the Framework Programme for Research and Innovation (2014–2020) under grant agreement 643808 Project MARIO "Managing active and healthy aging with use of caring service robots".

References

1. Bizer, C., Heath, T., Berners-Lee, T.: Linked data - the story so far. Int. J. Semantic Web Inf. Sys. **5**(3), 1–22 (2009)

---

5 https://github.com/diegoref/ESWC-CLSA/blob/master/task1Challenge_testGold. zip.

6 http://wit.istc.cnr.it/stlab-tools/sentilo.

2. Cai, K., Spangler, S., Chen, Y., Zhang, L.: Leveraging sentiment analysis for topic detection. IEEE/WIC/ACM Int. Conf. Web Intell. Intell. Agent Technol. **1**, 265–271 (2008)
3. Consoli, S., Mongiovì, M., Nuzzolese, A.G., Peroni, S., Presutti, V., Reforgiato, D., Spampinato, D.: A smart city data model based on semantics best practice and principles (2015)
4. Gangemi, A., Presutti, V.: Towards a pattern science for the semantic web. Semantic Web **1**(1,2), 61–68 (2010)
5. Lin, C., He, Y., Everson, R., Ruger, S.: Weakly supervised joint sentiment-topic detection from text. IEEE Trans. Knowl. Data Eng. **24**(6), 1134–1145 (2012)
6. Recupero, D.R., Nuzzolese, A.G., Consoli, S., Presutti, V., Peroni, S., Mongiovì, M.: Extracting knowledge from text using sheldon, a semantic holistic framework for linked ontology data (2015)
7. Recupero, D.R., Presutti, V., Consoli, S., Gangemi, A., Nuzzolese, A.G.: Sentilo: frame-based sentiment analysis. In: Cognitive Computation, pp. 1–15
8. Saif, H., He, Y., Alani, H.: Semantic sentiment analysis of twitter. In: Cudré-Mauroux, P., Heflin, J., Sirin, E., Tudorache, T., Euzenat, J., Hauswirth, M., Parreira, J.X., Hendler, J., Schreiber, G., Bernstein, A., Blomqvist, E. (eds.) ISWC 2012, Part I. LNCS, vol. 7649, pp. 508–524. Springer, Heidelberg (2012)
9. Titov, I., McDonald, R.: Modeling online reviews with multi-grain topic models. In: Proceedings of the 17th international conference on World Wide Web, WWW 2008, pp. 111–120. ACM, New York (2008)

Supervised Opinion Frames Detection with RAID

Alessio Palmero Aprosio[(⊠)], Francesco Corcoglioniti, Mauro Dragoni,
and Marco Rospocher

Fondazione Bruno Kessler, Trento, Italy
{aprosio,corcoglio,dragoni,rospocher}@fbk.eu

Abstract. Most systems for opinion analysis focus on the classification of opinion polarities and rarely consider the task of identifying the different elements and relations forming an opinion frame. In this paper, we present RAID, a tool featuring a processing pipeline for the extraction of opinion frames from text with their opinion expressions, holders, targets and polarities. RAID leverages a lexical, syntactic and semantic analysis of text, using several NLP tools such as dependency parsing, semantic role labelling, named entity recognition and word sense disambiguation. In addition, linguistic resources such as SenticNet and the MPQA Subjectivity Lexicon are used both to locate opinions in the text and to classify their polarities according to a fuzzy model that combines the sentiment values of different opinion words. RAID was evaluated on three different datasets and is released as open source software under the GPLv3 license.

1 Introduction

In the last years, analysis of sentiment and emotions in texts got increasing attention in the research community, and big companies started to release commercial tools whose purpose is to analyze opinions in products reviews, blog posts and social contents. See, for example, business tools such as IBM Watson Analytics[1] and SenticNet,[2] or academic tools like Stanford Sentiment tool[3].

Unfortunately, most of the commercial tools available for sentiment classification are limited to a small set of emotions, and can only manage explicit expressions, without being able to understand implicit opinions. In particular, they cannot deeply understand the frame outside the opinion expression itself, including the identification of the different roles involved in the expression. In contrast with this, opinion mining techniques capture, along with the sentiment expression, the subject(s) and the object(s) of the opinion, and its strength (intensity). This paradigm, which is the focus of this work, has great potential in gathering political trends, brand perception and business intelligence.

---

[1] http://www.ibm.com/analytics/.

[2] http://business.sentic.net/.

[3] http://nlp.stanford.edu/sentiment/.

© Springer International Publishing Switzerland 2015
F. Gandon et al. (Eds.): SemWebEval 2015, CCIS 548, pp. 251–263, 2015.
DOI: 10.1007/978-3-319-25518-7_22

Given a sentence, our task is to identify each *opinion frame* in it, extracting its *expression* span, *polarity, holder* and *target* text spans.[4] For example, in the sentence:

> *Conservative Justice Minister Kenneth Clarke said Britain's exit from the EU would be disastrous.*

token 'disastrous' is an expression that clearly denotes an opinion whose polarity is negative, holder is 'Minister Kenneth Clarke' and target is 'Britain's exit from the EU'.

Early works on opinion classification used very simple lexical features [18], following the general idea that adding complex (and computationally expensive) features leads to a small increment of performances. This approach worked well for sentiment classification, but is not enough powerful when the task consists in extracting the whole opinion frame with its expression, holder, target and polarity. For this complex task, which involves relations between entities, tools for *deep* Natural Language Processing (NLP) such as dependency parsing and semantic role labelling (SRL) are used due to their capability of extracting semantic relations between entities mentioned in texts.

In this paper, we present RAID, a tool for identifying opinion frames in texts leveraging deep NLP and semantic features extracted from text. RAID extraction algorithm consists of a number of processing steps organized in a pipeline:

- first, we use a Conditional Random Field (CRF) tagger to identify the opinion expressions in a sentence, using features extracted from NLP tools and resources such as SenticNet [3] and the MPQA Subjectivity Lexicon;
- then, target(s) and holder(s) for each expression are extracted using a combination of Support Vector Machine (SVM) classifiers, employing features that convey lexical, syntactic and semantic properties of the candidate target/holder and that leverage a syntactic and semantic role labelling (SRL) analysis of the text;
- finally, we classify the polarity of the expression using fuzzy logic for modeling concept polarities, combining it with a knowledge graph built on top of SenticNet.

We evaluated RAID on three different datasets using the intersection-based precision-recall measures [10], as well as the evaluation measures used in the ESWC2015-CLSA[5] challenge where RAID was a participant system. RAID is released under the GPLv3 license and is available as a module of Pikes,[6] a free knowledge extraction suite that includes also a NLP pipeline based on Stanford CoreNLP[7] and Mate Tools,[8] as well as a rule-based application capturing and

---

[4] In literature, terms defining roles in opinions may vary: in particular, the holder can also be expressed as *source*, and the target as *topic*.
[5] https://github.com/diegoref/ESWC-CLSA.
[6] http://pikes.fbk.eu/.
[7] http://nlp.stanford.edu/software/corenlp.shtml.
[8] https://code.google.com/p/mate-tools/.

formalizing in RDF important linguistic aspects, and a set of tools that allows a user to access and query common Semantic Web and NLP resources. The source code[9] and a working demo[10] of RAID are available online.

The remainder of the paper is organized as follows. Section 2 contains an overview of related work and describes the resources used for training and evaluation. Section 3 illustrates the approach for opinion expression, holder and target extraction, along with polarity classification. Section 4 reports the performances of our system over the three considered datasets. Finally, Sect. 5 sets out conclusions and possible future works.

2   Related Work

In this section we provide a brief overview of related work in opinion frame extraction (Sect. 2.1) and we describe three relevant datasets annotated with opinion frames that we use for training and testing RAID (Sect. 2.2).

2.1   Approaches for Opinion Frames Extraction

There are several works dealing with the extraction of opinion frames including opinion expression, holder, target and polarity.

In [5], opinion expressions are extracted using CRF-based sequence taggers and extracting the n-best sequences, while the opinion holder is identified using a Maximum Entropy relation classifier. Evaluation is performed against the MPQA corpus [15] (400 manually annotated documents at that time, see Sect. 2.2).

The work by Ruppenhofer et al. [12] describes how the perfect annotated resource should deal with subjective expressions, both direct and hidden (i.e. a journalist showing his idea on a particular topic). They also show how SRL can help the task, and provide some examples where SRL is not enough.

The works described in [2,11] deal with the problem of extracting opinions from news. In [11], the authors use a FrameNet-based semantic role labeller: if the detected frame belongs to a selected list of frames, then manually crafted mapping rules are used to map some roles to the opinion holder/topic. Instead, [2] concentrates the effort on quotations extracted from news, identifying holder, target and expression using various external resources (such as WordNet-Affect and SentiWordNet), without the help of semantic role labelling.

In [16], holder extraction is performed by using convolution kernels, by identifying meaningful fragments of sequences or trees by themselves.

Sentilo [8] extracts opinion holders, topics (the targets) and sub-topics in a sentence, where a sub-topic is an entity related to the actual main target of the opinion.

Johansson et al. [10] extract opinion expressions using relational features between different opinions contained in the text. They also increase accuracy using a reranker and evaluate the performances of their system over the MPQA corpus.

---

[9] https://github.com/dkmfbk/pikes.
[10] https://knowledgestore2.fbk.eu/pikes-demo/.

Recently, the work in [1] describes an approach that projects opinion extraction on different languages using a running system in a source language and a word-aligned parallel corpus.

A good general overview of opinion mining can be found in [4,21].

2.2 Datasets Annotated with Opinion Frames

We briefly describe three datasets containing text documents manually annotated with opinion frames, summarizing in Table 1 their contents.

Table 1. Statistics about the available datasets.

Dataset	Docs	Sents	Tokens	Opinions
MPQA Opinion Corpus (DSE+ESE)	691	15,883	387,390	24,475
News Texts with Opinion Annotations	434	580	12,020	816
Darmstadt Service Review Corpus	491	9,836	177,020	2,867
Darmstadt Service Review Corpus (challenge)	372	6,221	113,293	2,014

MPQA Opinion Corpus. One of the first datasets annotated with opinion frames is the Multi-Perspective Question Answering (MPQA) Opinion Corpus [15]. In its latest version, it consists of 691 news articles from various English news sources. The corpus is manually annotated with what the authors call "private states", i.e. opinions, emotions, sentiments, speculations, evaluations, and internal states that cannot be directly observed by others. The annotations are at expression (subsentence) level and each expression is connected with its corresponding source (holder). Each source is in turn connected to a coreference chain, that can end to a real span in the text, or to the writer. Otherwise, the holder is considered as "implicit". Expressions are finally enhanced with other properties such as intensity (low, medium, high, extreme), polarity (positive, negative, neutral) and even confidence of the human annotator. Targets of opinions are annotated only in particular cases (for attitudes), but an effort in that direction can be found in [13]. The MPQA annotation scheme distinguishes between direct subjective expressions (DSE), expressive subjective expressions (ESE) and objective speech events (OSE). For example, in the sentence:

"The report is full of absurdities," Xirao-Nima said.

the token 'said' is a direct subjective expression where the intensity is 'neutral', the source is 'Xirao-Nima', the attitude (polarity) is 'negative', and the topic is 'report'; the expression 'full of absurdities' is an expressive subjective expression, where the intensity is 'high', the source is 'Xirao-Nima', and the attitude is 'negative'.

News Texts with Opinion Annotations (NTOA). This dataset has been produced as part of the OpeNER EU project[11] and consists of 471 pieces of text

---
[11] http://www.opener-project.eu/.

extracted from political news. It is freely available online.[12] The annotation does not cover the whole text, but only some sentences. For each article, a sentence containing an opinion is chosen and annotated; an additional "non opinion-ated" sentence is selected, just to include negative examples in the set useful for training. Sentences are then annotated with opinion holder, target, expression (distinguishing between *direct expression of attitude* and *indirect expression of attitude*), polarity (positive, negative, neutral) and strength (normal and strong). For example, in the sentence:

> *Germany wants a looser arrangement among national bank-resolution authorities.*

the token 'wants' represents the expression, 'Germany' is the holder, 'a looser arrangement' is the target; the polarity is 'positive' and the strength is 'normal'.

Darmstadt Service Review Corpus (DSRC). The Darmstadt Service Review Corpus [14] consists of consumer reviews annotated with opinion related information at the sentence and expression levels. In particular, word spans for opinion expressions, opinion targets and holders are marked. The data consists of 474 reviews collected from various review portals, and related to the universities and online services domains. For instance, in the sentence:

> *I don't know why this site seems to attract people who have sour grapes with respect to Capella.*

the span 'sour grapes' is annotated as the expression, 'people' as holder, 'Capella' as target; the polarity is 'negative' and the strength is 'weak'.

3   The RAID Pipeline

Opinion extraction in RAID consists of a number of processing steps organized in a pipeline. An input text document is pre-processed by running a number of NLP tools on it, in order to obtain the necessary NLP annotations (Sect. 3.1). Opinion expression spans are identified on a per-sentence basis (Sect. 3.2). For each identified expression, the corresponding holder and target spans are then extracted (Sect. 3.3). Finally, a positive / negative / neutral opinion polarity is assigned to the expression (Sect. 3.4). These steps are detailed in the remainder of the section.

3.1   Pre-processing

Starting from the raw document text, we apply a set of linguistic tools whose output is used to extract the features needed for opinion extraction. In particular, we use Tintop, the NLP pipeline included in the Pikes suite (see Sect. 1). It performs tokenization, sentence splitting, part-of-speech tagging, dependency parsing, semantic role labelling (SRL), named entity recognition, word sense

---

[12] https://github.com/opener-project/opinion_annotations_news.

disambiguation and supersense tagging with respect to WordNet 3.0. (using the UKB[13] tagger).

3.2   Extraction of Opinion Expressions

The task of extracting opinion expressions from a sentence is formulated as a sequence labelling problem and consists in tagging each token of the sentence as being either *inside, outside* or the *beginning* of an opinion expression, according to the popular IOB2 format.[14] We use as supervised classifier a Conditional Random Field (CRF) trained with the Passive-Aggressive [6] algorithm, using the implementation provided by CRFsuite, a very fast classification tool publicly available on the author website.[15] The features used to train the CRF include the word form, lemma and part-of-speech tag of each token, as well as whether the token is included in the SenticNet [3] and Subjectivity Lexicon [17] resources. A sliding windows of size 2 is used, meaning that each token is classified using features of the two preceding and following tokens in the sentence. Finally, the gold column is added using the IOB2 format.

3.3   Extraction of Opinion Holders/Targets

For each identified opinion expression span, the extraction of the associated holder and target spans in the enclosing sentence is done in three phases described next.

Identification of Candidate Holder/Target Head Tokens. The opinion expression is shrinked or enlarged, if needed, until a unique noun, verb, adjective or adverb head token e can be identified inside it.[16] The head token e is used as an anchor for identifying two sets of *candidate* tokens H_e and T_e, whose elements can possibly be the heads of holder and target spans for e, respectively. We build H_e and T_e as the largest sets satisfying the following conditions:

- tokens in H_e must be nouns or pronouns (as holders are agents);
- tokens in T_e must be nouns, pronouns or verbs (as targets can also be events);
- tokens in H_e or T_e cannot be or syntactically depend on modifier tokens, unless the token beign modified is e (e.g., in 'he likes beers from Germany' with e ='likes', T_e contains 'beers' but not 'Germany');
- tokens in H_e or T_e cannot be part of noun or verb phrases coordinated with e or an ancestor of e in the dependency tree (e.g., in 'he likes beer and she loves wine' with e ='likes', H_e and T_e cannot have tokens in 'she loves wine');
- $e \notin H_e$ and $e \notin T_e$.

---

[13] http://ixa2.si.ehu.es/ukb/.

[14] https://en.wikipedia.org/wiki/Inside_Outside_Beginning.

[15] http://www.chokkan.org/software/crfsuite/.

[16] This normalization does not affect the expression returned by the system and is required as expressions extracted in Sect. 3.2 might not be aligned with parse tree constituents.

Selection of Holder/Target Head Tokens. Given e, H_e and T_e, we select the sets of holder head tokens $\hat{H}_e \subseteq H_e$ and target head tokens $\hat{T}_e \subseteq T_e$ as described next for target tokens (the same approach applies to holder tokens). For each token $t \in T_e$, we apply a supervised linear classifier to compute a score $s(t, e)$ that quantifies the likelihood of $t \in \hat{T}_e$, with $s(t, e) > 0$ if t is predicted to belong to $\hat{T}_e$. We train the classifier with the LIBLINEAR[17] software, using logistic regression as loss function and the score returned by the classifier as $s(t, e)$. The following features are used:

- *Lexical features*: lemmas of t and e.
- *Syntactic features*: (i) part-of-speech tag of t and e; (ii) dependency relation to parent token for t and e; (iii) verb voice of e, either active, passive, or none, if not a verb; (iv) whether t is a proper noun. (v) encoding of path p linking t to e in the dependency tree, simplified by removing COORD and CONJ coordination links; (vi) whether the length of p is not greater than c, for each $c \in 1 \ldots$ max path length.
- *Semantic features*: (i) WordNet 3.0 synsets of t and e, including hypernyms; (ii) WordNet 3.0 supersenses of t and e; (iii) BBN entity type[18] of t, if any, such as person, organization or location; (iv) path linking t to e in a semantic graph having a node for each token and an edge for each predicate-argument SRL relation (head tokens are connected), labelled with the thematic role.

To compute $\hat{T}_e$ we impose that candidate tokens in T_e that are coordinated one to another (e.g., 'beer' and 'wine' in 'they like beer and wine') are either all selected or not selected. To this end, for each cluster $C \subseteq T_e$ of coordinated tokens, and for each token $t \in C$, we alter the token score by setting $s(t, e) = \min_{t' \in C} s(t', e)$. We then compute $\hat{T}_e$ as the set of tokens having the largest non-zero score (if any), i.e., $\hat{T}_e = \{t \in T_e \mid s(t, e) > 0 \land \forall t' \in T_e, s(t, e) \geq s(t', e)\}$.

Selection of Holder/Target Spans. Although the selection of head tokens uniquely identifies holder and target entities in the text (e.g., 'crowd' and 'Obama' in 'the crowd acclaimed president Barack Obama'), it may be unsuitable to applications and evaluation metrics that expect the selection of longer spans of text (e.g., 'the crowd' and 'president Barack Obama'). We thus expand each selected head token to a longer span of text, using a supervised technique able to adapt to different, corpus-specific selection criteria (e.g., select 'Barack Obama' vs 'president Barack Obama').[19]

Our expansion algorithm is based on a linear SVM classifier (we use the LIB-SVM[20] software package) that, given a currently *selected span* S and a disjoint

---

[17] http://www.csie.ntu.edu.tw/~cjlin/liblinear/.

[18] https://catalog.ldc.upenn.edu/docs/LDC2005T33/BBN-Types-Subtypes.html.

[19] The choice of a supervised approach in place of hard-coded rules is motivated also by observing that none of the datasets considered in Sect. 2.2 provides clear guidelines for marking holders and targets, resulting in heterogeneous and sometimes inconsistent annotations.

[20] https://www.csie.ntu.edu.tw/~cjlin/libsvm/.

candidate span S_c dominated by some token in S, decides whether S_c can be added to S. We apply the classifier iteratively starting from an initial selected span consisting of the holder/target head token only. At each iteration, we consider (if it exists) a topmost token t in the dependency tree that is dominated by tokens in the currently selected span S, skipping prepositions and conjunctions. We build the candidate span $S_c(t)$ for token t by including all the tokens of named entities overlapping with t (e.g., 'Barack Obama' for t = 'Obama') and of auxiliary and main verb tokens belonging to the verb 'catena' of t (e.g., 'would have been' for t = 'would'). We apply the classifier to S and $S_c(t)$ and, if the outcome is positive, we add $S_c(t)$ to S. The process is iterated until a fix point is reached. The employed classifier features are listed below, where S is the selected span, $S_c(t)$ is the candidate span with head token t, $S_c^*(t)$ is the span with descendant tokens of t in the dependency tree, and p is the nearest ancestor of t that belongs to S:

- *Lexical features*:   lemmas of p and t.
- *Syntactic features*:   (i) part-of-speech tags of p and t;   (ii) whether p and t are proper nouns;   (iii) dependency relations from and to t;   (iv) token distance between $S_c(t)$ and S (adjacent, very near, near or far, based on number of tokens separating the spans);   (v) token distance between $S_c^*(t)$ and S (same categories).
- *Semantic features*:   thematic role of the SRL relation between p and t, if p is a predicate and t is the head token of an argument of p.

We train two separate classifiers for holder and target expansion if there is enough training data, otherwise a joint classifier is used. Optionally, the system can merge multiple holder (target) spans for the same expression by adding missing tokens (typically, punctuation and 'and' tokens), so that a unique holder (target) span is extracted.

3.4   Polarity Classification

The polarity module aims at computing the sentiment value from the extracted opinion expressions (see Sect. 3.2). This module is based on a model trained by using the Blitzer dataset[21] combined with information contained in SenticNet [3]. For each concept contained in SenticNet, the model contains a fuzzy membership function [19] describing the polarity of the concept and the uncertainty associated with it.

Model Construction. In a preliminary learning phase an estimation of the polarity of each concept is inferred by analyzing explicit information provided by the training set. This phase allows to define the preliminary fuzzy membership functions associated with each concept. Such a value is computed as

$$\text{polarity}^{(LP)}(C_i) = \frac{k_{C_i}}{T_{C_i}} \in [-1, 1] \qquad \forall i = 1, \ldots, n,$$

---

[21] http://www.cs.jhu.edu/~mdredze/datasets/sentiment/.

where LP means "Learning Phase", C is the concept taken into account, n is the number of concepts contained in the model, k_{C_i} is the arithmetic sum of the polarities observed for concept C_i in the training set, and T_{C_i} is the number of instances of the training set in which concept C_i occurs. The shape of the fuzzy membership function generated during this phase is a triangle with the top vertex in the coordinates $(x, 1)$, where $x = \text{polarity}^{(0)}(C_i)$ and with the two bottom vertexes in the coordinates $(-1, 0)$ and $(1, 0)$ respectively. The rationale is that while we have one point (x) in which we have full confidence, our uncertainty covers the entire space because we do not have any information concerning the remaining polarity values.

After this, we compared the value computed through the training set with the one defined in the SenticNet ontology. This comparison shapes the fuzzy membership function of each term in the following way (see Fig. 1):

$$a = \min\{\text{polarity}_i^{(LP)}(C), \text{polarity}_i^{(SN)}(C)\},$$
$$b = \max\{\text{polarity}_i^{(LP)}(C), \text{polarity}_i^{(SN)}(C)\},$$
$$c = \max\{a - ((b - a)/2)\},$$
$$d = \min\{b + ((b - a)/2)\}.$$

where SN refers to the polarity contained in SenticNet. Figure 1 shows a picture about an example of the final fuzzy trapezoid.

Opinion Polarity Computation. For each SenticNet concept identified in the opinion text, the correspondent fuzzy polarity is extracted from the model. The fuzzy polarities of different concepts are then aggregated by a fuzzy averaging operator obtained by applying the extension principle [20] in order to compute fuzzy polarities for complex entities, like texts, which consist of a number of concepts and thus derive, so to speak, their polarity from them. Details about how the set of membership functions are aggregated can be found in [7].

The result of the polarity aggregation phase is a fuzzy polarity, whose membership function reflects the uncertainty of the available estimate obtained by the

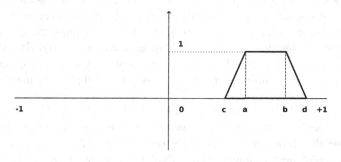

Fig. 1. The fuzzy trapezoid generated after the comparison between the polarity computed during the preliminary learning phase and the one contained in SenticNet.

system. Therefore, for extracting a crisp polarity value a defuzzification method, consisting in the conversion of a fuzzy quantity into a precise quantity, is needed. At least seven methods in the literature are popular for defuzzifying fuzzy outputs [9], which are appropriate for different application contexts. The *centroid method* is the most prominent and physically appealing of all the defuzzification methods. It results in a crisp value

$$y^* = \frac{\int y \mu_R(y) dy}{\int \mu_R(y) dy},$$

where the integration can be replaced by summation in discrete cases. This method is the one that we used for computing the value of the opinion polarity.

Finally, in the RAID system polarity is considered positive when $y^* > 0.2$, negative when $y^* < -0.2$, neutral otherwise.

4   Evaluation

We evaluate RAID on the MPQA, NTOA and DSRC datasets described in Sect. 2.2. We divided their documents into training and test sets according to a 75/25 ratio, except for the DSRC dataset where we reused the splitting given by the ESWC2015-CLSA challenge organizers. Then, we applied the RAID pipeline to extract opinion expressions, polarities, holders and (with the exception of the MPQA dataset) targets.

To compare the extracted expression, holder and target spans we use the state-of-the-art *intersection-based* precision and recall measures defined in [10]. Due to space reasons, we refer the reader to [10] for a detailed definition of these measures, only mentioning here that intersection-based measures evaluate extracted spans (of expressions, holder and targets) by giving them a reward proportional to the number of their tokens that intersect the ones of gold spans. This contrasts with *exact* measures, which require an exact match between extracted and gold spans, and *overlap-based* measures, which consider an extracted span as correctly marked if it overlaps with just one token of the gold standard (thus unfairly favoring longer extracted spans). Note that extracted and gold holder (target) spans are compared only when the corresponding expressions can be successfully matched, so to give credit only to holders (targets) of correctly extracted opinion expressions. Polarities are instead evaluated by comparing extracted and gold expressions that have been tagged (in gold and extracted data) with the same polarity, so that, e.g., the polarity precision measure corresponds to the amount of extracted opinion expressions whose span and polarity match the ones of gold expressions.

Table 2 shows RAID performance on the datasets described in Sect. 2.2 using the intersection-based measures. Concerning the identification of opinion expressions, the results show how the size of the dataset (and thus of training data) can result in different performances. The MPQA dataset, where RAID gets the best scores, is the biggest one, and this results in a high recall (0.501). On the contrary, NTOA is very small, that is the system has to be trained on a smaller set of expressions, resulting in high precision (0.819) and low recall (0.333). Finally, the DSRC dataset has some inconsistencies in the annotation of expressions, resulting in low scores overall. Similar considerations can be drawn for holder and target identification, noting that holder scores are generally (artificially) better for datasets such as DSRC whose opinion frames contain only few holder spans, as RAID successfully (and correctly) learns not to extract them.

To conclude the section, we report in Table 3 the performances of RAID on the DSRC dataset using the ESWC2015-CLSA evaluation measures, which are a form of exact precision-recall measures. In this setting, spans like "the teacher" and "teacher" are considered completely different, resulting in a decrease of precision and recall.

Table 2. RAID evaluation where precision (p), recall (r) and F_1-measure (f) are calculated for each dataset of Sect. 2.2. According to [10], polarity is considered wrong when the extracted expression cannot be matched to a gold expression. Accuracy for polarity detection without this limitation is 74.39 for MPQA, 83.67 for NTOA and 80.14 for DSRC.

	MPQA			NTOA			DSRC		
	p	r	f	p	r	f	p	r	f
expression	0.671	0.501	0.573	0.819	0.333	0.473	0.459	0.276	0.344
holder	0.584	0.584	0.584	0.710	0.647	0.677	0.952	0.952	0.952
target	-	-	-	0.416	0.431	0.424	0.596	0.588	0.592
polarity	0.419	0.305	0.353	0.620	0.283	0.389	0.321	0.195	0.243

Table 3. RAID evaluation using the ESWC2015-CLSA dataset and evaluation metric. Overall scores are the average of respective scores for expression, holder, target and polarity extraction.

	Expression	Holder	Target	Polarity	Overall
precision	0.261	0.839	0.310	0.189	0.340
recall	0.416	0.964	0.452	0.302	0.534
F-value	0.321	0.897	0.368	0.232	0.455

5   Conclusions and Future Work

In this work we have presented RAID, a supervised tool for extracting opinion frames from texts. RAID first extracts the opinion expressions inside a sentence and, for each expression, it identifies the associated holder and target (if any) and assigns a positive / negative / neutral polarity to the opinion. RAID has been evaluated on three different datasets and its open-source code and a working demo are publicly available online.

We plan to improve RAID opinion extraction algorithm in the future, as well as the quality of the data used for training and evaluation of RAID. The latter aspect is motivated by the heterogeneous performances shown by RAID on different datasets, which have two explanations. First, the annotation guidelines differ among datasets, making difficult for a system to perform well on all datasets. For instance, the sentence 'Cameron called the crisis in Algeria a difficult, dangerous and potentially very bad situation' contains 5 different expression frames in NTOA, because its guidelines ask for splitting expression (as well as holder and target) spans when a conjunction ('and', 'or', ...) is found. On the contrary, the MPQA dataset would consider them as a single opinion expression, unless different polarity values are involved. Second, datasets differ also regarding the completeness of their opinion annotations: while every opinion expression is guaranteed to be annotated in the MPQA dataset, this does not happen for DSRC, which includes many sentences where only part of the opinions are annotated.

Since the performances of a system depend on the size, consistency and quality of the training dataset, we deem useful to merge different opinion datasets into a single dataset with consistent annotations. This is something we would like to investigate in the future, so to increase the performances of RAID and other opinion extraction tools.

References

1. Almeida, M.S.C., Figueira, H., Mendes, P.: Aligning Opinions : Cross-Lingual Opinion Mining with Dependencies (2012)
2. Balahur, A., Steinberger, R., Kabadjov, M., Zavarella, V., Van Der Goot, E., Halkia, M., Pouliquen, B., Belyaeva, J.: Sentiment analysis in the news. In: Proceedings of the Seventh International Conference on Language Resources and Evaluation (LREC 2010), pp. 2216–2220 (2010)
3. Cambria, E., Olsher, D., Rajagopal, D.: Senticnet 3: a common and common-sense knowledge base for cognition-driven sentiment analysis. In: AAAI, pp. 1515–1521 (2014)
4. Cambria, E., Schuller, B.B., Xia, Y., Havasi, C.: New avenues in opinion mining and sentiment analysis. IEEE Intell. Sys. **28**(2), 15–21 (2013)
5. Choi, Y., Breck, E., Cardie, C.: Joint extraction of entities and relations for opinion recognition. In: Proceedings of the 2006 Conference on Empirical Methods in Natural Language Processing, EMNLP 2006, pp. 431–439. Association for Computational Linguistics, Stroudsburg (2006)
6. Crammer, K., Dekel, O., Keshet, J., Shalev-Shwartz, S., Singer, Y.: Online Passive Aggressive Algorithms **7**, 551–585 (2003)
7. Dragoni, M., Tettamanzi, A.G.B., Pereira, C.C.: Propagating and aggregating fuzzy polarities for concept-level sentiment analysis. Cogn. Comput. **7**(2), 186–197 (2015)
8. Gangemi, A., Presutti, V., Recupero, D.R.: Frame-based detection of opinion holders and topics: a model and a tool. IEEE Comput. Intell. Mag. **9**(1), 20–30 (2014)
9. Hellendoorn, H., Thomas, C.: Defuzzification in fuzzy controllers. Intell. Fuzzy Sys. **1**, 109–123 (1993)

10. Johansson, R., Moschitti, A.: Relational features in fine-grained opinion analysis. Comput. Linguist. **39**(3), 473–509 (2013)
11. Kim, S-M., Hovy, E.: Extracting opinions, opinion holders, and topics expressed in online news media text. In: Proceedings of the Workshop on Sentiment and Subjectivity in Text, SST 2006, Association for Computational Linguistics, pp. 1–8, Stroudsburg (2006)
12. Ruppenhofer, J., Somasundaran, S., Wiebe, J.: Finding the sources and targets of subjective expressions. In: The Sixth International Conference on Language Resources and Evaluation (LREC 2008), **2** (2008)
13. Stoyanov, V., Cardie, C.: Annotating topics of opinions. In: Proceedings of the Sixth International Conference on Language Resources and Evaluation (LREC 2008), European Language Resources Association (ELRA), Marrakech, May 2008. http://www.lrec-conf.org/proceedings/lrec2008/
14. Toprak, C., Jakob, N., Gurevych, I.: Sentence and expression level annotation of opinions in user-generated discourse. In: Proceedings of the 48th Annual Meeting of the Association for Computational Linguistics, ACL 2010, Association for Computational Linguistics, pp. 575–584, Stroudsburg (2010)
15. Wiebe, J., Wilson, T., Cardie, C.: Annotating expressions of opinions and emotions in language. Lang. Res. Eval. **39**(2–3), 165–210 (2005)
16. Wiegand, M., Klakow, D.: Convolution kernels for opinion holder extraction. In: Human Language Technologies: The 2010 Annual Conference of the North American Chapter of the Association for Computational Linguistics, HLT 2010, Association for Computational Linguistics, pp. 795–803, Stroudsburg (2010)
17. Wilson, T., Wiebe, J., Hoffmann, P.: Recognizing contextual polarity in phrase-level sentiment analysis. In: Proceedings of the Conference on Human Language Technology and Empirical Methods in Natural Language Processing, HLT 2005, Association for Computational Linguistics, pp. 347–354, Stroudsburg (2005)
18. Yu, H., Hatzivassiloglou, V.: Towards answering opinion questions: Separating facts from opinions and identifying the polarity of opinion sentences. In: Proceedings of the 2003 Conference on Empirical Methods in Natural Language Processing, EMNLP 2003, Association for Computational Linguistics, pp. 129–136, Stroudsburg, (2003)
19. Zadeh, L.A.: Fuzzy sets. Inf. Control **8**, 338–353 (1965)
20. Zadeh, L.A.: The concept of a linguistic variable and its application to approximate reasoning - i. Inf. Sci. **8**(3), 199–249 (1975)
21. Zhang, L., Liu, B.: Aspect and Entity Extraction for Opinion Mining. In: Chu, W.W. (ed.) Data Mining and Knowledge Discovery for Big Data. SBD, vol. 1, pp. 1–40. Springer, Heidelberg (2014)

Author Index

Printed in the United States
By Bookmasters